100 THINGS
ROCKETS FANS
SHOULD KNOW & DO
BEFORE THEY DIE

100 THINGS
ROCKETS FANS
SHOULD KNOW & DO
BEFORE THEY DIE

Jonathan Feigen

TRIUMPH
BOOKS

Library of Congress Cataloging-in-Publication Data upon request.

This book is available in quantity at special discounts for your group or organization. For further information, contact:
    Triumph Books LLC
    814 North Franklin Street
    Chicago, Illinois 60610
    (312) 337-0747
    www.triumphbooks.com

Printed in U.S.A.
ISBN: 978-1-62937-586-1
Design by Patricia Frey

For Houston, a city that takes on the best times and toughest challenges with the heart of a champion.

Contents

Foreword

There's nothing like a great sports team in a city. All great cities have them, but not every city is fortunate enough to have all three sports and not every city is fortunate enough to have had champions.

The Rockets won the first two major championships in this city. There's only been three. This team has been a competitive team for 40 years. The goal of ownership of this team has always been—from Charlie Thomas to Leslie Alexander to myself—we're here to win rings. We're going to be a champion and we're going to bring more championships to the City of Houston.

If you name the greatest athletes who played in the City of Houston, it's Hakeem Olajuwon, it's Elvin Hayes. And it helped that they played college ball here and they're icons.

Everybody plays basketball. It's a sport that's played all over the world. Boys play it. Girls play it. And I love owning a basketball team.

This isn't just a business venture. This is my heart and my soul. I want to live by that. This team will always have "The Heart of a Champion," as Rudy T said. That's something we'll never lose.

—Tilman Fertitta

1 Fit to a T

Twelve months later, Rudy Tomjanovich would deliver the most iconic address ever given in a trophy presentation ceremony. "The Heart of a Champion" address will be forever part of his legacy, repeated by players, fans, and coaches of teams across the globe.

The previous spring, however, he was every bit as on target. He spoke directly to the hearts and emotions of Houston sports fans, with understanding of the dues they had paid and the long road the Rockets had traveled to that moment.

"Houston has wanted this for so long," Tomjanovich said after the Rockets defeated the Knicks for the first championship in Houston team sports history, "and you've finally got it."

More than most, Tomjanovich had been there every step of the way. He was the young former All-American when the Rockets landed in Houston from San Diego as no more than an experiment (now so anachronistic that it's difficult to believe) to determine if professional basketball could work in Texas.

He was part of the barnstorming days when the Rockets played "home" games from the University of Houston's Hofheinz Pavilion to Waco, El Paso, and San Antonio.

He felt the promise and ultimate disappointment of the 1980s, when the Rockets twice reached the NBA Finals, only to fall apart around Hakeem Olajuwon as drug suspensions broke up a team with championship potential.

Finally, having reluctantly taken over as coach, after years as a player, scout, broadcaster, and assistant, he had guided the Rockets to that first championship. Though he is from Hamtramck, Michigan, and has long been a Los Angeles resident since his brief run as Lakers coach, he considered himself a Houstonian.

He knew of the pain from the Phi Slama Jama loss in Albuquerque and the Oilers collapse in Buffalo. He also knew that when the Rockets pulled away from the Knicks in Game 7, the Rockets had more than become champions. They had lifted the city above all the disappointments along the way, replacing the pain with elation few beyond the echoes of the honking horns and delighted shouts on Richmond Avenue could entirely understand.

Tomjanovich had instilled his determination into his championship teams. He had plenty to spare.

Tomjanovich grew up in a blue-collar factory town now cleaved by a highway since built through what had been his neighborhood. His father's chronic back problems often kept him from working, with the family getting by on government food with generic labels as Tomjanovich grew more driven with every indignity along the way.

He was doubted in his first high school tryout and even when he arrived at Michigan as one of the most highly touted offensive talents in the state. In his first varsity game, he had 27 rebounds and 13 blocked shots against Kentucky. By his last, he was the leading rebounder in school history, averaging 25.1 points in his career.

Yet, when the San Diego Rockets chose him with the second pick of the 1970 Draft, he was greeted with outrage from San Diego fans who wanted the Rockets to choose Pete Maravich. Criticism drove him. The negative press that he insisted on reading was his fuel. The hunger he kept from Hamtramck to the "Heart of a Champion" never left him, pushing him through obstacles great and small, on and off the court.

After a rookie season in which he rarely played, Tomjanovich heard a television report that the Rockets would move to Houston and expected to see cattle and tumbleweeds, rather than the

Rudy Tomjanovich is surrounded by his team as they hoist the Larry O'Brien Trophy following the Rockets 113–101 victory over the Orlando Magic in Game 4 of the 1995 Finals. (AP Photo/Pat Sullivan)

rapidly-growing metropolis that would come to mean so much to him. Coach Alex Hannum was fired, replaced by a college coach, Tex Winter, who not only helped drill Tomjanovich into the player he would become, but provided much of the foundation of Tomjanovich's beliefs as a coach.

Tomjanovich did not play much in his first season in Houston, but he continued to develop the shooting touch that would make him a five-time All-Star. He played with that determination to overcome doubts and obstacles. He joked often that power forwards hated him for too often going over their backs, a sentiment Tomjanovich said with his familiar laugh, a laugh that Wilt Chamberlain never forgot after their first meeting, when Tomjanovich was too out of control for The Stilt's liking.

Tomjanovich's high-release jump shot made him an All-Star, and he averaged 21.6 points in the 1976–77 season. But on December 9, 1977, teammate Kevin Kunnert was locked up with the Lakers' Kermit Washington. Players ran toward them. Washington and teammate Kareem Abdul-Jabbar fought with Kunnert. Washington saw Tomjanovich, turned, and landed the punch that changed both their lives.

Tomjanovich immediately knew his nose was broken, but at the hospital, Tomjanovich was told he had a fractured skull, broken jaw, and two broken cheekbones. Worst of all, spinal fluid was leaking and Tomjanovich was told he might not survive.

Tomjanovich spent four days in intensive care. Doctors repaired the fractures. Tomjanovich's lifelong determination swelled again. Asked if he was concerned in the months that followed that the damage might end his career, Tomjanovich said, "I would not let it."

Seven months after the punch, Tomjanovich was playing in summer leagues. He was hurt that next season and was moved to coming off the bench, but he still averaged 19 points per game. But by the 1980–81 season, when the Rockets reached the NBA Finals, Tomjanovich was out of the rotation, playing just 31 postseason minutes.

He understood, Tomjanovich said years later. He also hated it.

When it became clear that nothing would change before the next season, a trade to the Utah Jazz was discussed. Tomjanovich decided he would rather retire than move his family or spend a season without them. His playing career ended after 11 seasons at 32 years old. When he wrote his autobiography, he named it *A Rocket at Heart*.

He could not have known then how those experiences would inform the years to come, from the way he drove the Rockets past "Choke City" one year and past "the non-believers" the next, to his own battles with alcoholism and the bladder cancer that led to the end of his Rockets coaching career.

Yet, as much as Tomjanovich would prove to be the right man at the right time, he didn't believe that himself and did not want the job. Don Chaney, the 1991 Coach of the Year, had been fired with a 26–26 record. Carroll Dawson was the obvious choice, but that was the year Dawson had been struck by lightning. His blood pressure was still an issue. His job became convincing Tomjanovich to take the job.

Tomjanovich told Dawson, "I'm not coaching. I hate coaches." He and Dawson went outside for 15 minutes, with Dawson pledging to teach Tomjanovich everything he'd need to know, saying that the 30 games left would give him a chance to see how he liked it and most of all, that if Tomjanovich did not take the job, someone else would come in and fire them all. Tomjanovich went inside and told general manager Steve Patterson he'd take the job.

"We came into the office," Tomjanovich said, "and Steve said, 'I know what you guys are going to say. You can't save him.' I had no idea what was coming next. Carroll said, 'If you don't do it, we don't have jobs.' I had to take the job."

The Rockets went 16–14 the rest of the season. Owner Charlie Thomas removed Tomjanovich's interim tag. Dawson and Tomjanovich spent the spring and summer studying and preparing with Tomjanovich's now-familiar and often-destructive obsessiveness.

"He became one of the best coaches in the league," Dawson said. "Let me tell you something about Rudy. It doesn't matter what he's doing, and I told people this before he started coaching. People said, 'Will he be a good scout?' I said, 'Are you kidding? If you tell him go mop that whole warehouse floor, you'd get the best job ever done by Rudy. He takes everything and overdoes it.' He did the same thing in scouting. He did the same thing as a coach."

That quality made him a success, but it also tortured him. Tomjanovich always believed he could work so hard and care so deeply that he couldn't be stopped.

In many ways, Tomjanovich's career as a coach echoed his 11 seasons as a player. The Rockets became driven by defeat and doubts. Fueled by the Game 7 overtime loss in Seattle the previous season, the Rockets began the 1993–94 championship season 15–0. Defiant in the face of the "Choke City" collapse against the Suns, the Rockets rallied back, all the way to the title. Responding to the criticism the next season when they struggled and broke up the championship team with the trade for Clyde Drexler, they became the only team to win a title as a sixth seed.

Even after Hakeem Olajuwon began to fade and Charles Barkley could not be a star, Tomjanovich sought to rebuild the Rockets, rather than move on, seeking to make Steve Francis the next foundational star.

The Rockets, however, did not make the postseason in Tomjanovich's final four seasons. By the end of the 2002–03 season, Tomjanovich took a leave of absence to treat bladder cancer. That May, he and Rockets owner Leslie Alexander settled the final two seasons of his contract, ending his 33 years with the team.

Tomjanovich returned to coaching briefly with the Lakers, but stepped down barely halfway through the 2003–04 season when he believed it was too soon after his cancer battle to take on the stress and all-nighters of coaching again. He worked as a scout and consultant with the Lakers, a role closer to the collaborative work he preferred before becoming a head coach, until May 2017. Living in Los Angeles, he declared in 2014, "Right now, I think I'm the happiest person I know."

His influence as a coach goes far beyond the championship banners in Toyota Center. Tomjanovich's use of range-shooting power forwards Robert Horry and Matt Bullard, and the spacing that created, influences the offenses now used throughout the NBA. Never a pick-and-roll coach, he used it against the Knicks in the 1994 Finals to reduce the wear-and-tear on Olajuwon, and in the 1995 season against the Magic to attack Shaquille O'Neal.

Decades removed from the titles, his greatness has come to be understood.

"Based on personal experience, T was the greatest NBA coach," Horry, a seven-time champion who also played for Phil Jackson and Gregg Popovich, wrote in The Players' Tribune. "I know he doesn't have nearly as many championships, but sometimes we give one person too much credit for titles."

Still, when the pursuit of titles is reduced to two teams, and the broadcasts of The Finals offers a montage of unforgettable moments, Tomjanovich's voice still resonates with the words "Don't ever underestimate the heart of a champion."

Rockets fans, however, know just what he meant a year earlier when he spoke of their long, trying journey to the championship, as if before Tomjanovich could send a message that would be universal, he first had to speak to them and the road they had traveled together.

2 The Dream

There is gray in the beard now, but it is not difficult to see Hakeem Olajuwon in retirement and picture that powerful, young athlete with the quick-twitch explosiveness of a lightning strike.

He offers only glimpses of the Dream Shake, giving lessons to students ranging from NBA stars to wannabes that watch silently trying to learn its secrets. But it remains easy to see Olajuwon, at the height of his powers, "bamboozle" David Robinson, conquer Patrick Ewing, or flummox Shaquille O'Neal.

Olajuwon takes his place in his front row seat at Toyota Center and accepts the roars when he is introduced to the crowd, still seeming slightly embarrassed, but understanding of his place. He has long since become Rockets royalty and still wears the crown as gracefully as he moves in the memory of anyone that saw him block shots, drain soft jumpers, or, as he once said of his initial NBA goal, "dunk, dunk, and dunk."

With each image, whether spinning or still, working on practice courts or waving to crowds, there is a manner with which Olajuwon still carries himself.

More than two decades removed from the NBA mountaintop, that bearing, the dignity he displayed and serenity he found, still tells of how he got there.

For Olajuwon, it all came together when he was most at peace, when he embraced his faith and let that bring together everything that made him among the greatest players in the history of the sport.

From his years playing soccer and team handball in Nigeria before he discovered his basketball calling at 15 years old, to the University of Houston and the Phi Slama Jama triumphs and disappointments, from the Twin Towers to the lean years, to the battles with Charlie Thomas and ultimately to the years when he had mastered his craft and his priorities in life to become a champion, Olajuwon's climb to the top might have needed every step.

"I believe it is my duty to do my best and prepare my best," Olajuwon said during the 1995 Finals, days before winning his second championship, speaking of a spiritual obligation that drove him. "That concept to stay humble and stay hungry is not because we won a championship or we are winning. We demonstrated professionalism, even when we were on top. And we are still humble. That is very important."

That never changed. The road to Olajuwon's uncanny balance of who he was as a person and as a player, and how those parts of his life came together, was like no other.

Olajuwon, which translates to "always on top," was the third of six children in a middle-class family in Lagos, Nigeria, where his parents owned and ran a cement business.

His years playing team handball and soccer helped develop the footwork he would bring to basketball courts long after he had switched sports. When Olajuwon's high school, the Muslim Teachers College, sent a team to a basketball tournament at the All-Nigeria Teachers Sports Festival in Sokoto, the coach asked to borrow the towering handball star. Olajuwon was immediately hooked.

Just two years later, Akeem Abdul Olajuwon showed up on the University of Houston campus, famously taking a cab from the airport, and spent three years under Guy V. Lewis, blocking shots and mastering the fundamentals of drop steps. The Cougars of Olajuwon, Clyde Drexler, Larry Micheaux, and Michael Young reached the NCAA Final Four three straight seasons—making it to the championship game back-to-back years—but falling short each time.

Olajuwon, who dropped Abdul after his junior season and would become Hakeem for good in 1991, was the automatic first pick of the 1984 Draft, a choice so obvious it was considered a no-brainer even with Ralph Sampson already on the roster and Michael Jordan in the same draft.

"I never did understand," said former Rockets assistant coach and general manager Carroll Dawson, who helped Olajuwon perfect his counter moves, "how a guy almost seven feet tall could be that fast, that quick, and could jump that high."

As a rookie, Olajuwon averaged 20.6 points and 11.9 rebounds. He had been working with Moses Malone at Fonde Recreation Center in Houston, developing his shooting touch along with the toughness it would take to battle Malone on the court he ruled. By Olajuwon's second season, the Rockets were in the NBA Finals, defeated in six games by the 1986 Celtics, considered among the greatest teams ever assembled. The Rockets were thought to be on their way.

That team fell apart, broken by suspensions and Sampson's knee, hip, and back injuries. But Olajuwon kept honing his craft, mixing all that athleticism with off-the-charts competitiveness.

"It was an awesome experience just watching some of the things he could do on the court," Rudy Tomjanovich said. "He was a combination of quickness and finesse combined with strength and power."

Even in the Rockets' lean seasons, Olajuwon became increasingly dominant. In 1990, he became the third player with a quadruple double, getting 18 points, 16 rebounds, 11 blocks, and 10 assists against the Bucks just weeks after another Olajuwon quadruple double was removed from the record books when the NBA ruled he was given one too many assists.

"What made him great was the passion," Sampson said. "He wanted to be the best and he obviously was."

That all could have come apart for the Rockets when Olajuwon battled owner Charlie Thomas. Olajuwon would cite a hamstring injury for sitting out. Thomas would charge that Olajuwon was seeking a contract extension. Olajuwon would call Thomas "a coward" and "a fool." Olajuwon was not traded, but it had become a very real possibility.

They made their peace on a long flight to Tokyo. Olajuwon received his contract extension late in the 1992–93 season. Much of the championship team had been assembled around Olajuwon. Rudy Tomjanovich had been elevated to Rockets coach. In July of 1993, Thomas sold the Rockets to Leslie Alexander.

Most significantly, however, in 1992, Olajuwon made his first trip to Mecca and rededicated himself to his Islamic faith, as he had been taught as a child. He would travel with a prayer rug and a compass (to point toward Mecca) for his daily prayers. When the Rockets moved practices to Westside Tennis Club, a prayer room was installed just off the court for Olajuwon.

"It changed everything," Olajuwon said. "The whole outlook changed. You believe in just doing the best you can. Once you are doing the best you can, you leave it up to God to decide. If there is an opportunity for me to win a championship, then it will happen."

He had the team, coach, and ownership, but also serenity. He became a more eager passer, with greater belief in his teammates. Still driven as ever, he came to view doing his best as part of his commitment to his faith.

"I think it was a combination of experience and maturity, not to mention the desire to win," says Olajuwon. "My recommitment to Islam helped me develop the mindset that I needed to reach that."

The greater the confidence Olajuwon had in his teammates, the more they had in themselves. When the Rockets knocked off the Clippers in the first round of the 1993 playoffs, it was their first postseason series win since 1987. They dropped the second-round series in Seattle, losing in overtime in Game 7, but the Rockets knew what was possible.

Olajuwon was still a physical marvel, but he'd also mastered every possibility of his footwork, of his jump hooks and counters, and most of all, the Dream Shake.

When he was given the MVP Award, NBA commissioner David Stern said, "You do it with an elegance and a grace that is spectacular." As the crowd in The Summit roared, Olajuwon called his teammates to join him, raising the trophy with him.

The Rockets by then firmly believed they alone had the NBA's best player. Even after the Choke City collapse against the Suns, the Rockets could look to Olajuwon, eliminating doubt.

"He was very confident," Kenny Smith said. "You could see it in him. When your captain and your leader has that kind of feeling, it spreads throughout the team."

The Rockets beat the Suns in seven games and knocked out the Jazz in five games. The Rockets took their first championship by topping Ewing, who had beaten Olajuwon for the NCAA title 10 years earlier. The Rockets took Game 6 when Olajuwon blocked John Starks' final shot.

When the Rockets took the title, Olajuwon took the ball and took a seat, watching the celebration around him, soaking it all in as if considering, or at least feeling, all it took to get there.

The following season cemented his legacy. The Rockets struggled with injuries, traded for Drexler, and began the playoffs as the sixth seed. But from Olajuwon's demolition of Robinson in one of the greatest series ever played to the tip that won Game 1 of The Finals, sending the Rockets to a sweep of O'Neal and the Magic, Olajuwon had realized all that potential, mastered his game, and stood at the top of his sport.

The Rockets could not remain at that level. They lost to the SuperSonics in the second round of the 1996 playoffs. They traded for Charles Barkley to help inside and try to keep Olajuwon's championship window open longer. They twice fell to the Jazz, first in the Western Conference Finals and then in the first round.

By the summer of 2001, when Olajuwon was a free agent, he chose the three-year, $17 million contract with the Raptors, deciding that the Rockets were negotiating to keep him out of a sense of "obligation." The Rockets worked out a sign-and-trade deal with Toronto, where Olajuwon played one season before retiring.

He never lost his affection for Houston or the fans' appreciation for him. He would help the Rockets recruit free agents, work with young players, and accept the adulation at games, doing it all with the sensibility that helped make him a champion.

"Some people have that aura," Rockets forward Luc Mbah a Moute, who had been inspired by Olajuwon as a young African with NBA dreams, said. "Hakeem is one of those guys, man, when you see him, he just warms up the room. Whether it's a smile, the way he talks, the way he carries himself. It's great to have him around. When you talk to him and spend some time with him, as amazing as he was as a basketball player, I think he's an amazing person."

He was also the greatest player in franchise history, as iconic as he was revered in his adopted hometown and far beyond.

"If I had to pick a center [for an all-time best team], I would take Olajuwon," Jordan told NBA.com. "That leaves out Shaq, Patrick Ewing. It leaves out Wilt Chamberlain. It leaves out a lot of people. And the reason I would take Olajuwon is very simple: he is so versatile because of what he can give you from that position. It's not just his scoring, not just his rebounding, or not just his blocked shots. People don't realize he was in the top seven [in NBA history] in steals. He always made great decisions on the court. For all facets of the game, I have to give it to him."

3 The First Championship

As Hakeem Olajuwon drove to The Summit as he had countless times before, his mind wandered. The route was the same. The feelings that day were very different.

Olajuwon thought about Game 7, as of course he would, but he also imagined Houston if the Rockets won. He knew the history, knew that the city had never celebrated a major sports team championship, knew of the heartache that came the many times Houston teams had teased with possibilities, only to have them vanish, often in the most agonizing of ways.

Olajuwon tried to imagine how Houston would feel with that first title. Imagination, however, could not match reality.

"You play both sides," Olajuwon said 20 years later. "When I was driving down to the game, you play, 'Man, to win...' Every once in a while you think you could lose that game so you know you might. To see that finally it's over, that we won it, and to see the excitement of the whole city at the same time celebrating... unbelievable. I mean, unbelievable. Even after the game, I just got my stuff and jumped in the car, the limo. I tried to get on Richmond."

He, as with so many other Houstonians, hit the happiest gridlock ever. In an era in which so many celebrations around the nation turned bad, with parked cars turned to kindling and partiers into combatants, Houston gave itself a hug.

"The whole city was celebrating," Olajuwon said. "The whole city jumped in their car. I mean, unbelievable. I've never seen anything like it."

Cities typically embrace champions. Bandwagons fill. Longtime fans feel elation multiplied by the years invested. But Houston had

Hakeem Olajuwon goes up over Anthony Mason in Game 7 of the 1994 NBA Finals. (AP Photo/Tim Johnson)

suffered to earn its celebration. It had gone through the Oilers' Luv Ya Blue near misses and the collapse in Buffalo. It had watched the airball dunk and Jim Valvano dash around the court in Albuquerque. It lost in the frozen Cotton Bowl and the ninth inning collapses in the Astrodome.

Houston had never finished on top, never had a champion's parade, much less the spontaneous celebration that had the city thrilled to be stuck in traffic, horns blaring.

The 1994 NBA Finals would be remembered elsewhere for many reasons. There was the showdown of sublime centers, Olajuwon and Patrick Ewing, revisiting the national championship game matchup 10 years earlier. There was the physical, suffocating defenses that helped lead to rule changes to remove the stifling hand checks. There was the unforgettable drama of the O.J. Simpson slow-motion car chase playing out during Game 5.

There was also a long, tough series that filled seven tense games.

The teams had split the first two games in Houston, before the Rockets broke through in Madison Square Garden with Sam Cassell, who had moved past Scott Brooks in the rotation late that regular season, scoring the game's final seven points, including the game-winning three off a pass on the move from Olajuwon.

The Knicks overwhelmed the Rockets with defense in Game 4. The Rockets faded badly down the stretch in Game 5 as the nation was transfixed by the television coverage from Los Angeles.

Back home for the final two games, however, the Rockets regained their footing. Ewing had been sensational in Game 5, setting a Finals record with eight blocked shots. Game 6 was Olajuwon's turn, as the NBA's all-time blocked shots record holder sealed the win when he rotated out of pick-and-roll coverage and closed to John Starks just in time to get a piece of Starks' shot for the championship.

"When you are on the road, you don't want to go to Game 7," Olajuwon said. "Game 6 is your best opportunity to win. We were at home. We couldn't wait. We couldn't sleep until this game was decided."

By Game 7, the Rockets guards—Kenny Smith, Vernon Maxwell, and Cassell—who had taken turns taking over throughout the postseason, all came alive at once, combining for 45 points on 14 of 24 shooting. Starks could not make a shot, going 2-of-18 as he missed all 11 of his three-pointers and Knicks coach Pat Riley stuck with him, playing Starks for 42 minutes despite his struggles.

Olajuwon outscored Ewing in all seven games, averaging 26.9 points on 50 percent shooting while holding Ewing to 18.9 points on just 36.3 percent shooting. When Ewing became a Rockets assistant coach, he spent four years forced to recall those Finals with a large photo of Olajuwon blocking Starks' shot taunting him in the players' lounge, reminding of the defeat that would torment Ewing as the one that got away.

"It was a great series," Ewing said. "It went seven games. We had our opportunities to win. Unfortunately, they were able to prevail. Hakeem had an outstanding playoff run. It just wasn't in the cards."

For all the trials in years past, the Rockets had been certain it would be their year. They believed in their potential when they opened the season 15–0, capped by a win in Madison Square Garden. They became confident when they made their way through the Western Conference playoffs. They were certain when they won Game 3, ensuring the series would end in Houston.

"When we got to The Finals, we had been through so much," Rockets coach Rudy Tomjanovich said. "It wasn't just when things went right. We went through some tough times that season, too. We had the streak to start the season, but people forget we slid in the middle of the season, too. We had the whole Choke City/ Clutch City thing. When we played the Knicks, we were ready."

Elsewhere, the series was lampooned for its low scoring, diminished for delivering a championship in a season Michael Jordan did not play. To Houston, however, it was about much more than even the celebration of a title.

In Houston, 1994 will forever be the first championship, the claim no title to follow could ever share.

As much as Tomjanovich would be remembered for his "Heart of a Champion" comment while receiving the trophy a year later, that admonition was directed to others, to the "non-believers."

When he took that stage in 1994, he was a Houstonian, speaking to his elated adopted hometown with an understanding others might not have shared.

"Houston has wanted this for so long," he said after Game 7, "and you've finally got it."

Soon after, when Tomjanovich, Olajuwon, and the Rockets left The Summit to find Richmond Avenue packed, they found the party had already begun. Houston had been pained and patient and finally rewarded. It could wait no longer.

"There's nothing like it," Olajuwon said. "You have to go through it to know. Everybody is a part of it. Unbelievable."

4 From Choke City to Clutch City

The large-type, bold-faced headlines in both Houston newspapers screamed:

"CHOKE CITY"

Rudy Tomjanovich kept seeing those words. Even as he studied the tape of the Rockets' loss to the Phoenix Suns the night before:

"CHOKE CITY"

As he boarded the flight to Phoenix and weighed what he would say to his team to rebuild confidence:

"Choke City"

The headline was about more than the 20-point lead the Rockets let slip away in the final 10 minutes of Game 2 of the 1994 Western Conference Semifinals against the Suns. It was a reminder of their place alongside the Oilers, Cougars, and Astros, all having similarly gone through their nights of ignominy that would never be forgotten.

Tomjanovich, however, did not care about any of that the morning after. He would have to pick up the pieces. He would have to seize the opportunity that the Rockets' predecessors in collapses never had, not after the second-half failure in Buffalo, the ninth-inning collapse in the Astrodome, the icy loss in the Cotton Bowl, or the airball dunk in Albuquerque.

He just kept seeing those words haunt and taunt him.

"Choke City"

"What crossed my mind was, *That's going to be my legacy,*" Tomjanovich said. "*That's how people are going to remember me.*

"I was thinking I was going to be part of Houston sports history as the dummy who got us into Choke City. I was surprised by the reaction in the paper, how big it was. It was the full page, the headlines. I thought, *This could be stuck to me the rest of my career.* That was the thought that went through my head."

The Rockets were outscored 40–13 in the final 15 minutes and lost in overtime, 124–117. It was, at the time, the largest lead ever blown in a playoff game loss.

"It was very sad," Hakeem Olajuwon said. "That team, we lost that game, we were ahead by 20 points and lost and it was Choke City. It wasn't because of that team. We went back to our old habits of not sharing the ball, not playing together. We thought we were up 20 points, the game was over. We thought it was going to be an easy series."

Tomjanovich used the flight to Phoenix to consider how to bring his team back, running through and rejecting every motivational speech and ploy he considered. Then it hit him. He would show the video of all that went wrong, of 10 minutes with little ball movement and just one field goal, a Sam Cassell three-pointer, in a 20–4 Suns run to close the fourth quarter.

Then he would present video evidence of all that went right to build the lead.

If the Rockets could dominate one game, they could another.

"I showed them how we got the lead and guys were taking shots, fading away, and playing with confidence," Tomjanovich said. "After a while, it was, 'These… can't guard us.' It went from barely looking up to the edge of their seats saying, 'We can do this.'"

Kenny Smith wrote the words "Two Wins" on his shoes as a reminder of the goal of the trip to Phoenix. Mario Elie wrote "Choke City." But beating the Suns would still not be "easy," as the Rockets assumed when they built their Game 2 lead.

The Suns led by 16 midway through the second quarter when the Rockets player that struggled most in those first two games took off. Maxwell had gone 1 of 9 in the Game 1 loss, committing a crucial late-game turnover. After the game, he angrily vented about the lack of a Mother's Day sellout, "Our fans are the worst. To hell with them."

After Game 2, however, Maxwell was defiant. The doubts and criticism fueled him. "I was so focused that night on the game. I am sure we had words. It was a great night for our team. I think that turned it around. That was one of the biggest moments of my NBA career.

"I think everyone was really down, and I thought it wasn't over."

Maxwell scored 31 of his 34 points in the second half. The Rockets rose from the ashes in Phoenix, winning Game 3 by a score of 118–102 on Friday the 13th to stay alive. By Game 7, Olajuwon dominated and the Rockets started a roll, built on confidence and determination that had been driven by Choke City, that would take them to two championships.

After Game 3, that mentality got a name. Former Rockets owner Leslie Alexander told his team president, John Thomas, "I think they got the wrong car part. Its Clutch City, not Choke City."

The name stuck not just as a marketing slogan or even a rallying cry, but as a definition of a team and a time. Mail could be sent to the post office at Clutch City, Texas. The organization became Clutch City Sports & Entertainment. The mascot bear was named "Clutch."

The Rockets had not won despite Choke City; they won because of it, emerging transformed into champions.

"Nothing that ever took place, the first championship and especially the second, would've happened without 'Choke City,'" Tomjanovich said. "It became the last thing that made us a team. It drove us."

5 The White Bronco Game

The details of the game have largely been lost, blurred in memory or obscured by the unforgettable events that overshadowed everything.

The Knicks pulled away to win Game 5 of the NBA Finals, 91–84, sending the series back to Houston with the Knicks holding a 3–2 series lead. Patrick Ewing had his best game of The Finals. The Rockets' backcourt struggled. John Starks excelled. Almost no one remembers.

It was more than the passage of time that stole attention from that stop on the way to the Rockets' first championship. Even during the game in Madison Square Garden, focus was drawn away from the court to the low-speed car chase in Los Angeles.

In one of those "where were you when" moments in American history, O.J. Simpson was a fugitive from justice, with his friend A.C. Cowlings driving him in his white Ford Bronco as the Los Angeles police followed and the nation watched.

In the days before smart phones and instantly available information in the palm of every hand, fans in the Garden turned away from the court to look at the television screens in the suites behind them. Many rushed to the concourses to watch on the televisions next to concession stands. Others crowded around the courtside monitors to look over the shoulders of reporters and broadcasters.

The day—June 17, 1994—was filled with monumental sports events. The New York Rangers held a tickertape parade through Manhattan to celebrate their first Stanley Cup championship since 1940. Arnold Palmer played his final round of a U.S. Open. The World Cup opened in Chicago. But as the Rockets and Knicks battled, a "modern tragedy and drama of Shakespearean proportion" as NBC News anchor Tom Brokaw called it, unfolded, culminating in Simpson's arrest on murder charges following the death of his ex-wife Nicole Brown Simpson and Ronald Goldman.

The game went on without interruption. Rockets forward Robert Horry said that the team saw monitors on the way back to the locker room at halftime, but players were generally unaware of the details behind the images on those television screens.

"We had too much other stuff on our minds," former Rockets guard Sam Cassell said. "I was worried about Derek Harper and John Starks. Hakeem [Olajuwon] was worried about Patrick Ewing and Anthony Mason and Charles Oakley. The O.J. situation, we found out about that after the game."

Viewers, however, turned away from the game. The 7.6 rating was one of the worst in Finals history and the worst since 1986. The combined viewership on other networks was worth a Super Bowl–like 48.4 Nielsen rating.

After a few updates during stoppages of play, NBC was compelled to break away from the game.

"It is our professional obligation to cover the ballgame tonight in what we hope is a professional fashion," NBC's Bob Costas said. "We are, of course, mindful of the O.J. Simpson situation and we will apprise you of any developments."

By the end of the second quarter, NBC put coverage of the chase and the game on split screen with Marv Albert and Matt Goukas, who were calling the game, giving way to Brokaw's reporting on Simpson.

"It was almost impossible to concentrate on the game," said Hannah Storm, who was reporting for NBC that night, taking on duties covering both teams when Ahmad Rashad, a longtime friend of Simpson's, had to leave the arena.

"It was a surreal convergence of sporting and news events, and our producers were scrambling with all manner of issues."

It was a night like no other, offering a glimpse at the way the Simpson case and trial would provide compelling drama long after the Rockets and Knicks left the stage. As Costas put it two decades later, before ESPN's retelling, it was "a shared event, for better or worse."

6 How Sweep It Is

The Rockets had done everything else. They had rallied from near-impossible deficits. They had won a classic series against the Knicks for the first championship for the franchise and City of Houston. They had lived up to the legacy of "Clutch City," rising from the sixth seed to return to the NBA Finals.

The final step in the two greatest seasons in franchise history was to take a worthy opponent and destroy it, leaving no remaining doubt about the Rockets' place in NBA history.

They had become champions, not just as the holders of the 1994 NBA title, but as the embodiment of the qualities associated with their reign. By the time they arrived in Orlando for the 1995 Finals, they were unbeatable.

The Magic had seemed to be the team ready not just to supplant them as champions, but to begin a long run on top. They had vanquished Michael Jordan and the Bulls. They were built around the prodigious talents of Shaquille O'Neal and Penny Hardaway. They, like every Rockets opponent that postseason, had home-court advantage.

The Magic had put outside shooting from Nick Anderson and Dennis Scott next to Hardaway's playmaking and O'Neal's interior power. They had added Horace Grant as a final piece, a veteran presence with a championship past.

They had their chance to take Game 1. More than a chance, the game was within their grasp. It had everything—a spectacular battle between Shaquille O'Neal and Hakeem Olajuwon, a Rockets comeback from a 20-point deficit, and the clutch three-point shooting of Kenny Smith, who nailed a Finals record five three-pointers in the third quarter. Still, the Magic went into the closing seconds with a three-point lead and Anderson going to the line.

Anderson missed both free throws with a chance to clinch the win, but the Rockets could not control the rebound. They fouled Anderson again, sending him to the line with two more chances to secure Game 1. He again missed both free throws, leaving just enough of an opening.

Smith grabbed the rebound. The Rockets called time out. Rudy Tomjanovich set up a high screen, but Smith pulled up, pump-faked, and waited long enough for Hardaway to sail by before nailing his game-tying three-pointer with 1.6 seconds remaining.

Once in overtime, the Rockets were more convinced than ever they could not be beat, but the Magic did not go quietly. Scott tied the game at 118 with 5.5 seconds remaining. Clyde Drexler drove for the game-winner, but had to put his runner high over O'Neal. He missed, but with O'Neal having moved over to pick up Drexler, Olajuwon batted in the rebound with three-tenths of a second remaining. Olajuwon took a moment to survey the scene initially without realizing that the Rockets had finally secured Game 1, before he saw his teammates celebrate in the suddenly silenced arena, raising his arms in triumph.

The Rockets had overcome the Jazz, Suns, and Spurs, and rallied back from a 20-point deficit to win Game 1, earning a feeling of invincibility that Tomjanovich would not allow. In one more master stroke typical of Tomjanovich's feel for his team and its mentality, he ripped into his players the next day at the Magic training facility in a tirade that thoroughly moved them past Game 1.

The Rockets rolled to a 22-point halftime lead and headed home with a 2–0 series lead after a 117–106 win, the Rockets' record seventh-consecutive postseason win on the road and their record eighth that season.

Game 3 was considerably tougher. Though Olajuwon had 31 points and 14 rebounds and Drexler finished with 25 points and

13 rebounds, the Rockets secured the 106–103 win when Robert Horry nailed a three-pointer with 14 seconds left.

The Rockets pulled away in the fourth quarter, allowing them to finish Game 4 and the series celebrating. If the 1994 Finals was a physical, tough, low-scoring battle, the repeat was earned with a team retooled to shoot threes and put up numbers far beyond the clash with the Knicks. So before Olajuwon would take his second-consecutive MVP Award, he added a fitting, final exclamation point, nailing a corner three to give him 35 points in the clincher.

"It was just wonderful winning the back-to-back champion-ships at home," Olajuwon said. "It's wonderful to win at home, because you can celebrate that with the rest of the city. That was special."

Moments after the victory was complete, with confetti pouring down, Tomjanovich defined his team.

"We had nonbelievers all along the way," Tomjanovich said, "and I have one thing to say to those nonbelievers: Don't ever underestimate the *heart of a champion!*"

A year earlier, he had shared the feelings of the city finally breaking through, citing the long wait for the first championship. After the 1995 Finals, Tomjanovich considered all that it had taken to repeat, all his team had overcome.

"I don't have a word to describe how I feel about this team," Tomjanovich said that night. "Their character. Their guts. No one in the history of the league has done what this team has done."

The Rockets had gone through the 60-win Jazz, the 59-win Suns, and the 62-win Spurs just to get to the Magic, a team still getting better after a 57-win season. They became the first and still only team to win a championship without home-court advantage in any round. They were then just the fifth repeat champion, and just the sixth to win The Finals in a sweep.

They had pulled off the stunning February trade for Drexler, drastically changing their rotation and style. They had overcome

Shaquille O'Neal attempts to block Hakeem Olajuwon's shot during the first quarter of Game 3 of the 1995 Finals. (Tom Spitz/KRT/ Newscom)

injuries and doubts and turmoil. They triumphed not just with Olajuwon at his peak, the return of his Phi Slama Jama running mate and a team perfectly built around him, but with determination and, as Tomjanovich put it, heart that could not be beat.

"I always had a perspective of looking at the positives they did and tried to create things out of that—what kind of people they were to do the things we did," Tomjanovich said. "I don't know if it will ever be duplicated, coming from the sixth spot, winning 10 elimination games in a row."

That earned the 1995 champions their place in league history. For Houston, it was proof, validation of the '94 title, and the long-sought championship that escaped Olajuwon and Drexler at the University of Houston. So before he left the court that night, Drexler took the microphone and borrowed Gene Peterson's customary radio broadcast adage after Rockets wins, shouting, "How sweet it is!"

7 The Heart of a Champion

With a microphone in his face and the cameras moving in for one last close-up, Rudy Tomjanovich did what he always had before. He spoke from the heart.

He had not prepared the comments that will never be forgotten. He did not mean to produce the phrase now a part of motivational speeches and rallying cries in every sport and beyond.

Rudy T was just Rudy T, ever defiant in the face of doubts as he always had been, endlessly proud not just of the talent, but of the character of the team he had taken to consecutive championships.

Asked to share his thoughts, he uttered perhaps the most iconic, most unforgettable, most widely appropriated phrase ever in a trophy presentation.

"We had non-believers all along the way, and I have one thing to say to those non-believers," Tomjanovich said. "Don't ever underestimate the heart of a champion!"

With that, the Rockets became role models for every team or player aspiring to have the "heart" the Rockets had demonstrated.

The phrase is still tossed around regularly.

"We showed the heart of a champion."

"It's tough to beat the heart of a champion."

A season rarely passes in which it is not brought up. The broadcasts of the NBA Finals usually begin with a video montage that includes Tomjanovich on that podium. But the joyful admonition was very specific to that team and that time.

"The thing that was so good about our guys, when our backs were against the wall, nobody was better," Tomjanovich said. "It was like a fairy tale, it really was."

The Rockets had struggled in the defense of their first title. On Valentine's Day, they traded their starting power forward, Otis Thorpe, for Clyde Drexler, a move celebrated in Houston but panned nationally.

They entered the playoffs as a sixth seed, holding a middling 47–35 record, further removed from the upper echelon of the standings than any team had ever been on its way to a title.

In the first round best-of-five series against the Jazz, the Rockets trailed by 13 in the fourth quarter and rallied to the win.

In the second round, they trailed the Suns 3–1, just as they'd trailed them 2–1 the year before, and again rallied to win in seven games.

In the Western Conference Finals, they faced a Spurs team that had swept them in the regular season and were going against the newly crowned MVP, David Robinson. The Rockets won in six games, with Olajuwon at the height of his powers.

By the time the Rockets swept the Spurs for a second-consecutive title, they were more certain than ever they could not be stopped. There were still doubts about them with the Magic loaded with the abundant youthful talent of Shaquille O'Neal and Penny Hardaway and a team masterfully built around them.

When the Rockets took Game 1 in overtime, they were on a roll the Magic were not ready to stop. The Rockets rolled to the title and Tomjanovich's unforgettable description about them.

The line, however, was adopted from one of the players the Rockets had defeated along the way, Suns point guard Kevin Johnson.

"Actually, I stole it from Kevin Johnson," Tomjanovich told the *Houston Chronicle* years later. "After we came back to beat Phoenix in one of those early playoff games, I remember reading his comments. He said, 'Those guys are like cockroaches. You keep trying to step on them, but they always scurry away and come back. They have the heart of a champion.'

"In that moment up there after we clinched, it just came back to me. It was my response to all of the doubters. It said everything about us."

Tomjanovich said friends often told him he sounded like a scolding parent with the term, "Don't ever…" But the sentiment spoke to the quality that meant the most to Tomjanovich.

"Being a champion just doesn't happen," Tomjanovich said in the NBA-TV video *Clutch City*. "You've got to go through a war. I don't know any team that doesn't—just like any family—that doesn't have to go through some adversity, some difference of opinion, some hard feelings, some tears.

"But the team that doesn't let that stuff bother them, and they go through the storms, they tie things down when things get tough, and they get through it… to me, that's what a champion is."

More specifically, is the measure of "The Heart of a Champion."

8 The Real MVP

David Robinson was a deserving MVP. Whether he was the most deserving could be debated as long as his selection was not unanimous, but he had led the Spurs to the best record in the NBA and a regular-season sweep of Hakeem Olajuwon and the Rockets.

When David Stern handed him the MVP trophy, with roars and MVP placards filling the Alamodome, Olajuwon watched silently from the other end of the court. The Rockets had won 47 games that season, the Spurs 62. But Olajuwon was, until that moment, the reigning MVP. He was a champion. He was intently proud and at the height of his powers.

Robinson was humble and gracious as always as he made his acceptance speech, but he also made an error as damaging as leaping for one of Olajuwon's pump fakes. He cited former MVPs. He did not mention Olajuwon.

"I was standing right there," former Rockets forward Tracy Murray said in the *Clutch City* documentary. "Kenny Smith was hyping up Dream like Don King hyping up Mike Tyson, telling him that Robinson was stealing his trophy."

On Olajuwon's other side, Clyde Drexler told his friend it was disrespectful for the Spurs and NBA to hold the ceremony in front of him, and then stomped away, feigning anger at the insult.

Olajuwon grabbed Drexler by the arm and said, "Do not worry. We will get the big trophy."

Olajuwon's own feelings have long been debated. He has always insisted that he understood the choice of Robinson. The numbers were close that season with Olajuwon averaging 27.8 points, Robinson 27.6; Olajuwon averaging 3.4 blocked shots,

Robinson 3.2; and both averaging 10.8 rebounds. But the Spurs' record crushed the Rockets', as Olajuwon pointed out.

Olajuwon's teammates, however, will never believe that Olajuwon, ultra-competitive and supremely focused, was not driven to make a point.

"We all saw the look on Dream's face, and I think Dream considered the whole ceremony to be disrespectful," Rockets forward Chucky Brown told the *Houston Press*. "He just went to work."

Olajuwon had everything working, mercilessly hitting Robinson with drives to dunks and soft-touch jumpers. He rapid-fired head fakes and spin moves until the league's MVP was "bamboozled," as iconic Rockets broadcaster Bill Worrell put it. Olajuwon put up 41 points with 16 rebounds as the Rockets took a 2–0 series lead.

"Who are the idiots who voted Hakeem fifth for MVP?" Rockets guard Sam Cassell said that night.

The Spurs did not go quietly, winning both games in Houston to even the series. But when Olajuwon returned to the floor in San Antonio's football stadium, he dominated again. By then, it was apparent, Robinson and the Spurs were powerless to stop him.

Olajuwon put up 42 points with nine rebounds, eight assists, and five blocked shots in Game 5. In Game 6, Olajuwon rolled again, demonstrating signature moves that had Robinson nearly leaping from his path. Olajuwon had 39 points on 16-of-25 shooting, adding 17 rebounds. Robinson, uncharacteristically tentative, made just 6 of 17 shots for 19 points.

When the series was over, he was right on target.

"I don't know how I can say this with a straight face," Robinson said, "but I thought I defended him pretty well. He played at a level I haven't seen often."

He was right. Robinson did not play badly. He was not an undeserving MVP. He had pushed Olajuwon to his most spectacular. Olajuwon averaged 35.3 points on 56 percent shooting in the series, along with 12.3 rebounds, five assists, and 4.2 blocked shots. Robinson averaged 23.8 points, 11.3 rebounds, 2.7 assists, and 2.2blocked shots.

"I had to give him one, two, three, and four fakes, just to get my shot off, because he [always] recovered," Olajuwon said. "It was a true championship series. I don't think I've ever played better than that, because nobody pushed me to that level before."

When the Rockets swept Shaquille O'Neal and the Magic in the NBA Finals, Olajuwon was proved correct. He received another Finals MVP Award. He also got the "big trophy" he told Drexler they would claim on the night Robinson was handed the MVP.

Whether he was offended or driven by that will never be entirely clear. He could have used it. He might have been lifted by the respect he had for his opponent. He made it clear, however, that when someone else was the MVP, he was still better.

"They sorta owned us all season," Tomjanovich told NBA. com. "They felt they had our number. Then there was that MVP ceremony and this is how I see it in my mind's eye: I see them presenting that trophy to David Robinson. I had to look right through Hakeem, who was standing in my line of vision. My thought was: *I wonder how he feels about that?* It wasn't a big thing. Just, *I wonder what's going through his mind right now?* Then we found out."

9 Happy Valentine's Day

The image remains a symbol of triumph and joy, a partnership at last rewarded for its greatness.

Amid the celebration of the Rockets' run to the 1995 NBA championship, completed with the sweep of the Orlando Magic, Hakeem Olajuwon found Clyde Drexler. With beaming smiles shining a light on all they'd shared, from the shocking disappointment in Albuquerque with the University of Houston and through Hall of Fame careers, they slapped a high five as the camera clicked and rolled, as if the moment had been scripted to provide 1,000 words worth that unforgettable picture.

Four months earlier, on Valentine's Day, Drexler made his way through the mid-court entrance to the court, the trade from the Trail Blazers home to Houston complete, for a lovefest at The Summit.

The reaction around the country, however, was very different. Had there already been the explosion of social media that would come in the decades ahead, the Rockets would have been roasted through the remainder of the season.

They broke up the starting lineup of a championship team. They dealt Otis Thorpe, who was not only their rock-solid power forward, but a reliable backup behind Olajuwon. They had, the argument elsewhere went, panicked.

In Houston, however, they had landed a hometown hero and put him in position to complete the championship chase he and Olajuwon could not finish as members of Phi Slama Jama. When Drexler was introduced during the game that night, the roars would rival the celebration to come four months later.

"I couldn't be happier," Drexler said that night. "This is the one place that I'd rather be than anywhere else [in the league]. I was raised here, and I've got all my family here. I talked to my mom when I got here, and she was so ecstatic, she started to cry. It's a tremendous feeling."

The deal delivered the proven No. 2 scorer the Rockets had sought for years. The Rockets had tried to trade for Sean Elliott the previous season, but negated the deal when Elliott failed his physical. A season (and a championship) later, they became unwilling to include Robert Horry in a deal, as they had in the Elliott trade, making it difficult to find the scorer they wanted.

"It's too good to be true," Olajuwon said after the trade was complete. "I can't believe it. Now our team is going to be different. We'll have more speed. Clyde is a natural athlete who creates so many opportunities."

In Drexler, the Rockets not only landed the sort of second star they had long sought, they signaled the mindset that would guide Rockets owner Leslie Alexander throughout his tenure.

Alexander always sought stars, from Charles Barkley and Tracy McGrady to James Harden and Chris Paul, even if he had to gamble greatly and give up large packages of talent. Never did that work out as well as with Drexler.

Initially, however, the Rockets struggled, increasing the criticism of the deal. The Rockets went 17–18 the rest of the season, finishing as the sixth seed in the Western Conference. But Rockets coach Rudy Tomjanovich increasingly moved to the smaller, range-shooting lineups that would help change NBA offenses. He moved away from Pete Chilcutt and Carl Herrera as Thorpe's successors and Chucky Brown and the postseason starter, to using Horry as a power forward to close games.

Drexler, meanwhile, took off when the postseason began, living up to all those hopes and promises from the night of the trade. In the first-round series against the Utah Jazz, Drexler averaged 25.2 points per game, including 41 and 31 in the final two games to complete the comeback from a 2–1 deficit in the best-of-five series.

Against the Phoenix Suns, before Mario Elie's "Kiss of Death" three-pointer to win it, Drexler scored 29 points as the Rockets moved to the Western Conference Finals. Drexler averaged 20.5 points, five assists, and seven rebounds in that postseason, and 21.5 points, 6.8 assists, and 9.5 rebounds in The Finals. He played just 3½ seasons with the Rockets, but was so revered, his number was retired in in 2000. He returned as a broadcaster in the 2005–06 season.

Most of all, he delivered on the promise made on Valentine's Day, 1995.

When the Rockets swept the Magic, Drexler and Olajuwon shared that high five and a hug, champions together at last, just as they had envisioned when they were teammates long before, and especially on the night they reunited in Houston.

"The Dream is the best in the game," Drexler had said that night. "All he needs is a little help and we can win another championship."

10 Moses Malone and "Four Guys from Petersburg"

Moses Malone did not intend to be talking about himself, much less to define his role with the Rockets, but no one ever put it better.

Malone famously said, "I could get four guys off the street in Petersburg" and beat the 1981 Celtics. He was wrong. He couldn't. The Rockets lost the 1981 NBA Finals in six games to Larry Bird, series MVP Cedric Maxwell, and the Celtics. But Malone had established himself as the quintessential carry-the-team superstar.

The Rockets had gone 40–42 that season, trying to run through much of a season before a late-season loss to the Celtics convinced Del Harris to hit the brakes and put the Rockets' post-season chances on Malone's broad back.

Malone had been built to carry a team, with a relentless drive that made him so brutish a rebounder he could miss shots— intentionally, some still argue—and power his way to the rebound. He averaged a career-best 27.8 points that season, to be topped by his career-high 31.1 the following season, while grabbing a league-best 14.8 rebounds.

The Rockets beat the Lakers in the first round before emerging from a tough seven-game series against the Spurs. When they rolled past the Kansas City Kings, in five games, the Celtics were waiting.

The Rockets had some talent with Billy Paultz, Tom Henderson, Mike Dunleavy, and Bill Willoughby, but even with Calvin Murphy still scoring away late in his career, they did not have the Hall of Fame–bound collection of the Celtics. Rudy Tomjanovich had been hurt during the season and rarely played in The Finals of his last NBA season.

When the Celtics played the 76ers in the Eastern Conference Finals, Maxwell had called the series the real NBA Finals, inspiring Malone to label the Celtics "chumps" and to say, "They ain't that good." By Game 1, the Rockets showed they could make it a series, leading much of the way, before Bird made one of the most memorable shots of his career, rushing in for the rebound of his own missed 18-footer and shifting the ball from his right hand to his left to flip in a one-motion, running jumper.

The Celtics took a three-point win, but the Rockets evened the series in Game 2, with Malone scoring 31 points with 15 rebounds. Allen Leavell scored late to give the Rockets the win, their eighth postseason game on the road, a record that stood until the Rockets' 1995 run to the title.

The teams split the games in Houston, with Malone his dominating best on the boards in Game 4, when he grabbed 22 rebounds.

With that, Malone's "four guys" quote was blasted in bold type headlines. His hometown might have had great basketball talent, but the Celtics were deeper. With Bird struggling with the defense of Robert Reid, Maxwell took over, scoring 28 points with 15 rebounds in the Celtics' 109–80 rout.

With the series back in Houston, the Celtics rolled again, before a stunning comeback brought the Rockets from down 17 to within three. Bird, however, found his shot, keying his late run with his only three-pointer of the series. The Celtics pulled away. Boston took the series in six games.

The next season might have been the most dominant of Malone's career. He averaged 31.1 points and 14.7 rebounds with 6.9 of those boards coming off the offensive glass.

Moses Malone (24) tries to knock the ball from Larry Bird, while Bill Willoughby (32) comes in to assist during Game 1 of the 1981 NBA Finals. (AP Photo)

That was Moses Malone of the Rockets, outworking opponents to—and on—the offensive boards. He did not have a pretty game. He did not rely on grace. Though he'd added a soft shooting touch over the years, Malone in Houston was about his brutish determination to pound opponents and push himself to exhaustion with competitive drive few could ever match.

He played 19 seasons in the NBA. His top five seasons on the offensive boards were all in Houston.

"More than any player I've watched or worked with closely, nobody did more to fulfill his responsibility to try to win a game than Moses," former Rockets general manager Carroll Dawson told the *Houston Chronicle* in 2006. "He absolutely loved to play the game and did it to his physical limits every time he ever played.

"I used to sit on the bench and watch him work like nobody else to get rebounds, to put in follow shots. I'd see him play 48 minutes and then come into the locker room and literally collapse in his locker. It would actually take five or 10 minutes before he could even move."

After the 1981–82 season, however, the Rockets were sold to Charlie Thomas. Malone had won his second MVP, but the Rockets lost in the first round of the playoffs to the Seattle SuperSonics. A restricted free agent, Malone signed with the 76ers. Several clauses in the deal were not permitted by the league, but the deal was considered so great, paying Malone $2.2 million a year, that the Rockets worked out a trade to send Malone to Philadelphia.

That began the Rockets rebuilding toward the Twin Towers era. Malone won another MVP and issued another postseason declaration, with "Fo, fo, fo," his prediction of three playoff sweeps that was nearly met, even more celebrated in NBA history than his "Four guys" boast. Over the years, Malone mentored Hakeem Olajuwon, Dominque Wilkins, and Charles Barkley. At Malone's funeral, after his passing at just 60 years old in 2015, Barkley referred to Malone simply as "Dad." The court at Fonde

Recreation Center, the Houston proving ground where Malone ruled well into his fifties, was named in his honor.

"He made you smile," Barkley said. "He made you laugh. And he loved everybody. He helped everybody. From the rookies on, he treated everybody great. He was a wonderful man."

Rockets teammates Tomjanovich, Murphy, John Lucas, and Major Jones attended the service in the church that had been The Summit, the Rockets' home when Malone played. Julius Erving and Maurice Cheeks, with whom Malone won the 1983 NBA championship with the 76ers, were there, along with Wilkins, Ralph Sampson, Clyde Drexler, George Gervin, Artis Gilmore, Alex English, and Tracy McGrady.

"He did it his own way," Erving said, comparing basketball's "Chairman of the Boards" to another. "You have to compare him to Frank Sinatra, a guy who did it his own way and in the process, changed everything. Moses wasn't the smoothest. He wasn't the most articulate. There's a short list of things he wasn't and a long list of things that he was.

"I feel like he completed his mission. He always had a mission, the message that he carried around in his bible. He did what it said. He was a man who loved his family, loved life to the fullest, and got the most out of his time here."

With the Rockets, his mission was to carry his team to greater heights than anyone else thought possible. He did not win that title in 1981, but in a sense, his mission was accomplished.

11 The Trade That Wasn't

Robert Horry still has his Pistons uniform. It has never been worn in an NBA game. It never hung in a locker room waiting for him to pull it on. But it has a place of honor in his game room, a reminder of the trade that never happened and the way it transformed him.

Matt Bullard kept his, too. Though a player that for more than two decades has been identified by his career in Houston, he had wanted to wear the Pistons colors.

For a few hours, Bullard and Horry felt like Pistons. The Rockets had traded them to Detroit to make Sean Elliott the perfect-fit small forward they lacked. But Bullard and Horry never officially were members of the Pistons.

They went to Auburn Hills. They met with coaches and players. They sat in a suite, eating popcorn and drinking beer. They saw the Pistons retire the number of former sixth man and star Vinnie Johnson. But the deal never went through, with Rockets doctors unwilling to sign off on Elliott's physical because of a kidney condition that several years later would lead to a transplant, returning him to the Pistons and bringing Horry and Bullard back to the Rockets.

It was the best thing that could have happened to them. Though they felt very differently at the time and neither could have known how fortunate they were.

When the trade was rescinded, Elliot was indignant, Bullard disappointed, and Horry determined.

Bullard had welcomed the change. Coming back from a knee injury, he saw a chance to advance his career.

"I get to Detroit and Don Chaney was the coach," Bullard said. "He was my first coach with the Rockets. As soon as I got there, I went to his office. He said, 'We're so happy to have you here. We're going to run these plays for you.' I was thinking, *You're going to run plays for me?* I went to practice, and Isiah Thomas came up to me, 'We're so glad to have you.' I was thinking, *This is going to work out just fine.*"

Horry was angry. The Rockets were 32–11. They had matched the best start in NBA history, winning their first 15 games. He had been a willing role player, defending and rebounding and taking only the occasional shots that came his way while playing with Hakeem Olajuwon.

"We hit a little hiccup there, but I felt like everything was meshing," Horry said. "We had a great defensive team. Sean wasn't going to be the defensive player they wanted him to be. For me, I was like top 10 shot-blocker, top 10 steals, and you get rid of me. I'm what you need."

Both had sensed there was a deal coming. When they were told that they would be sent back to Houston, they reacted very differently. Bullard, who would become far more tightly associated with the Rockets by finishing his career in Houston and becoming a longtime analyst on the television broadcasts, was disappointed. Horry, who would win championships with the Lakers and Spurs, was defiant, determined to be the sort of player the Rockets wanted in Elliott, to show the team that had drafted and traded him they were wrong about him.

"When we got the call and were told we were going back to Houston, I was mad and Robert was happy," Bullard said.

Elliott was despondent. He had wanted the trade and considered retiring. He did not blame the Rockets for rescinding the deal, but wanted out of Detroit, signing with the Spurs as a free agent the following summer and winning a championship in 1999.

Bullard became Rudy Tomjanovich's first range-shooting four, leading to the changes in NBA offenses since. Horry, with an attitude adjustment that came straight from the trade, became Big Shot Bob.

"I came back with a fuck-you attitude," Horry said. "I said 'I'm probably the only player in the history of basketball that got traded for not shooting the ball.' There was one game I came back they told me, 'Can you pass the ball a little more.' I was like, 'No, y'all traded me for not shooting. I'm going to show you.' I came back focused on offense.

"It changed me…. I'm going to just play, have fun, enjoy the game."

Four months after that night spent in a Palace of Auburn Hills suite, Horry and Bullard were part of the Rockets' first championship team. A season later, the Rockets traded Otis Thorpe, and Horry became their late-game power forward, ushering in the change of NBA offenses, and becoming a key to the Rockets second title.

Horry won three more championships with the Lakers, two with the Spurs. But it all started when he was told he was traded, but never officially was.

"I let it go," Horry said. "I viewed it as a couple days off and the Rockets making a huge mistake. I didn't look at it as any more than that. Bull came back and kind of held a grudge. I said it was the nature of the beast. It didn't bother me at all.

"I told Rudy, 'Dude, trust me. I knew this was a business from Day One. I knew when you wouldn't pay me more than that bum [Adam Keefe] who was drafted in front of me. I ain't stupid. I'm just going to go out and prove to you I can score.'"

He proved that and more, with an attitude that helped make him one of the most clutch shooters of all time. He might have become all that even if not sent the message of a trade that never happened, but it helped, with a reminder still hanging on his wall with the artifacts from all the success that followed.

12 Thunder and a Lightning Strike

Rockets general manager Daryl Morey had made his final offer and knew that it was enough. But he was no more optimistic that he would land James Harden than he had been in all the times he had pursued a star only to fall just short.

He had made his pitch to Oklahoma City general manager Sam Presti for more than a year and knew what would get the deal done. Talks had picked up four months earlier around the draft and weeks later when Morey landed the first-round pick from Toronto that would be key to the deal. But he doubted there would be a deal at all, with the Thunder still negotiating to sign Harden to a $52 million, four-year contract extension.

Morey was convinced Harden could be a face-of-the-franchise star, but could only wait. The call came at about 1:00 PM on October 27, 2012, with Presti saying he would make the trade.

Harden was out to dinner with his family that night when he was told and was in Houston by noon the next day, stunned by how his life had changed. He said he was confident he could live up to the job, but also cautious as he took in everything that had changed.

He'd wanted the job of franchise star and got it, and three days later he'd also have the $80 million contract to go with it. But on the day Morey finally made the sort of deal he had pursued for years, he never thought it would happen.

"I absolutely thought they were using our interest to pressure the completion of a deal with James," Morey said. "[The deal to trade for Harden] was done at that point. We had finished what deal we were going to do. They were just going to call back me if they were in."

Gersson Rosas, the Rockets' vice president and Morey's front-office right-hand man, had sent a text message, knowing how Morey was suffering. Morey is nearly always the pessimist. As many deals as he had completed, never letting a trade deadline go without making a move, he almost never thinks he will succeed. Rosas tends to be more optimistic.

"I told [Morey], 'This is it. This one has got to go through,'" Rosas said. "I felt really good."

The Rockets had chased franchise players for years since injuries shortened the runs of Yao Ming and Tracy McGrady. They nearly landed Dwight Howard at the trade deadline. When that failed, they made the deal to send Kyle Lowry to Toronto for a first-round pick, believing a lottery pick would be a stronger trade asset. They again fell short, with the Magic choosing a three-team deal in which they would get Aaron Afflalo rather than the Rockets' offer with Kevin Martin.

Finally, that pick would be a key to the offer with the Thunder. The Rockets would add Martin to give Oklahoma City, considered a championship contender, a sixth man to replace Harden. They would add the first of the three players they had just taken in the draft, Jeremy Lamb, to give the Thunder the sort of prospect they would be unlikely to draft themselves while picking late in future first rounds.

Oklahoma City was coming off a Finals run, having already locked up Kevin Durant, Russell Westbrook, and Serge Ibaka, making it difficult to sign Harden, too. The Rockets gave them an option.

Presti made his final contract offer to Harden's agent, Rob Pelinka, now the Lakers' general manager. Morey made his final trade offer to Presti. Then, they waited.

When Harden turned down the last offer from the Thunder, Presti chose the Rockets' package rather than allow Harden to become a free agent after the following season. He called Morey, then found a stunned Harden to tell him the news.

The Thunder would select Steven Adams with the pick from Toronto, and Mitch McGary and Alex Abrines with the picks from the Rockets. Oklahoma City did not make the expected postseason run, with Westbrook hurt in the first-round series against the Rockets. Martin left as a free agent. Lamb never carved out a place in the Oklahoma City rotation.

Rather than the four-year, $52 million deal offered by the Thunder, he was signed to a five-year contract worth nearly $80 million days later, receiving super-max contract extensions twice since. From his first game with the Rockets, against the Pistons, when he had 37 points with 12 assists and six rebounds, he has been the dominant face of the franchise.

"We definitely thought franchise-level player," Morey said. "Runner-up MVP, that's a very hard thing to forecast. That's really unfair. We decided he could be the best player on a championship-level team."

Harden had gotten all he wanted. He had seen stardom up close playing with Durant. He grew up a devoted fan of Kobe Bryant. He had his chance to join them.

"I've always been confident, but when things come your way, you sit back and try to figure out your surroundings," Harden said. "Being in Houston, I was confident I would be successful. When the trade happened, I thought I was going to be good, but I was trying to figure this thing out."

Morey, meanwhile, had finally completed the biggest trade of his career. Less than a week later, he was in the front row in Auburn Hills, Michigan, watching the first of many games Harden would own.

"That," he said, "is why we got that... guy."

13 The Beard

James Harden wanted it all. Before he or anyone else thought that possible for him, he wanted greatness and all he imagined that comes with that, from the perks to the pressures.

From growing up with Kobe Bryant for a hero, to leaving a note for his mother, Monja Willis, when he was only 12 years old that ended "Imma be a star," to his three-year apprenticeship for stardom with the Oklahoma City Thunder, Harden had envisioned the NBA stardom that he later found with the Rockets.

He had to become a greater player, better even than the pick-and-roll master that he had been, according to Rockets general manager Daryl Morey's data analysis. He had to learn all that comes with being the face of a franchise, responsibility that had largely fallen to Kevin Durant in Oklahoma City with the remainder spilling over to Russell Westbrook. He had to become a leader.

Harden, however, had arrived in the NBA as the third player taken in the 2009 Draft and got to Houston, following the stunning trade days before the 2012 season, determined to take all that on.

"It's going to take some time," Harden said that day, "but I think I'm ready for it."

Looking back, he called those days "a whirlwind," from turning down a final Thunder offer $6 million shy of the maximum, to a Saturday night flight on former Rockets owner Leslie Alexander's jet, to those heady first games with the Rockets just days later. He scored 37 points with 12 assists in his first game with the Rockets and 45 points in his second game, knowing from then on he could rise to the new demands placed on him.

"It happened very quick," Harden said. "One minute I was at dinner with my family. The next minute I'm heading to Houston.

Moving to a different city, a different role, a different organization, it was completely new to me.

"I get traded to a younger organization trying to find its identity. For me, it was, *How am I going to do? How am I going to find my way in this league? How am I going to make my name in this league, put my stamp on this league?*"

Harden had drilled himself into a top player. Growing up in Compton, California, he played constantly and chased the best competition he could find around Los Angeles. The courts were, he said, his "safe house." He led Artesia to consecutive state championships and brought Arizona State to the NCAA Tournament.

"Wherever there were games, there was basketball, good competition, I would go," Harden said. "There were too many I got whipped. That's what made me who I am. There were older guys, guys more physical, guys that were better than me. My competitive nature came out. Most of the time, I didn't win. That's what made me.

"There's been plenty of situations I was the underdog and didn't win. Sometimes I won. Sometimes I got my [butt] kicked."

Even after nine NBA seasons, Harden searches for summer runs in the Drew League. He has added more drill work to his regimen. He remains devoted to his routine, when he shoots, the shots he takes. But for all that had changed, all the ways he is viewed, he still is drawn most to the time on the courts.

"It just shows the passion, the love I have for it, I've been having since I was a little kid," Harden said. I think every basketball player has had it. It changes. As you get older, some people fall out of love with the game or lose touch with the game. For me, that connection that was there from when I was a little kid got even better. I think it got even better because of the things I've seen in the game. It's everything."

Along the way, Harden would develop a modern mix of the streetball magic and a professional's mastery of the game. He would

January 30, 2018, Houston, Texas: P.J. Tucker hugs James Harden after Harden's historic 60-point triple-double led the Rockets past the Magic, 114–107. (Erik Williams/USA TODAY Sports)

lead the league in assists one year, scoring the next. He would set records for everything from the only 60-point triple double in NBA history to his four-year, $228 million contract extension signed in the summer of 2017.

Harden had averaged 29.1 points, 11.2 assists, and 8.1 rebounds the previous season, the first player since Oscar Robertson to averaged 29 points, 11 assists, and eight rebounds in a season, finishing as the MVP runner-up for the second time in three seasons. He averaged 30.4 points, 8.8 assists, and 5.4 rebounds in 2017–18, joining Michael Jordan as the only player to average at least 30 points, eight assists, five rebounds, and 1.7 steals in a season.

"He's… the best offensive player I've ever seen," Rockets coach Mike D'Antoni said. "He's got everything."

The Rockets won a franchise record 65 games that season with Harden seeming more at ease with the role and responsibilities that came with his place as the focus of everything the Rockets do.

"These last few years are probably when I've been most comfortable," Harden said. "I worked hard, I always put the time in, but the trust and having the guys around me and the coaching staff to encourage me to go out there and not worry about anything but being me is probably the most confidence that I've had since I've been here."

More than the Rockets franchise player, Harden had become one of the NBA's signature stars, with dozens of sponsorship deals and commercials and other ad campaigns. That too was part of the plan, or at least his idea of the life of an NBA star.

"This is what I dreamed of," Harden said. "This is one of the reasons I play basketball, to market myself, to show the world what kind of person I am, what kind of player I am."

Harden had often said his goal as a player was simple. "I want to be great," he said, even before he truly was. Off the court, he wanted that kind of status as well.

"That everyone loves James," Harden said. "Whether it's his personality, whether it's his game on the court, whether it's how he markets himself, James is someone I would look up to."

Over the years, he became less interested in how he is viewed. Friends say he pays little attention to outside praise or criticism. With Harden, there is so much of both it would be difficult to keep up. But by then, he had all that he dreamed of. He was unquestionably a star, among the world's best and most recognizable players. He had a coach, Mike D'Antoni, that had given him his offense and respect, teammates assembled to play with him, and an organization that staked its future on him.

"It's rare that you feel so welcome, that you feel like you're at home and feel like every single day you wake up to go to work and have people around you to motivate you, that push you to be better, that you love to be around," Harden said.

"I don't want to go anywhere. I know where home is. I know where I want to be. I know where I want to retire ultimately. And I know where I want to win a championship. Everything is going to happen in Houston."

14 Trade Day

The deal was not made during a pair of free throws, but that's where it started.

With the Rockets facing the Los Angeles Clippers in a late-season game, James Harden asked Chris Paul about joining him. Paul had carried the Clippers' offense long enough. Harden needed help. As in the first meetings retold in romantic comedies, they met cute.

Work had to be done, however. The Rockets did not have anywhere near the cap space to add another max player, though Rockets general manager Daryl Morey was convinced he could move the contracts if he had to.

Instead, Paul told the Clippers he was gone, either in a trade to the Rockets or as a free agent.

The Clippers had been around Paul long enough to know he would not be sweet-talked to change his mind, so the work began to build a package of players the Clippers would want to fill their roster, and for the Rockets to bring in non-guaranteed contracts in the frenzy of deals needed to ship west.

The start of the deal made sense. Patrick Beverley had gone from happy to sign any minimum NBA contract to underpaid with a four-year, $25 million deal. He wanted the ball in order play his way to a richer contract and let the Rockets know of his dissatisfaction. With Paul in Houston, it made sense to send Beverley to Los Angeles.

Lou Williams was a known commodity, an instant-offense reserve that would bring scoring punch. Montrezl Harrell and Sam Dekker, both still on their initial deals, had shown enough potential to be worth a look. They headed to the Clippers with Beverley.

From there, the Rockets had to pile up non-guaranteed contracts.

They started with Kyle Wiltjer off their own roster, then went shopping, bringing in a few pieces to move on to Los Angeles, and a few more as they spent their last bits of 2016–17 trade cash.

They acquired Ryan Kelly from Atlanta, DeAndre Liggins from Dallas, Darrun Hilliard from Detroit, and Tim Quarterman from Portland, all for cash considerations. They picked up Shawn Long from Philadelphia in exchange for a future second round pick and cash considerations.

When they were through, they sent Beverley, Dekker, Harrell, Hilliard, Liggins, Williams, Wiltjer, a future first-round pick, and, of course, cash considerations to the Clippers for Paul.

In one day that tested the stamina of NBA lawyers through a series of trade calls, the Rockets made six trades involving 10 players, two picks, and several mountains of cash.

A day later, as if treating a hangover with some hair of the dog, they made another similar deal, picking Jarrod Uthoff from Dallas for a bit more cash.

The Rockets pulled off more deals than necessary to complete the trade for Paul, but once they started talking, they had trades lined up and took the opportunity to check out some prospects.

Of the players other than Paul acquired on that long, crazy day, only Quarterman made it to camp. Only Hilliard and Liggins spent much time on NBA rosters in the subsequent season.

CP3

Before he had celebrated his first win in a Rockets uniform, Chris Paul had run fundraisers to benefit Harvey victims. Before he truly knew his way around town, he battled Houston traffic on his long commute to work. He teamed with James Harden in a Drew League game. He threw out the first pitch at an Astros game. He helped organize the Rockets' Bahamian mini-camp.

He had barely enough time to get sweaty on the Rockets practice court before he fit in as if he had always been in Houston, always shared a backcourt with Harden and run Mike D'Antoni's offense.

Shoot more threes? Check. Take turns at the point? No problem. The idea that he would have to adjust to shooting more often, an issue NBA players generally overcome, ended as quickly as the questions many had for how he and Harden would mesh.

The Rockets won the first 15 games Paul played, taking the season opener as he limped through a win at Golden State, and then the first 14 after he returned from the bruised knee he picked up in the final preseason game. The Rockets were so giddy to have him back, they put up a 90-point first half in his first healthy game, the romp in Phoenix.

Paul, however, had gotten together with Harden, initially discussing it during a late-season game in 2017, to chase the championship neither had won. He would eventually tell the Clippers

Chris Paul shoots over Steph Curry during his heroics during Game 5 of the 2018 Western Conference Finals. (AP Photo/Eric Christian Smith)

that he would go to Houston as a free agent if they did not trade him there, a move that would require that he opt in to the final season of his contract to help the Rockets make subsequent moves. When he was introduced in Houston, Paul quoted the motto of Will Ferrell's race car driver, Ricky Bobby, "If you're not first, you're last."

"We talked about the ultimate goal, and that's winning," Paul said of his nearly daily conversations with Harden in the weeks after the trade went through. "Neither one of us has had the opportunity to do that. We talked about how good that will feel. That's what I'm most excited about, to be on this journey with somebody else that wants it as badly as I do."

Even he thought there would be an adjustment period, but there really wasn't. He had developed his mid-range game to work in the tight spaces from his years with two big men—Tyson Chandler and David West in New Orleans, and DeAndre Jordan and Blake Griffin in Los Angeles—on the floor with him. That gave him another weapon when teams mimicked the Spurs' defense against the Rockets in the 2017 playoffs, keeping defenders tight at the three-point line and protecting the rim, but Paul flourished off the ball and on the ball with extra shooters around him.

"I never played with three guys around the three-point line, just spacing the court," Paul said. "I know I can shoot it. I know I can score and stuff like that. I don't have to. I've just always been a guy that takes what the defense gives me. If you're off me, I'm a shooter. If there's two guys on me, I'm going to find the open guy.

"I'm going to find you. I always say, 'There ain't but so many things you can do on a court.' I'm going to find you. I always heard that I like to dribble, dribble," Paul said. "But I'm loving this. I love it. For me, who loves finding guys open shots, it's been a lot of fun."

Paul's 2.5 three-pointers per game in his first season with the Rockets were a career high. Even sharing the load with Harden, his 21.1 points per 36 minutes were the third most in his career.

"He just reads it," D'Antoni said. "He's unbelievable in mid-range, maybe the best in the game. He could always shoot threes. He was over 40 percent [in his last season with the Clippers]. He's just taking more of them.

"He's just smart. He just plays. He's always thinking the game, smart, never taking anything for granted. He's not getting in the Hall of Fame just because he's pretty. He's going there for a reason."

He also went to Houston for a reason. It was not to enjoy the style of offense. Paul often said he hates losing more than he enjoys winning, and it was quickly clear how much he enjoyed winning more often than he ever had. The goal was not even about those wins. It was about the playoffs.

It was fitting then that when his first season with the Rockets ventured beyond any of his first 12 in the NBA, it was Paul who brought the Rockets there. He had perhaps his finest game with the Rockets to clinch his first trip to the Western Conference Finals, scoring 41 points, including 22 in the fourth quarter, to carry the Rockets on a night Harden was sick.

Paul had been tantalizingly close before. After he scored 27 points on his 33rd birthday during the series against the Jazz, he said things "went bad real quick" the previous time his team held a 3–1 lead in the Conference Semifinals, before the stunning 2015 collapse against the Rockets.

With the Rockets, he fit in immediately, won, and kept on winning. When he took the Rockets to the showdown with the Warriors, he was serenaded with a long and loud chant of "CP3, CP3!"

Along the way, he believed he had found a home. He would become a free agent, the result of his decision to complete his contract rather than sign a new one with the move. But from the start, Paul fit in as if his career had led him to the Rockets, the decision on his career path already made.

"That's what happened when the trade happened," Paul said. "I love it here. I love it here."

16 The Coin Flips

The Rockets had done everything that it seemed they could to get the most obvious of No. 1 picks. They lost. They lost a lot, more than any team in franchise history. But that was not enough.

They also needed good fortune to land the life-changing talent they needed. But once they discovered their winning formula, they did it again, paired Ralph Sampson and Hakeem Olajuwon, and changed the way the NBA determines the order of the draft forever.

The Rockets began the long road to the 1983 No. 1 pick when they traded the Most Valuable Player, Moses Malone, betting on a rebuild rather than the expense of keeping him. They had dutifully collapsed, losing their first 10 games and trusting a "process" long before anyone outside the Hinkie family heard of former Rockets vice president Sam Hinkie or the radical tanking system he executed in Philadelphia.

The Rockets, however, still needed good fortune. The trade of Malone had brought them the Cleveland Cavaliers' pick at a time when the worst teams of each conference would flip a coin to determine the draft order. When the Rockets bombed in Charlie Thomas' first season as owner, they thought they would have the top pick no matter how the coin landed, using either the woeful Cavaliers' pick or their own.

Instead, the Indiana Pacers sunk even lower than the Cavaliers, giving them an equal chance at drafting Ralph Sampson.

With a 50/50 chance to land the top pick and no chance anyone would be selected before the 7'4", three-time college player of the year should the Rockets slip to the second pick of the draft, the Rockets even offered the Indiana Pacers a package of players, picks, and a pile of Thomas' cash to assure that the pick would be theirs.

The Pacers turned that down, so a cadre of Rockets officials headed to New York for the coin flip that would determine if it was all worth it.

The night before the coin toss, Thomas, team president Ray Patterson, media relations director Jim Foley, and an entourage of friends and family gathered at Jimmy Weston's, a legendary Manhattan supper club. They dipped lucky silver dollars into glasses of Irish Whiskey. Weston had a clock in the shape of Ireland, with 12 Irish coins representing each hour, removed from the wall and gave it to Foley to bring to the NBA offices for luck.

The next day, Thomas called heads as his daughter Tracy had advised. The silver dollar bounced twice and off a wall before it landed face up on the carpet in commissioner Larry O'Brien's office. The group from Houston that had packed the room, with the spires from St. Patrick's Cathedral seeming to peak in through the windows to watch, celebrated wildly. Foley pulled open his shirt to reveal a t-shirt with the word "Ralph." Champagne corks popped with more waiting back at Weston's and Patterson broke records for hyperbole.

"Sampson is not going to be the player of the decade. He is going to be the player of the century," Patterson said. "Ralph will dominate the league and change basketball. Forget about every other big man you're ever heard about. This is the guy who will be better than them all."

The Rockets giddily selected Sampson with the first pick—the Pacers took Steve Stipanovich as a consolation prize—and chose Rodney McCray, rather than hometown hero Clyde Drexler, with the third pick, believing McCray more of a ready-made contributor than Drexler, who went 14th. The Rockets, however, faded badly down the stretch of Sampson's rookie season, going 3–14 to close the season at 29–53, again the worst record in the Western Conference.

They returned to New York, retracing each step from the year before. They went back to Weston's. They dipped the coins in the whiskey. They commandeered the Irish clock. The next morning, they returned to that same office, this time with new commissioner David Stern to toss the coin. Tracy Thomas again advised her father to call heads, but he never got the chance.

The first coin flip determined which team would make the call for the coin flip to determine the first pick. The Trail Blazers won that flip and made the call: "Tails." Just as it had a year before, the coin landed face up. Once again, Foley opened his jacket and unbuttoned his dress shirt to reveal the one-word plan: "Akeem."

Though they had Sampson in place to revolutionize big man play, the Rockets never hesitated after they won the first pick of the draft again, selecting Hakeem Olajuwon and putting him at center. The Trail Blazers famously chose Sam Bowie, rather than Michael Jordan. In Olajuwon's second season, the Rockets reached the NBA Finals. Less than a decade later, he led them to consecutive championships, becoming the greatest player in franchise history.

He also was the last to have been the target of an NBA coin flip. After the Rockets' consecutive wins, the NBA instituted the lottery system to determine the draft order. Thomas would sell the team in 1993. Ray Patterson had stepped down in 1990, handing the team over to his son Steve, who years later would become the general manager of the Trail Blazers. By 1990, Jimmy Weston's was closed.

The Rockets, however, remained the champions of coin flips, with twin towers to prove it.

17 Ralph

No amount of hyperbole was enough. No player had ever been, or probably could ever again be more heralded than Ralph Sampson when he became the Rockets center.

He was the three-time college player of the year, an idea unthinkable now. He was 7'4", with skills and grace previously thought impossible for a player with that size. He was to make the suffering of the Rockets' 14-win season in 1982–83 all worth it. But much, much more than that was predicted, building expectations impossible to reach.

"Sampson is not going to be the player of the decade; he's going to be the player of the century," Rockets president Ray Patterson gushed, with few arguments. "Ralph will dominate the league and change basketball. Forget about every other big man you've ever heard about. This is the guy who will be better than them all."

Patterson, of course, was charged with selling tickets. He had reason to rave. Marty Blake, the longtime NBA scout, with 30 years of history evaluating talent and nothing at stake, put Sampson in the class with the greatest players he had ever seen, and he saw them all.

"I've seen George Mikan, Wilt Chamberlain, and all the great ones," Blake said the day after the draft. "Ralph Sampson can do more coming into pro ball than any center I've ever seen."

Simpson was such a no-brainer after the Rockets won the coin flip that gave them the rights to the first pick over the Pacers that, upon announcing the actual selection, commissioner Larry O'Brien mocked the idea that there could be any suspense.

"I have a big surprise for all of you," O'Brien said. "The Houston Rockets select Ralph Sampson, University of Virginia."

Sampson showed all that promise quickly. He was Rookie of the Year. He was an All-Star in his first four seasons. He was the All-Star MVP in his second year and second-team All NBA his second and third seasons.

When he joined forces with Hakeem Olajuwon, forming the Twin Towers frontcourt, the Rockets seemed on their way to the greatness expected when they began winning coin flips. Olajuwon would bring interior ferocity. Sampson could employ all those offensive skills without being forced into a round hole of a traditional center, freeing him to play more as he wished, ball-handling and facing up to shoot jumpers.

"I was excited to have another seven-footer, but also a guy who could play and had a passion for the game," Sampson said. "You now had two seven-footers who had multiple skills, shoot the ball, dribble the ball, understand the game. Now, everybody had to compete with us. Between Robert Reid, Rodney McCray, myself, and Hakeem Olajuwon, we band together. Everybody had to ante up. No matter who you were, you had to come to the game ready to play, and we did."

By Sampson's third season, he hit the turning, twisting, re-directed jumper that eliminated the Los Angeles Lakers and sent the Rockets to the NBA Finals against the Celtics.

"When you win a game like that, it takes you to the next level," Sampson said. "It's very emotional."

The Rockets took the Celtics to six games, with Sampson famously fighting with the Celtics' Jerry Sichting in Game 5. Sampson had thrown two rights at Sichting and a left at Dennis

Ralph Sampson (50) goes for a loose ball along with Mark Eaton (53) and Hakeem Olajuwon (34) during a 1985 playoff game. (AP Photo/Ed Kolenovsky)

Johnson before Bill Walton brought him down to the floor. Sampson and Sichting were ejected, but the fight seemed to spark the Rockets, up three at the time, to take a 15-point win and send the series back to Boston.

The Rockets lost the series, with Boston fans all over Sampson, who faded badly in the clincher. But throughout the NBA, even in Los Angeles, the Rockets were thought to be on their way to much more.

The following season, however, when the Rockets returned to Boston Garden, Sampson went up for a rebound between Walton and Scott Wedman and landed hard on his back. He hit his head in the paint under the Rockets basket with a thud that silenced the Garden. He reported temporary paralysis in his right leg, but the damage to his hip would last much longer.

He came back in a week, overcompensating for the hip injury and exacerbating his knee problems. He slipped on a wet spot in Denver and needed arthroscopic surgery, putting him out for eight weeks. When Sampson returned, he had lost much of the agility that made him so special. He lost his explosiveness. He could not cut and turn as he once had. So many of the things he needed to play forward with Olajuwon at center were gone.

By December of 1987, only 18 months after Sampson and the Rockets had taken down the Lakers, the Rockets traded him to Golden State for Sleepy Floyd and Joe Barry Carroll. He had shown all that promise, but never could fulfill it, never quite fitting with the style and tastes of Bill Fitch, never escaping the expectations, but also never being anything but unique and, in his own way, special.

18 Twin Towers

There was never a question the Rockets would draft Ralph Sampson when they got the chance. They failed hard to get that coin-flip chance to get him. Any team would have made him the first pick of the 1983 NBA Draft.

There was nearly as little doubt a year later. The Rockets had their center, but they also had the first pick of the draft again. Enter Hakeem Olajuwon and the "Twin Towers" were born.

"It's time," Rockets general manager Ray Patterson declared that first season with Olajuwon and Sampson together, "to win more than coin flips."

Sampson was to revolutionize big-man play, with agility and skills thought impossible from a 7'4" player. Rockets coach Bill Fitch had tried to mold him into a more traditional center, but when the Rockets added Olajuwon and his rim-to-rim ferocity in the 1985 Draft, Sampson's versatility allowed him to shift to the perimeter, passing from the top of the key and shooting from the wings.

Michael Jordan was in that draft class, eventually going third to the Bulls. But the Rockets never hesitated in pairing Olajuwon, the centerpiece of Guy Lewis' Phi Slama Jama University of Houston teams, with Sampson.

"The fans in Houston would have burned down our building if we hadn't drafted Olajuwon," Fitch said. "What is going to make this thing work is Ralph. I know Ralph can play forward. I never would have drafted Akeem [as Olajuwon's name was then spelled] if we weren't going to play him, too. He is very intelligent and he learns quickly."

The pairing immediately took off. The Rockets won the first eight games of their first season together. Sampson, in his second season, was the All-Star Game MVP. The Rockets jumped from 14 wins in 1982–83 and 29 wins in 1983–84 to 48–34 in 1984–85, Olajuwon's rookie season. Sampson averaged 22.1 points and 10.4 rebounds. Olajuwon averaged 20.6 points and 11.9 rebounds.

By just their second season together, and in a rotation that included Rodney McCray, Robert Reid, Mitchell Wiggins, Lewis Lloyd, Allen Leavell, and John Lucas, who returned to Houston after a six-year absence to run the Rockets offense at the point, the Rockets had grown to a 51-win team and a championship contender.

They took down the reigning-champion Lakers in five games, completed with Sampson's twisting, redirected jumper in The Forum. The Rockets moved to The Finals against Fitch's former Celtics team, with the Twin Towers taking on the Boston skyline frontcourt with Robert Parish, Kevin McHale, Larry Bird, and Bill Walton off the bench.

The Celtics, on the short list among the greatest teams ever, won that series in six games, but the Rockets believed they had built a champion. There were cracks, however, in that foundation.

Lucas had been suspended after a failed drug test. Wiggins and Lloyd would be similarly sent away the following season. In March of 1986, months before Sampson would help take the Rockets to The Finals, he had fallen in Boston, slamming his left hip to the floor. When he overcompensated for the pain in his hip, he developed the knee issues that would send him to three surgeries and rob him of some of that remarkably athletic grace.

The Twin Towers became more about Olajuwon's brilliance, as he averaged 23.5 points in the 1985–86 season and 23.4 in 1986–87. That season, Olajuwon's third, the Rockets went 42–40 and were eliminated in the second round, with Olajuwon scoring 49 points with 25 rebounds in a double-overtime loss in Seattle.

The Twin Towers lasted just 19 more games. Sampson was traded to Golden State for Joe Barry Carroll and Sleepy Floyd, delivering the Rockets the point guard they had lacked since losing Lucas. Olajuwon became the greatest player in franchise history, going from the Twin Towers to twin championships a decade later.

Sampson, his knees deteriorating quickly, played in only 150 games over five seasons (just three more playoff games), before he retired at 31-years-old.

The experiment itself, however, was a success. The pairing worked. Circumstances, from the collapse of the backcourt to the condition of Sampson's knees, ended the Rockets' Twin Towers prematurely, an unsatisfyingly brief era that ironically fell short.

19 The Lottery Win

Steve Francis, so much the face of the Rockets' franchise that he comfortably carried the convenient nickname "Franchise," mingled easily in his lavender suit on the Secaucus stage for the unveiling of the 2002 Draft order.

The Rockets were slotted to pick fifth in the draft that season with an 8.9 percent chance to move to the top pick. They had already decided, though they would not announce it before or after the draft lottery, that they would select Yao Ming, the towering star of the Shanghai Sharks, if they ended up with the first.

Rockets coach Rudy Tomjanovich had called Francis back to Houston to view video of Yao in action before Francis would represent the Rockets on the draft lottery stage, with Rockets director of media relations Nelson Luis in the backroom where the ping pong balls bounce and the actual lottery is held.

Yao Ming holds his Rockets jersey following a news conference after his arrival in Houston. (AP Photo/Brett Coomer)

"Everyone was talking about how they were going to get Yao if they got the first pick," Francis wrote in the Players' Tribune in the days before Yao's Hall of Fame induction in 2006. "He was all the GMs and owners were talking about. Before the show, I just minded my own business because I didn't really know anyone.

"That's when my competitiveness kicked in.

"I'll never forget it, I was sitting up there on stage and Bulls GM Jerry Krause was next to me.

"Chicago had passed on me with the No. 1 pick in '99. I looked over at him like, *You should've drafted me, Krause.*"

In the backroom, where the cell phones are confiscated and the participants and observers are sequestered until the results are revealed, the team representatives received their list of lottery numbers and then watched as Luis celebrated with a brief, subtle fist pump when the numbers on the ping pong balls matched one of the sequence of numbers assigned to the Rockets.

When the second set of numbers was uncovered to determine which team would pick second, they again came up with one of the Rockets' list of numbers as Luis felt every eye in the room turn toward him.

The Rockets had just one lottery pick and had already won the right to pick first so the ping pong balls went through the machine again.

"I'm not a superstitious person, but as the lottery balls were coming out, I think some outside forces were at work," Francis wrote. "It was my chance to go toe-to-toe with Krause at the draft.

"The Rockets made it into the top 10. Then the fifth pick got drawn and we were still alive. Then it came down to the last two picks. It was just me and Krause.

"I'm telling you, something was in the air that day. When the second pick went to the Bulls, it was time to celebrate.

"Bingo. Got it."

When the lottery was over, word spread that Dawson's phone was ringing off the hook. He had left his cell phone in the car and without it was struggling to arrange plans for a group to attend Larry Dierker Day at an Astros game. But the mixup sparked a rumor that he was getting and considering offers for the pick.

He wasn't. He just planned to celebrate at a baseball game.

Five weeks later, the Rockets made Yao the first pick of the draft, just as they always intended. Whether they earned that right from destiny, as Yao believed; karma, as Francis thought when he was seated next to Krause; or the lottery luck of Luis or lavender, the Rockets got their man.

20 The Great Wall

Yao Ming had told the story often, but it never ceased to amaze him. Perhaps the night in Shanghai that in hindsight seemed to portend so much about his life to come was filled only with coincidence. He preferred to consider it fate.

The first time Yao saw a live broadcast of an NBA game came in the 1994 NBA Finals. Rockets vs. Knicks. Hakeem Olajuwon vs. Patrick Ewing.

His teammates all pulled for the Knicks. That was reason enough for Yao, always a trailblazer, to choose the Rockets.

The years passed, nearly eight before the Rockets would own the first pick of the NBA draft. Yao would become the star of his hometown Shanghai Sharks and a champion of the China Basketball Association. He would play in the Olympics and World Championships. He would be the certain first pick of the NBA draft when the Rockets won the lottery to choose him, refusing all offers to move the pick, to instead add him to their proud lineage of franchise centers.

Less than a decade after he saw an NBA game live for the first time and decided he was a Rockets fan, the Rockets made him the first Chinese player taken in the first round of the NBA draft, the first international player taken with the first pick without playing college basketball in the United States.

When his career was complete, his brief time as the world's best center interrupted and then ended by injuries, his global impact on the sport extended beyond even the expectations of former Rockets owner Leslie Alexander (who has said based on numbers Yao would become the world's most popular athlete), the announcement came—in Houston—that he would be a Hall of Famer.

Even that seemed more like fate than fortuitous coincidence, with the 2016 Final Four (the site of the Hall of Fame announcement) in Houston in the year that the selection process was amended in a way that moved up his induction.

"You talk about coincidence; I talk about destiny," Yao said. "It goes back to the '94 Finals, Houston against New York. I'm the only guy who supported the Rockets on my team. It's like destiny.

"I feel very peaceful. I'm glad it all can be connected with Houston."

From the day he arrived in Houston, with politicians, dignitaries, and documentarians waiting at the airport, Yao had a career like no other.

It was about so much more than basketball, with a role far larger than the 7'6", 310-pound shadow he cast.

Yao was to be a bridge between nations and cultures, the symbol of China's still-new outreach to the West.

"When I joined the NBA in 2002, it was only one year after China joined the WTO [World Trade Organization]," Yao said.

"The WTO was so big for China. We had to open our gates to the entire world for trade, for culture exchange, for sports exchange, for everything. That's why everything I experienced was very, very new to China. I'm such a lucky guy to have such good timing."

Even the process of bringing him to the United States was unprecedented, with a delegation of general manager Carroll Dawson, general counsel Michael Goldberg, and coach Rudy Tomjanovich in Shanghai and Beijing for difficult negotiations with the Sharks, the CBA, and the Chinese government.

"This is the biggest individual sports story of all time," Alexander said in 2002, the day after Yao was drafted. "When they drafted [Michael] Jordan, or Shaq, or all the guys in baseball, nobody had the aura around him that this guy does. This is an international story before he plays a [NBA] game. He will be the biggest sports story in the world for years to come."

When he arrived, Yao knew his every move and utterance would be closely watched in China, with Western media flocking to document his every stop along the way, with Yao armed with a quick wit and his confidence that he needed only to be himself.

"I tried to stay simple," Yao said. "I knew, but I tried to keep that out of my mind. I knew my job, and I tried to stay focused.

"I just keep flowing. When you are in water, very strong water, you don't fight it. You are in the flow. You let the water carry you. That is my philosophy. Sometimes, you keep yourself in a very narrow area to keep your mind clear and keep your mind focused. You do your job, your part. To think about too much does not help."

Every step brought a harsh spotlight and harsher rapid evaluations. At the daily media sessions, he was treated as a curiosity more than a player. The Rockets hired an interpreter, Colin Pine, to ease the transition, with Pine helping Yao adjust to everything from local cuisine to learning how to drive. By his second season,

Yao spoke easily with teammates, coaches, and media, though still with Pine's translation when on the record. He took to learning something about each NBA season so when he was inevitably asked if he was in any way familiar with the site of that night's game, he was ready with an answer.

He joked easily. When asked one day in Minneapolis what was discussed in a team meeting, he looked both ways, leaned forward, and in the clearest English he had at the time, said, "I don't know. I don't speak English."

He remained dignified, not allowing himself to be treated as a prop. He would constantly pose for pictures, but would not be objectified by disk jockeys standing on chairs or comparing hand sizes.

When Shaquille O'Neal, who would become a friend and fellow member of the Hall of Fame Class of 2016, spoke in mock Chinese about their first meeting, Yao calmly explained that he took no offense, having never experienced any form of racism, understood those that were insulted, and then said, "Chinese is a hard language to learn."

O'Neal always appreciated Yao's grace that day. His father, Phillip Harrison, instructed him to stop mocking a young player that looked up to him, so he learned a few words to share before tipoff of their first meeting. (He was taught Cantonese, however, so Yao, who speaks Mandarin and Shanghainese, did not understand him.) Their meeting that night was epic, with Yao blocking O'Neal's shot twice early in the game, O'Neal dominating for a stretch, but Yao eventually finishing the overtime win with a dunk.

"Yao's a fabulous player, one of a kind, 7'7" with excellent skills," O'Neal said the day before they were inducted into the Hall of Fame. "Nobody blocked my shot. Nobody, and I played against the best. The first time I played against Yao, he blocked it three times in a row. I had to get angry and start dunking.

"But you can't stop Yao. You just have to stay in front of him and hope he'll miss. He'd get it, look at you, and shoot it right over you. He was probably my toughest matchup."

Yao played for just seven full seasons, averaging 19 points and 9.2 rebounds. By his fifth NBA season, he averaged 25 points and 9.4 rebounds. He was hurt in the next season, but came back from his foot injury in time to play for China in the Beijing Olympics, carrying his nation's flag for the second time in a clear demonstration of how much he had come to mean to the world's most populous nation.

"When the Olympics finally came to our country, that was a dream come true," Yao said. "Somehow, you have that feeling that your life, no matter how old you were, you prepared your life for that moment. We felt like we didn't know what to do tomorrow, almost like our life was finished that night."

Yao led the Rockets to the only playoff series win of his career the next season, but was hurt in Game 3 of the second round against the Lakers. He played just five more games.

"He got hurt when he was getting to his prime," Dawson said. "It kills me when you think about what he could have been. His career was just 8½ years. He was just coming on."

Yao will admit he misses the game and competition and especially the camaraderie. He bought the Sharks and has become the CBA president. He graduated from Antai Economics and Management College of Shanghai Jiao Tong University business school. He works with NBA China. He is extraordinarily involved with his philanthropic efforts, including his own foundation, a concept new to China when he started it in 2008. He returns to Houston each season.

"I did have disappointment, some frustrations about the injury keeping me away from the court and that it stopped my career,"

Yao said. "But I'm a guy that likes to look forward instead of looking back."

When he does, he will see a world he helped change. The NBA has become the most popular sports league in China, with NBA players each off-season making the trip to be with fans as loyal as those in Boston or Los Angeles, and the league holding preseason games there every year.

"Every player in the NBA owes a debt of gratitude to Yao Ming," Rockets CEO Tad Brown said. "He's opened up incredible doors on the marketing front. He's opened up incredible opportunities for the league to continue to expand and grow.

"The way the game has exploded in China is a direct relation to Yao Ming's skills and Yao Ming's ability to handle all the pressures when he first came into the league and throughout his career."

His career did not last, but he touched greatness, and made that just a part of his story, fulfilling a mission like few others. To consider his own legacy would be looking back, but Yao can no more deny it than others could mistake his impact, as if it were all his destiny that night in Shanghai when he decided to be a fan of the Rockets.

"Life is my guide," Yao typically said on the day he retired. "Just follow it and it will open doors. Out of each door, there will be a beautiful world outside. Since I am retired, one door is closed. But a new life is waiting for me."

21 15–0

The Rockets arrived in Madison Square Garden that night with a 14-game winning streak to start the season, one shy of matching the NBA record, but also with something to prove.

The game was not quite billed as the NBA Finals preview it would become, but as a chance for the Rockets to validate their dominance of the opening month of the season.

Knicks forward Anthony Mason declared, "They're coming to the wrong place." The Garden crowd chanted, "14–1, 14–1!"

The Rockets, however, brought more than a need to prove something that even the first 14 games of the 1993–94 season had not, or a desire to claim a share of the record.

The Rockets remained hungry from the previous season, driven to ease the pain from the Game 7 overtime loss in Seattle as only a championship could. Long before the Rockets reached New York, before they ran the table on the way to the showdown with the Knicks or put together late-game comebacks to keep the streak alive, they had gathered in Galveston for training camp a changed team.

There had been some additions. Forward Mario Elie was signed in the off-season. Guard Sam Cassell was drafted to join the backcourt with Vernon Maxwell, Kenny Smith, and Scott Brooks. But mostly, the Rockets were powered by the loss that ended the previous season and fully engaged in Rudy Tomjanovich's system.

"The streak started from practice," Elie said. "We were very competitive, man, me and Vernon going at it, Scott, Kenny, and Sam competing for minutes. When I got down there, I saw, we hung out together, we ate together. It was a good job on Rudy's part to get the team out to Galveston. We did a lot of stuff together and it showed on their court."

When the season began and the streak rolled on, the qualities that would mark the Rockets' first championship season—defense, tenacity, and Olajuwon at his peak—would become repeatedly and increasingly evident.

After solid wins against the Nets, Trail Blazers, Warriors, and Timberwolves, the Rockets finally had a close game, edging the Suns by four in a sign of things to come months later in their incredible postseason series.

The streak faced its greatest threat in another playoff preview in Utah. Elie sank a pair of free throws to tie the game with 2.1 seconds left and Olajuwon stole an inbounds pass to send the game to overtime. He would finish with 29 points, 17 rebounds, and seven blocked shots to herald his mastery of the Jazz in the postseason.

After the overtime win against the Jazz, the Rockets won in Sacramento on a Robert Horry jumper with 55.3 seconds remaining. With the lead down to one, Olajuwon swatted a Walter Berry shot to preserve the win. Against the Clippers, Olajuwon nailed a baseline jumper with 22.5 seconds left to complete a three-game road trip that the Rockets swept by a total of seven points.

After returning home to complete an unbeaten November with a win against the Bucks, the Rockets headed to New York in a game to test the credibility of their run.

There should not have been any doubt; Olajuwon was player of the month, Tomjanovich coach of the month. Going back to the end of the 1992–93 season, the Rockets had set a franchise record for wins in three consecutive months.

New York, however, was viewed as the heir apparent to Chicago as Michael Jordan dabbled in minor league baseball. Patrick Ewing had defeated Olajuwon for the NCAA championship. The Knicks were loaded with frontcourt muscle with Ewing, Mason, and Charles Oakley.

"I felt they were tough and if we were going to get this record, we were going to have to earn it," Tomjanovich said. "I remember coming in and the headline was, 'Not In Our House.' They had a lot of pride. We went in there and I don't think it was even close."

It wasn't. The Rockets led by 10 by halftime and easily pushed the lead to 19 in the second half. The Rockets had won nine road games to open the season, winning from one coast to the other in a span of six days.

"I remember them talking junk, saying the streak was going to stop in New York," Elie said. "We just smacked them."

The Rockets had nothing left for the Hawks the next night. They had arrived in Atlanta at 3:00 AM. The airport trams had shut down for the night so they had to carry the equipment through the airport. It got so late that the bus driver assumed they stayed in New York and left, forcing the team to take taxis to the hotel. The Rockets checked in at sunrise and lost by 22.

Relieved of the pressure to keep the streak going, they built another one. The Rockets won their next seven games to start the season 22–1. They had demolished the disappointment from the way the previous season ended. More than that, they armed themselves with the confidence they would carry all the way to the championship.

"We were playing well, but the games got more pressure-packed as the streak kept going," forward Matt Bullard said. "When we lost in Atlanta, it released our pressure and we could just carry on with our business. But we had that 15-game win streak in our memory bank, 'Hey, we can do this, we're good enough.' It was our foundation for the year to build on."

When that building was complete, the season ended even better than it began, with the first championship in franchise history.

22 The Streak

Every day, as the Rockets make their way to the Toyota Center home locker room, they pass the mural celebrating the championship seasons, complete with images iconic to Rockets fans and by now familiar to any Rockets player that has needed to change clothes before a game or practice.

Before games, however, they head the other direction to the court and make their way past a different mural, celebrating another triumph and bringing a very different message.

The Streak is commemorated on that wall, triggering memories of—or perhaps even inspiration from—the Rockets' blast of 22 consecutive wins in the 2007–08 season.

The run, at the time the second longest in NBA history, was special for the obvious reasons. From late January to early March in 2008, if the Rockets played, they won. From Steve Novak hitting a buzzer-beater to send the Rockets into the All-Star break with a win against the Kings to Shane Battier hounding Kobe Bryant to complete the run, the Rockets drove themselves beyond what seemed possible.

Yet, it is more than the final score in 22 consecutive games that earned that time a place of honor a few feet removed from the celebration of the greatest team and greatest time in Rockets history.

That team accomplished something normally only champions can achieve. They were the best they could have conceivably been. They overcame obstacles great and small, including the season-ending injury to Yao Ming 12 games into the run, and just kept winning. They came together to the point they were as close as any championship team, elevating one another beyond what seemed possible.

"The camaraderie of that group, guys you just love to be around day in and day out," Tracy McGrady said.

"I'm so proud of that streak," said Battier, "because nothing mattered but team."

The Streak, then the longest since the NBA-ABA merger, has since been surpassed by a 27-game run of the 2012–13 Miami Heat. But in many ways, that Heat run shed light on how remarkable the Rockets' streak really was.

The Heat were loaded, topped by the Big Three of Chris Bosh, Dwyane Wade, and LeBron James, the reigning regular season MVP and NBA Finals MVP. The Rockets had to replace Yao with 41-year-old Dikembe Mutombo and 6'6" center Chuck Hayes, and when more injuries hit, had to bring Mike Harris in from the China Basketball Association and plug him into the rotation before he could even get over the jet lag.

Rick Adelman was in his first season as Rockets coach, still putting in his motion offense. When the streak began, with McGrady out with an injury, the Rockets were 24–20. The Rockets would win by double digits in nine of their next 12 games, before Yao's broken foot ended his season.

The Rockets, however, just kept winning. McGrady kept filling stat sheets, but point guard Rafer Alston rolled through the best stretch of his career. Battier averaged in double digits after Yao's injury. Luis Scola, then a rookie, averaged 11.6 points during the streak. The Rockets won the final 10 games of the Streak, after Yao's injury, by an average of 14.5 points per game.

The win against the Lakers, completed with Alston's show of "Skip to My Lou" ballhandling and a flash of Mutombo's enormous smile and two raised fingers on each hand, completed the run. The Rockets hit a wall against the Celtics in the next game, leaving the floor with a 94–74 loss and a standing ovation. By the playoffs, the loss of Yao was too much to overcome, with the Rockets going out in the first round.

As the wall next to the locker room reminds their successors, the 2007–08 Rockets will always have the Streak and share the magic that came together in ways so inexplicable that it will be forever special.

"We knew back then that it was one of the most improbable runs in basketball history—maybe even in sports history," said Battier, who would be a part of the Miami run and two championship teams. "We were journeymen, a bunch of role players. When we were healthy—with Yao and Tracy—that team was pretty good. But we could never stay healthy.

"That was our championship."

23 The One and Only Calvin Murphy

At some point during every Rockets home game, most often in the middle of the second quarter, Calvin Murphy makes his way around the court toward the stands in the opposite corner from his nightly broadcast position.

Murphy climbs the stairs, still walking fast at 70 years old with a bounce in his step and his back straight as a flagpole, toward the suites to shake a few hands and pose for a few photos. Eyes immediately leave their focus on the game and follow him as he passes, always decked out in his impossibly dazzling, gaudy suits and shoes, his smile as irrepressible as he was on the floor.

Shouts trail him, as Murphy flashes that smile and waves, sometimes stops, and never disappoints with the outsized personality that might have seemed to be a made-for-television show, but was just typical Calvin Murphy.

Murphy still fills a room, as he always had. Though his stature at 5'9" had been attached to descriptions of him since his days filling it up in Norwalk, Connecticut, and then as a three-time All-American at Niagara, even that missed the point. Murphy did not become the player and personality he was despite his lack of size, but because of the way he was fueled by it.

"They had the audacity to tell me I was too small to be an NBA player," Murphy said of when he entered the 1970 NBA Draft. "They picked me first in the second round so I had something I had to prove to the world that they were wrong."

With a chip on a shoulder as large as he was, Murphy never stopped trying to prove the world wrong, 165 pounds of effervescent energy and determination. He played 13 seasons with the Rockets, averaging in double figures in all of them, 25.6 in 1977–78 and retiring as the Rockets' all-time leader in scoring and assists.

Hakeem Olajuwon would top the career scoring mark and James Harden bested Murphy's single-game franchise scoring record of 57 when he scored 60 against the Orlando Magic in the 2017–18 season. Murphy happily cheered Harden on that night and celebrated when Harden passed him, but had not forgotten what his accomplishment meant beyond the box score.

"I'm very proud of the fact that I held that record for 40 years," Murphy said. "Remember now, I was never supposed to be in this game. I was too short for the NBA and I held the record for 40 years. And it was broken by an individual who is eventually going to be a Hall of Famer who is quality. I have no qualms whatsoever. The fact that he broke it, he is going to take me along for the ride."

There were rocky times along the way to beloved Rockets icon, especially a month-long trial in 2004 when Murphy was charged with molesting five of his estranged daughters. Jurors took less than two hours to reach a not-guilty verdict, with Murphy's lawyers maintaining the charges were falsified because of a dispute over money.

Murphy had been taken off the air during the trial, but returned after 8½ years on the pre- and postgame and halftime studio shows. Though many fans longed for a return of his on-air partnership with Bill Worrell, the role suits Murphy well and he cherished his return to the air.

"I didn't solicit the job. I didn't become a drum major for it," Murphy, a champion baton-twirler, said. "But I am blessed that it has happened. It's like putting a period at the end of a sentence and going ahead.

"I've been looking for closure, and this does it. It makes me legit again, if I can use that phrase. I can start fresh now. I get a new beginning, and you can't get more blessed than that."

He had not changed. His laughter was as loud as his suits, his love for the Rockets unrelenting. The love Houston had for him had not been lost and would only grow in the years that followed.

"You start talking about the fans, the city of Houston saw me grow up," Murphy said. "The city of Houston has taken a little fella from Norwalk, Connecticut, and made him a native son."

Many of those fans might not have seen him stop at the elbow and fire up an impossibly quick jump shot. They might not have seen his Golden Gloves boxing skills on the floor when he was listed by *Sports Illustrated*, along with a handful of giants of his time, as one of "The Enforcers." They might never have seen his "HOF '93" medallion, the celebration of his induction to the Hall of Fame as the shortest player honored that he keeps close to his heart.

They can't miss the enthusiasm, energy, and joy he brings and always has.

"Coming in as the modern little guy in the game," Murphy said, "I had to set the world on fire."

He did that, and with every effervescent smile, every cell phone photo he takes, he still does.

24 T-Mac

More than most, or perhaps anyone ever had been, Tracy McGrady was expected to explain his worthiness for the Hall of Fame. It was the final, fitting contradiction in a career complicated by the conflict between what was and what could have been.

Even then, McGrady seemed to explain why his time in Houston was never simple, never just about his talent, from the time he arrived as a two-time scoring champion that the Rockets found to be capable of even more to when he departed with little left and a sense that all those hopes were as unfulfilled as they were, even in hindsight, justified.

"I'm damn proud of going into the Hall of Fame," McGrady said. "When I see myself play, there was no doubt I was one of the best players playing. There's no doubt about that. Now, if you take what I did and put me on a winning team, now you're talking about one of the best of all times. So yes, I was one of the greats."

That was all true. It was impossible to watch McGrady and not see greatness. When he teamed with Yao Ming, brought to the Rockets in a trade that sent Steve Francis, along with Cuttino Mobley and Kelvin Cato, to Orlando, the Rockets believed they had the inside-out pairing of a championship contender.

McGrady believed it, too. By his third season with the Rockets, he declared "it's on me." That was the season the Rockets had their best chance, a first-round series against the Utah Jazz in 2007 with Yao healthy and in his prime. The season came to crashing end, however, with the Rockets repeatedly unable to secure offensive rebounds in the final minutes of Game 7 as the Jazz rallied for the win.

McGrady was spent and solemn, as if he knew that would be his best chance.

"I said this team was going to go as far as I take them," he said. "I tried my best. I tried, man. Maybe I could have made an extra play here. Maybe I could have got those loose rebounds I didn't get down the stretch of the game in the fourth quarter that we needed. Maybe I could have done more, but it didn't happen. I tried man, I tried."

A season later, with Yao out, the Rockets lost at home, and McGrady offered his "my fault" speech, seeming to tire of the expectations that he carry the Rockets.

"It's my fault," McGrady said. "It's my fault we're missing free throws. It's my fault we lost both games. It's my fault that we fouled to tie the game up with I think a minute left when Luis [Scola] fouled. That's my fault. It's my fault they're getting layups. It's my fault that we're not executing well. It's my fault that a couple people in the stands ordered Budweiser, but they got Heineken. It's my fault. I'm sorry."

McGrady had a good series that season, averaging 27 points. That was often overlooked when he was slapped for never taking a team past the first round. McGrady's numbers, remarkable as they were in the regular season, were better in the playoffs. He never once, however, could celebrate a series win until he hopped on the end of the Spurs bench at the end of his career.

In a final postseason irony, when the Rockets finally moved on from the first round for the first time since the Hakeem Olajuwon era, McGrady was not there, out with an injury as the Rockets topped the Trail Blazers in six games.

He never played for the Rockets in the postseason again. His final seasons in Houston became contentious, short-circuited by the injury issues that had held him and the Rockets back in the six seasons McGrady and Yao shared, and marked by acrimony in

Tracy McGrady yells after getting fouled in the final 16.2 seconds against the Seattle SuperSonics. (AP Photo/Jim Bryant)

the final months. After beginning his time in Houston with back issues that he solved, McGrady developed knee issues that stole his greatness.

He annoyed Rick Adelman by announcing his decision to have microfracture surgery to the media before telling the team and even before meeting with the specialist the Rockets set up to examine him and who would ultimately do the surgery. He angered Adelman when he grew tired of the wait to return and turned over the equipment trunks in Minneapolis in search of his uniform to force his way back on the floor.

Adelman did not relent. Weeks later, McGrady was sent home from New Jersey, having played brief first-half stints in six games, averaging 3.2 points, before leaving the team on a leave of absence while the Rockets sought a trade. He was dealt to the Knicks two months after his final game with the Rockets, coincidentally in Orlando, in a three-team deal.

The hopes that arrived with McGrady were gone before he was, but in the end, he was right. It was impossible to watch McGrady at the height of his powers and not see a Hall of Famer. The idea of what could have been was equally conspicuous.

McGrady, however, did win. He was made a Hall of Famer, and went in with one more career-defining, if characteristically widely-misunderstood statement.

McGrady said that "anybody" can win a championship, but not the Hall of Fame ring he earned. That drew strong rebuke, but he knew better than most how much good fortune plays into team success. Had the Spurs won Game 6 of the 2013 NBA Finals, McGrady would have won a championship without ever getting sweaty. McGrady could not play the Rockets to postseason success, but he did earn his place in Springfield.

"When I made that statement that anybody can win a championship but everybody can't get in the Hall of Fame, it was not to discredit the greats that have won championships," McGrady said.

"I'm saying if you want to talk about me getting in the Hall of Fame without winning a championship, I have to come at you and say, 'Anybody can win a championship,' which is so true.

"Anybody means any individual person. It doesn't mean 'everybody.' I was one shot [Ray Allen's corner 3] from winning a championship and I didn't even play. If you're offended by that, tough…"

McGrady's seasons with the Rockets could not be defined completely by his successes or failures, by the hopes when he arrived, or the disappointment when he left. But when he looked at his play, he saw the same thing anyone would.

"I didn't have the opportunity to win a championship," McGrady said the week of his induction. "I gave everything I possibly could. I tried to lead in the way I could, with my play. It didn't happen. I'm not happy I didn't win a championship, but very excited to be getting inducted into the Hall of Fame. This is my championship."

25. 13 in 33 Seconds

Ever the optimist, Gene Peterson, long the radio voice of the Rockets, said the words that few in Toyota Center—or those already in the parking lots heading home—would have argued.

Tony Parker passed to Tim Duncan for a dunk and a 10-point Spurs lead with 62 seconds remaining, and Peterson said, "Ballgame over."

He said it over the boos in the arena, his familiar baritone seeming just a bit deeper. "All we need here is a final score."

On the floor, a prescient Rockets coach Jeff Van Gundy shouted, "There's still time, there's still time!"

Yet, when a 33.3-second, 13-point burst of Tracy McGrady lightning strikes somehow delivered victory, Van Gundy called it "a miracle."

"That game was hopeless," Rockets center Yao Ming said. "T-Mac turned on his firepower."

When he did, the Rockets had the greatest comeback in franchise history and McGrady had authored a performance that would seem no more than a tall tale left over from a bygone time had it not come with video evidence.

The comeback began slowly, the way a locomotive that will eventually reach its top speeds begins to move.

Yao slammed home an offensive rebound. The Spurs barely seemed to notice. Scott Padgett stole a Parker inbounds pass and took it in for a dunk, reducing the lead to six. Still, there were just 47.3 seconds left.

Even then, the Spurs defense, then at its most powerful, had surrendered just 68 points in 47-plus minutes. Rockets-Spurs games in those years were brutal showdowns of Van Gundy's and Gregg Popovich's most suffocating defenses. The Rockets had scored 11 fourth-quarter points.

The Spurs pushed the lead back to eight when, with just 35 seconds left, McGrady put on a scoring exhibition for the ages, draining three-pointers as easily as tossing wadded up balls of scrap paper in a trash can.

"He was magical," Spurs forward Bruce Bowen said.

Lost in the history of the now legendary run was that the Spurs did not collapse. There were a few missteps, most of all the final turnover that led to McGrady's ultimate charge up the floor. But McGrady's shots were contested. The Spurs, a poor free throw–shooting team, made all six of their free throws after the Rockets' run began.

The Spurs did just enough to require McGrady, who had left the floor in the fourth quarter with stomach pain, to do more than seemed possible.

His run began unspectacularly. McGrady moved sharply to his right, used a Padgett screen and pulled up just past the center of the three-point circle to nail a three over Malik Rose, cutting the lead to 76–71 with 35 seconds left.

The Spurs led 78–71 when the comeback picked up steam. McGrady used a Yao screen a full three feet beyond the arc, turned, and pump-faked Duncan off his feet. Years earlier, when McGrady was with the Magic, he had copied his deadly pump fake from former Rockets guard Sam Cassell, mastering it over the years. It would never be more useful.

"He pump-faked me and I went for it, and he jumped into me," Duncan said. "It was a great play by him."

McGrady glided his body into Duncan's as he shot-put his three up and in. When he sank his free throw, the Rockets had pulled within four—78–75, 24.3 seconds left.

"I knew he thought I was going to pull up when I came off that screen," McGrady said. "I knew I could bait him on the pump fake. He went for it. I don't know how I got the ball off. After that, every time I came up the court, I felt whatever I shot would go in."

The Spurs put in two more free throws, pushing the lead to a seemingly safe five points. If there ever were any doubt about where the ball would go, it was long gone, with McGrady seeming engulfed in Bowen's defense until reserve point guard Andre Barrett was forced to simply loft his inbounds pass in McGrady's general direction.

McGrady caught the pass near mid-court and took off toward his right with Bowen in his face every step of the way, reminding everyone that the Spurs had the NBA's best three-point defense that season. Three dribbles to the three-point line and McGrady elevated. Just as he needed all of the reach of his long-limbed 6'8" body to snare the inbounds pass, he relied on it to launch over Bowen. He banged home his three, cutting the lead to 80–78 with 11.2 seconds left.

The Rockets prepared to foul to stop the clock. Devin Brown, who had made four straight free throws in the final minute, turned toward the baseline, perhaps to work up a bit more clock, as Padgett closed to his right. Brown slipped, the ball rolling away from him, and headed as straight to McGrady in the lane as if it were a pass in pregame warmups.

With 6.9 seconds remaining, McGrady headed up the floor with one thing in mind.

"I knew we were down two," McGrady said. "The only thing I was thinking about was a three. I didn't want to get the ball and try to tie the ballgame up. I was going to take my chances going for the three and go for the win."

McGrady took off, veering to his left before pulling up from 26 feet in front of Brent Barry. When he drained one last three-pointer with 1.7 seconds left, he turned the other way and punched the air with an 81–80 lead. As Parker's desperate, running 30-footer missed, the Rockets mobbed McGrady.

"The way I was feeling those last couple seconds, I felt like anything I would throw up would go in," McGrady said. "The rim felt really big to me out there. To come back and pull out the game, all my teammates jumping on me, I swear I've never been a part of anything like that.

"That was the best feeling to me, to have my teammates embrace me, jumping on me like that. That was a great feeling. And for all those fans that left, gosh you missed a great game."

26 The Rockets vs. M.J.

The Rockets were often reminded that they never played Michael Jordan's Bulls in The Finals. The Rockets won their first title when Jordan was playing minor league baseball. They repeated after Jordan was eliminated by the Orlando Magic.

The argument of course ignored that many teams before and after the Bulls' run never played Jordan in The Finals. But the Rockets of the championship years have always made another point ignored by proponents of invisible banner asterisks.

When they did play Jordan's Bulls, the Rockets usually won.

In the regular-season meetings during the Bulls' first threepeat, the Rockets won five of six meetings. The Bulls had no one to match up with Hakeem Olajuwon, rotating Bill Cartwright, Luc Longley, and Scott Williams in those years. The Rockets had a guard not only willing to defend Jordan, but who relished those nights against the league's best player.

That might have been evidence that Vernon Maxwell deserved his nickname, "Mad Max." But he was so determined to compete with Jordan, he said, "I wanted to fight him."

More than two decades later, Maxwell was as convinced as ever that the Rockets would have won a series against the Bulls, with logic that was in no way insane.

"I always say 'Google it,'" Maxwell said. "Michael Jordan saying we wouldn't have won the championships the time he was out and tried to play baseball. I say just Google the times we played them. They couldn't beat us. Like we couldn't beat Seattle, if we could've beat Seattle, we'd have got a championship against Chicago because they couldn't match up against us.

"I hear what they said. I hear what everybody said. I don't believe it. Just Google it. The numbers don't lie."

Maxwell had become the face of the argument, but the teammate least given to hyperbole and overflowing with credibility shared the opinion.

"It's something that you will never know, but if you just go by the record, we never had a problem with Chicago," Olajuwon said in NBA-TV's *Clutch City* documentary. "We loved that, because we wouldn't just play against Chicago; we would dominate Chicago."

The Rockets did not get past the SuperSonics in Jordan's last season before baseball or in his first full season after his return. When the Rockets were their best, the Bulls did not reach The Finals. But when they played, especially in the Bulls' initial three-peat, the Rockets had a guard that loved playing against Jordan in ways the assorted Bulls centers at the time could never feel about facing Olajuwon.

"One time. I wish I could have got in a seven-game series," Maxwell said. "I would have loved to have that. I wanted that. That would have been a dream to me. I would have loved to have a seven-game series against Michael Jordan. He's a tough cat to guard. I just love to compete with him.

"When I came up, my grandfather always told me, 'Ain't no man better than you. He put his pants on just like you. Don't be scared of no man.' That's the way I took it. That's the way I lived my life. I loved playing against Michael. People back in my era wouldn't play against Mike, they didn't want to play against Mike. But I loved that because I wanted to play against the best. I wanted to see what the best got. I wanted to see where I'm at, where's I'm at on the totem pole. I love that. I wanted to fight Mike. That's what I wanted to do."

He and the Rockets never got that chance in The Finals. But for all the Bulls accomplished, it can also be said, they never got to take on the Rockets, either.

27 1986 and What Could Have Been

They'll never truly know what could have been, but that just adds to the pain of regret. They do know what they were in the spring of 1986 and how much seemed to be awaiting them.

The Rockets had rolled past the reigning champion Lakers in five games to reach the NBA Finals. They took a pair of games in The Finals when the Celtics were their most loaded, with Larry Bird and Kevin McHale at the height of their powers and Bill Walton coming off the bench. They were young and gifted, with Hakeem Olajuwon and Ralph Sampson bringing a two-fisted frontcourt combination few teams could match.

Then it was gone, wrecked before those Rockets could reach the potential on display that spring when they seemed to just be hinting at what could be.

"When you think about where we were, just a short time earlier, man," Robert Reid told the *Houston Chronicle* in 2006, 20 years after that Finals appearance. "The Celtics and Lakers still had their starting fives together and we were all broken up. It was all gone in a heartbeat."

That Rockets team had John Lucas, Lewis Lloyd, Mitchell Wiggins, and Allen Leavell in a backcourt; Sampson, Olajuwon, Rodney McCray, and Jim Peterson in the frontcourt; and Reid fitting in anywhere needed. Lucas was masterful at getting Sampson and Olajuwon touches where they could be unstoppable. Olajuwon was already off the charts as a rim protector. Sampson's outlet passes triggered fast-breaks, with Lloyd in particular a devastating finisher.

The Rockets clicked from the start, winning nine of 11 games to open the season. They were 40–24 when it began to slip away.

Rockets guard Lewis Lloyd shoots over Larry Bird during the 1986 NBA Finals at The Summit. (MPS/USA TODAY Sports)

Lucas, the first pick of the 1976 Draft, who had returned to the Rockets in 1984 after several drug-related suspensions, awoke in a downtown Houston street after a night of drinking and using cocaine. He failed a drug test and was released.

"I don't mean to be disrespectful to anyone or in any way put a knock on accomplishments of the organization," Lucas said in 2006. "But when I walk around Houston now and I hear people talk about winning those championships in '94 and '95, I just shake my head. I tell them, 'You've either forgotten or you have never seen the best Rockets team. I know. I was a part of it. And I was a big part of bringing it down.'

"I'm telling you, we'd have beaten Boston if I was there. You look at most teams that are put together like that one and they get about an eight- to 10-year window. We didn't know it, but our window was right there, and then it slammed shut."

The following season, Wiggins and Lloyd, both just 27 years old, failed drug tests and were banished from the league in January of 1987. Sampson began the battles with injuries that would mark the rest of his career.

Weeks after Lucas was released in 1986, Sampson had crashed to the court in Boston Garden, hurting his hip and back. When he returned, he was still limping. Compensating for those injuries led to knee issues. The season after The Finals trip, Sampson tore ligaments in his left knee. He played just 19 more games with the Rockets before he was traded in December 1987 to Golden State for Sleepy Floyd and Joe Barry Carroll.

The Rockets went 46–36 that season and were eliminated in the first round of the playoffs. In 1988, Fitch was fired, Reid was traded to Charlotte, and McCray and Petersen were dealt to Sacramento. It took the Rockets six seasons to win another playoff series.

Just two years after Sampson had hit the twisting buzzer-beater to beat the Lakers and send the Rockets to the NBA Finals, nearly all of the team that expected that Finals trip to be one of many was gone. Only Olajuwon and Allen Leavell remained, with the hopes and promise of the 1986 Rockets replaced by the haunting thoughts of what could have been.

28 John Lucas and the Full Circle

The ritual replays nearly every night as John Lucas begins his pregame work, getting Rockets players ready for each game. He sends passes to shooters and offers instructions, as so many assistant coaches and development specialists around the league do each night. But when Lucas has a moment, the routine is different, or at least more extreme than for others.

Scouts and coaches that have gotten to know him through the years stop him to chat. Players that he has mentored pay their respects and trade hugs before getting their work in. Front office executives exchange greetings.

Lucas can barely walk across an NBA court without being stopped, with relationships that speak to all the lives he has touched, skills he has shaped or sharpened.

This routine, however, speaks to more than his longevity or the jobs he has held in and around the NBA for most of the past four decades. It shines a light on something far more important.

Guiding others had become more than his calling; it was and remains his salvation. From his selection as the first pick of the 1976 Draft to his fall to tragic cautionary tale and his rise as the source of hope and inspiration for recovery and redemption for so many, Lucas' road brought him back to where his NBA journey began and to a role perfect for someone with such a disparate set of life experiences.

Lucas returned to the Rockets before the 2016–17 season to lead their development staff. He had long since devoted himself to his mission, working to guide others to recovery from everything from substance abuse to anger management issues. In doing so, he served his own care.

The Rockets, however, were family. Houston was home, with roots planted deep. With Mike D'Antoni taking over as Rockets coach, Lucas gave up most of his work with the John Lucas Wellness and Aftercare Program and John Lucas Enterprises. He would no longer train young prospects from around the nation. He would not prepare college players for the NBA Draft Combine. He would instead work each day on Clint Capela's jump hook, Eric Gordon's left hand, and James Harden's follow-through, but also on what they think and feel.

"People have tried to get me to do it before," Lucas said. "I did it because I live and breathe Rocket red. Before all these people, I consider myself one of the original Rockets, '76 and all the way through. This city and this organization loved me. I love them.

"I've been blessed. There are a lot of people in this city who raised me. I owe them something. I owe them everything. I love this city."

To the rest of the world, Lucas was born in Durham, North Carolina, on Halloween, 1953. He considers his hometown to be Houston, his birthday March 14, 1986, the date he at last hit his rock bottom.

That was the morning he woke on the street in downtown Houston, slacks soiled, still high on the drugs he'd taken the night before when they meant more to him than even his career as a wildly talented point guard, so gifted he had a side job as a professional tennis player.

The Rockets released him that day. That was the day, Lucas said, and has taught so often ever since, that he found his "gift of desperation."

"I fell in love with the game when it was gone, not when I had it," Lucas said. "That was the first day of my life—March 14, 1986. That was the year the Rockets went to The Finals. I wasn't a part of that. We ended up losing to the Celtics. It's almost second nature to have an issue with marijuana and alcohol now, but then,

I was the first athlete to admit to having a problem and struggling publicly with getting sober.

"When I came back to play and ended up playing in Milwaukee, I fell in love with the game. I always loved it, but I fell out of love with it. When I made it, it became, 'Now what?' I got there and I was like, 'Is that all there is?'"

When he took his gifts for granted, Lucas tried to fill the void with the voids, finding the luxury cars and fine jewelry not enough and leading him to drugs and alcohol. When he got sober, he gave all of that up, unwilling to even wear a watch, a reminder of the pursuits of his departed past.

"There's nothing worse than emotional and spiritual bankruptcy in a person," Lucas said. "They have a hole inside them. They try to use basketball, use sex, use everything they could to fill it up.

"Life intrigues me, just like basketball. I think a lot of people are scared to find out who they are. They say, 'I'm a lawyer. I'm a basketball player.' No. No. That's what you do. What makes you happy? What makes you cry? Is your self-worth making the game winning shot?"

When Lucas got well, he played four more seasons in the NBA, finishing his career where it began with the Rockets. He was a head coach with the Spurs, 76ers, and Cavaliers, an assistant with the Nuggets and Clippers. He would have been happy to remain the head of his extremely hands-on treatment and training programs.

He began working more closely with the Rockets when Ty Lawson was with them following his DUI arrests while with the Nuggets. The Rockets' coaching change led to a reworking of the staff, with Lucas getting players in the morning. Even on the many days the Rockets do not hold shootaround, Lucas puts the young players to work as he had for so many years in gyms around Houston.

"The way you play is a mirror of who you are," he said. "Helping players shape who they are can make them better players.

"I tell them all the time, 'I've been sober 30 years, but I know who I am.' I never woke up a day and thought, *I've forgotten my past.* I always tell them 'fail' means 'first attempt in learning.' Let's do it again. Here's your training ground so you can dance at the dance. That's on the court and off the court."

To Lucas, there is no living in between, no distinction between teaching and learning, helping and healing. The process never ends. It is a circle he travels each day, and in a life in the NBA that brought him back to where it began.

29 The Punch

Kermit Washington reached his hand—that right hand, the hand that changed everything—toward Rudy Tomjanovich. This time, Tomjanovich smiled, happy to see it.

Nearly 25 years after Washington turned and landed the punch that nearly killed Tomjanovich, changed both their lives, and forever altered the way the sport looked at the sort of on-court violence that had once been viewed as inevitable, Tomjanovich and Washington came together in Oakland to move on in the one, final way they had not.

For Tomjanovich, this was part of his mindset, gained through years of self-examination. Washington, then 50 years old, was still something of an NBA pariah and nervous, unsure how he would be viewed by the man he so badly injured all those years before.

Then they shook hands, clapped backs, and moved on. They joked that day about the way the game has changed, even mentioning the way teams in their time all had players labeled "enforcers" as if unaware of the irony of their sharing that conversation. Perhaps at last that no longer mattered to them. They had left that horrible night behind them.

"When something like that happens in a person's life, there has to be healing—physical healing and emotional healing," Tomjanovich said the day he and Washington finally met in 2002 outside the Golden State Warriors practice facility. "The physical heals. Nature and medicine take care of that. I have nothing to do with that. The emotional healing has everything to do with me."

It was a long, hard road, begun the night, December 9, 1977, when the Rockets played the Lakers in The Forum. Kareem Abdul-Jabbar and Kevin Kunnert became tangled. Washington joined the fracas. Players rushed toward the beginnings of a fight with Tomjanovich reaching them first. When Washington saw Tomjanovich, he turned and threw a hard right hand that landed just below Tomjanovich's nose.

Tomjanovich fell to the court, blood gushing, his face shattered in four places, spinal fluid leaking from his brain.

After Tomjanovich initially thought he had broken his nose and hoped to return to the game, he was rushed to a hospital, where he was told that the leaking spinal fluid made his condition life-threatening.

Tomjanovich spent four days in intensive care and underwent a series of surgeries. He returned the next season and even averaged 19 points per game, but he never fully recaptured his role as one of the Rockets' primary stars. Tomjanovich sued the Lakers and won a $3.25 million ruling. He reached a $2 million settlement before the appeal was heard. He played just three more seasons before he retired.

Washington was fined $10,000 and suspended for a record 60 days. The Lakers traded him weeks after the punch. After he finished that season with Boston, Washington played for the San Diego Clippers, Portland, and Golden State.

Tomjanovich's career in the years since would not allow him to be labeled as just a part of the most violent episode in NBA history. He became the coach of the Rockets' only championship teams and USA Basketball's gold medal–winning 2000 Olympic team. But for years, Tomjanovich had haunting visions of his own death. Even after he moved past that, he felt a need to forgive Washington, if only to rid the remaining bitterness, like the spinal fluid he tasted and will never forget, from his mouth.

After reading advance copies of John Feinstein's book *The Punch*, Tomjanovich and Washington began to talk, mostly about a prospect Washington had seen in China, Sonny Watson, for whom he hoped to find an NBA tryout. They had crossed paths over the years. Washington said he had apologized in 1987, at a chance meeting in Sacramento, blaming himself for the incident. But they never really had time to move past a few words of small talk.

Washington had been an assistant coach at Stanford for a few years. He helped run Pete Newell's legendary big man camp, working for the coach that had drafted Tomjanovich into the NBA. He had a radio show in Portland for a while. Despite many efforts, he never returned to the NBA, believing the incident forever marked him, despite Tomjanovich's ability to forgive him.

Tomjanovich, in Oakland for Yao Ming's national team game in the summer before his rookie season, agreed to check out Watson, also bringing him and Washington together. As plans were made to meet, they also knew they could finally take the last remaining step to move past the punch.

"Many, many years ago, I said to Rudy, 'I am sorry about what happened. I'm very sorry. It's my fault. Please forgive me,'" Washington said. "I didn't think he could be that forgiving."

Washington could not have known that Tomjanovich had come to believe that holding resentment is "a poison" people ingest needlessly.

"If I keep those other things, self-destructive things, a part of who I am, I'm missing a good life," Tomjanovich said. "All that matters is where people are today. For me, what happened in the past has nothing to do with where I am today. I have to live today. Analyzing, judging on the past doesn't do anybody any good. It's meaningless to me. What matters to me is how I'm going to live today. I made my choice.

"It takes time and it takes lessons and it takes pain. I've lived in a lot of self-constructed pain because of my thinking. It has nothing to do with other people. I have to live with me. When I'm happy in my mind and my conscience, and everything is clear, it's a good life."

Tomjanovich forgave Washington. That day in Oakland, he took Washington's right hand in his and they moved on together.

30 The Kiss of Death

The picture is still clear as if it had just happened, rather than a part of Rockets history. The image endures: Mario Elie in his defiant, chip-on-shoulder best, pressing two fingers on his right hand to his lips to blow a kiss to the Phoenix Suns bench and send a farewell as the Rockets moved on toward their second-consecutive championship.

The "Kiss of Death" never entirely leaves Elie, as he is asked again and again to relive it throughout his life in Houston, and happily obliges, having come to share the warm feelings that Houston fans associate with the memory.

It was, however, a different image, far more private and difficult to define, that stuck with Rudy Tomjanovich and made that shot on that day in Phoenix possible long before Elie took a pass from Robert Horry and hit a corner three from in front of the Rockets' bench in America West Arena.

Late one night after an East Coast game, Tomjanovich had gone out to unwind, but could not stop thinking about basketball and the qualities in a player he admired most. He kept watching the late game and in particular, kept his eyes on a tough Portland player who battled as if angry, playing with something to prove.

Tomjanovich was in his first full season as Rockets coach, but knew what he wanted in a player. Even on that small television across the room, he saw it. He saw a player that competed as he had. He saw a player, though without some of Tomjanovich's All-American and NBA All-Star size and skills, with the same tenacity and even determination to prove doubters wrong.

Elie had many doubters. He had gone from New York to play at American International, hardly a basketball power, and was the 160th player taken in the draft by the Milwaukee Bucks when the draft was long enough for Elie to be made a seventh-round pick.

He made his way through the Irish Superleague, which as a starting point for NBA players, was anything but super. He played in Argentina and Portugal. He toured the minor leagues of the time, playing in the CBA and USBL. He spent five seasons working his way to the NBA, and played for the 76ers, Warriors, and Trail Blazers before signing with the Rockets. But even then, many scoffed when new owner Leslie Alexander had said the team would make a major addition before revealing the move to bring Elie to Houston.

Tomjanovich, however, remembered that night when he saw those qualities he wanted on the Rockets. By that season's training camp, the additions of Elie and Horry helped fire up intense competition at practices and a 15–0 start to the season. Elie averaged

9.3 points per game, then a career high. The Rockets won the first championship in franchise, and the city's, history.

By the next postseason, Elie had a larger role. The trade of Otis Thorpe for Clyde Drexler put most of Elie's minutes at small forward, but also moved Horry to power forward to close games.

By the 1995 Western Conference Semifinals, the Rockets had rallied back from a 3–1 deficit and had taken Game 7 to the final minute.

With 21.6 seconds left, Suns guard Kevin Johnson, who had made his first 20 free throws, missed. The Rockets called time out with the game tied 110–110. Tomjanovich knew Suns coach Paul Westphal would trap Kenny Smith in the backcourt and had Horry come up to take the pass.

Horry found Elie in the left corner with a crosscourt pass. Suns center Danny Schayes, concerned with Hakeem Olajuwon in the low post, rotated late. Elie never hesitated, launching the shot that put the Rockets in front to stay and himself into franchise history.

"I told [Elie] he was a wicked man," Olajuwon said. "He didn't just go for two. He went for the three."

Elie swished his three-pointer with 7.1 seconds remaining. When he turned toward the Suns bench, he saw Joe Kleine, the center with whom he had traded trash talk for two games, inspiring him to blow a kiss goodbye.

"[Kleine] started that in Game 5," Elie said. "It started as fun, but I got the last kiss. It was just emotion, friendly competition, and us going at each other for the second year in a row.

"Everybody dreams about making the winning shot in a playoff game. With nobody on you and nobody in the park, I can make that shot all day. But being there with 19,000 people screaming and yelling, it's a different story. I've dreamt about something like that my whole career. Players like me don't get the publicity or the ink and, usually, we don't get the chances to even take those shots."

The Rockets, however, believed in Elie, and especially in his determination to compete, with the same qualities that brought him that long way to that moment, the same qualities that Tomjanovich saw that night as the late game flickered in the background, making his career-defining shot typical.

"Don't ever question that guy's guts," Tomjanovich said, hinting at the "Don't ever underestimate the heart of a champion" directive that would come a month later.

Elie had become celebrated as the embodiment of that, the "Junkyard Dog" of the championship teams. Decades later, he is still stopped, still asked to share the moment. Still living in Houston, and with another championship ring from his time with the Spurs—where he threw the pass to lead to another defining shot, Sean Elliott's "Memorial Day Miracle"—Elie will happily recount his place in Rockets history, and that indelible image of the Kiss of Death.

"Only about a million and one times," Elie said. "It's on YouTube, and they show it on TV during the playoffs each year, and it's cool to see. I have triplets, and my kids don't think the old man could play. I can show them on video that I was pretty good."

31 The Shot

The Rockets had rolled to three consecutive wins and the brink of the series victory, but they still had to knock out the champs. As well as they had played, doubts about them—or perhaps confidence in the power of the Lakers—remained.

Ralph Sampson, however, had a message as direct and on target as the shot that would follow moments later.

"Get the ball in to me," Sampson said in the timeout huddle. "I'll get the shot. I'm going to score."

These were the Lakers of Kareem Abdul-Jabbar and Magic Johnson in their Showtime prime. They were the reigning NBA champions, assumed to be on their way to a rematch with Larry Bird and the Celtics in the NBA Finals. The Lakers were so confident that before Game 5, they sent 200 copies of their playoff media guide to the Celtics to be distributed in anticipation of their NBA Finals meeting.

When Hakeem Olajuwon was ejected from the game for his part in a fight with Mitch Kupchak, a Lakers big man and future general manager, the Lakers' confidence seemed warranted. The Rockets trailed by four with 5:14 left when Olajuwon departed with 30 points, seven rebounds, and four blocked shots. The lead would swell to nine. The champs, who had led by 12 in the third quarter, seemed to be regaining their footing and certain to send the series back to Houston.

The Rockets, however, rallied. Sampson took over, scoring the Rockets' next eight points. After a Johnson jumper with 37 seconds left gave the Lakers a three-point lead, Robert Reid missed a three, but Rockets guard Mitchell Wiggins grabbed the rebound. Given another chance, Reid hit his three to tie the game.

Byron Scott missed a jumper and Rockets guard Allen Leavell grabbed the rebound in time to call timeout with one second left, giving the Rockets a last possession to tie the game.

With that, Sampson made one of the most iconic shots in Rockets history and the finest moment of his career.

With one second remaining, Rockets coach Bill Fitch had forward Rodney McCray, the player drafted to be the final piece on a team built around Sampson and Olajuwon, inbound. Sampson, who more than ever seemed to be fulfilling his enormous potential, rolled toward the lane with Abdul-Jabbar moving with him.

"That last shot we got Ralph was [Denver coach] Doug Moe's play," Fitch told the *Houston Chronicle* in 2001. "I stole it from him. If you look at the Denver game, they ran it and [Blair] Rasmussen got wide open but missed the shot.

"We went into that timeout and in the huddle I said, 'Guys, remember Denver? Here's what we're running.' And I drew up the play Doug Moe used against us. We never ran it before that, and we never ran it after that."

That series against the Nuggets had taken a toll on the Rockets, with the clinching Game 6 going to double overtime and leaving the Rockets drained and with no preparation time for Game 1 against the Lakers less than 48 hours later. The Rockets lost that game, but won the next three games and were one second from either overtime or the series win as Sampson moved into possession for the game-winner.

McCray was shocked the Lakers did not have a defender on the ball and demanded the ball from the official before the Lakers could adjust and challenge his pass.

"I was getting all excited trying to get the official to hurry up and give me the ball," McCray said. "I couldn't believe the defense they were showing us."

Facing the Lakers bench, Sampson took McCray's pass 12 feet from the rim and with no time to land and go back up, turned slightly and pushed a shot over his right shoulder with a touch impossibly soft for a 7'4" center. The ball bounced straight up and then short-hopped the rim before falling through the net.

"I saw the basket, I knew where it was," Sampson said. "But I thought the shot was short."

The buzzer had sounded between bounces on the rim. After the shot, Sampson ran toward the Rockets bench, with teammates swarming him, forward Jim Peterson wrapping him in a tight hug. Lakers forward Michael Cooper fell to his back, his hands raised to his forehead in shock.

"My heart just dropped to my feet," Johnson said. "I felt like crying."

The Rockets celebrated a return to The Finals. On his way off the court, Sampson stopped long enough for an NBA interview, offering the description that would remain as true throughout his career as it was in the moment.

"It was," he said, "probably the best experience I've ever had in my basketball life."

32 Big Shot Bob

For all the shots that have come to define his career, the moments that added up to championships and spawned the nickname that endures, Robert Horry at first would not shoot.

Horry would cut. He would dunk. He would block shots with gusto. He would put up a shot or take off on a drive if he had to, but before Horry became celebrated forever as "Big Shot Bob," he was "Reluctant to Shoot Robert."

Before the shot against the Spurs, or the Kings, or the Pistons, helping the Rockets, Lakers, and Spurs to titles, the Rockets traded Horry to Detroit and changed him forever. In the chain reaction of events to follow, he helped change his era of basketball history.

Horry, who was traded for not providing enough offense, took no offense to the trade. He was not angry at the Rockets for trading him in his second season or upset when the deal, to get the firepower from Sean Elliott that the Rockets were not getting from Horry, was voided. Elliott had failed his physical. Horry and Matt Bullard were sent back to Houston. Horry was determined, not just

Robert Horry carries the Larry O'Brien Trophy during a victory celebration following the Rockets 113–101 victory over the Orlando Magic. (AP Photo/ Rick Bowmer)

to prove the Rockets wrong, but to play as if freed from the hesitation that had held him back.

"When I got to Detroit, I was like, 'Okay, I'm going to change my whole mindset,'" Horry said. "People think of me as a defensive player. I'm going to go in there and look to score. I'm going to show I can be more than one-dimensional.' My mind was open. I didn't look at it as a negative thing. A lot of guys when they get traded look at it as teams not wanting them. I looked at it as a team wanting me to help them succeed and to be better. I didn't look at it as a negative.

"It changed me. I'm going to just play, have fun, enjoy the game."

Horry decided he already had been traded. Make shots? Miss shots? It didn't matter. There was nothing else a team could do to him. No matter what might be on the line through the rest of his career, he would take the biggest of shots with a care-free nonchalance that allowed him to not so much shrug off pressure, but to never notice it in the first place.

"The best thing for my team at the time was to go out and be me," Horry said. "I went from a guy who was reluctant to shoot the basketball to if I got an open J I'm taking it. We started running more plays for me. I started being more aggressive. The next thing I know, I'm feeling good, we're playing better, and we're winning championships."

By Game 1 of the 1995 Western Conference Finals, Big Shot Bob was so relaxed, he forgot for a moment that he was in the game after a timeout in the final seconds. The Rockets trailed by one. The ball worked its way to Hakeem Olajuwon in the low blocks, who made his move and drew Dennis Rodman off Horry. Olajuwon by then had grown into a masterful passer out of double teams and found Horry on the wing.

Horry faked a pass to Sam Cassell on his left, coolly took one dribble to 18 feet, and nailed his jumper for the 94–93 lead with 6.5 seconds remaining.

"Playing in that game, I didn't make a shot," Horry said. "Dennis Rodman backed off me because Dream was totally annihilating David Robinson in that series. I got a shot. I took it and I knocked it down. That's what it's about, believing in myself and more importantly, my teammates believing in me. It's about having the confidence factor."

He never lost it. A player that was drafted to a team whose fans wanted Harold Minor, who began his career upset that Adam Keefe, drafted one spot before he was taken 11th, was paid more and who would be traded in his second season, became defined as clutch in Clutch City and beyond.

Horry nailed a similar shot, a three-pointer, on the Rockets' final possession to seal their Game 3 win against Orlando in The Finals, head-bobbing as he back-pedaled back down the floor. He hit buzzer-beaters with the Lakers to beat the Trail Blazers and Kings, and with the Spurs to beat the Pistons, winning seven titles in his career.

"Clutch means getting it done," Horry said. "I'm happy for being known as one of the clutch players in the game because that means I got it done no matter what.

"You have to have a 'I don't care' attitude. You have to play, whatever happens, happens. I don't even think about making it. If I make it, I make it. If I don't, oh well."

When Horry learned that, and then mastered it like few others, the legend of Big Shot Bob was born.

33 The Jet

Kenny Smith arrived in Houston with at least as much attention paid to the player dealt away as the one coming in, which was telling because the player traded away would never play again.

John Lucas' career was over when the Rockets sent him, along with injured center Tim McCormick and a conditional first-round pick, to Atlanta to get Kenny Smith. Smith had been a first-round pick of the Kings, the sixth player taken in a draft. He was a McDonald's All-American, as well as a college All-American at North Carolina. He had a limited role in his half-season with the Hawks, coming off the bench for the first time in his career, but he was no afterthought in the deal that brought him to Houston.

There just was no way to know quite how vital he would become to the championship success to come.

He immediately started and scored reliably, averaging a career-high 17.7 points per game on a career-best 52 percent shooting in 1990–91, his first season with the Rockets. That probably should have offered a clue of what could follow.

He was entrenched as a starter, but by his third season in Houston, when Rudy Tomjanovich had taken over as coach, Smith had become the perfect complement to the threat of Hakeem Olajuwon in the low post, the catch-and-shoot point guard adept at getting the Rockets into their Olajuwon-centric offense and knocking down the threes that increasingly became a key to their style.

By the championship seasons, Smith would share the position, first with Scott Brooks and then with Sam Cassell, but was very much a key to the championships.

There is no disputing Smith's hand in Clutch City, no difficulty finding his definitive moment on the way to back-to-back titles.

For Smith, there will always be Game 1 against the Magic in the 1995 Finals.

The Magic, overflowing with youthful confidence as well and the prodigious talents of Shaquille O'Neal and Penny Hardaway, led by 20 in the first half, that night before Smith began pouring in threes on his way to breaking the record for a Finals game at the time with seven.

In the closing seconds, when Nick Anderson missed his fourth-consecutive free throw with a Magic win in Game 1 likely one made shot away, Smith grabbed the rebound and called time out. With the game on the line, he drove toward an Hakeem Olajuwon screen, pump-faked Hardaway off his feet, and nailed the three to tie the game and send it to overtime.

Smith finished with 23 points and nine assists that night. The Rockets took Game 1 on Olajuwon's overtime tip. But Rockets coach Rudy Tomjanovich always insisted that Smith's three with 1.6 seconds left in regulation changed the course of the series by keeping the young Magic from gaining the momentum they could have ridden to a much different series. The Rockets finished their run to a second consecutive championship in a sweep.

After the Rockets were swept in the second round of the 1995–96 playoffs, Smith was released. He played briefly for the Pistons, Magic, and Nuggets, just 48 games in that one remaining season of his career.

Always loquacious with the Rockets, and often the last voice in the pregame huddle before the Rockets hit the floor, he moved seamlessly to broadcasting with TNT's *Inside the NBA*. But, as he often reminds Charles Barkley as he sits to his right, there is no topping those championship seasons.

"To me," Smith said, "I'm still a Rocket at heart."

34 Mad Max

The reactions are always the same as Vernon Maxwell makes his way around NBA arenas.

He could stop in the visitor's locker room in Charlotte, chatting with kindred spirit Patrick Beverley, or wave to the crowd in Toyota Center, where the good times are remembered and cherished. It doesn't matter. The comments quickly follow that Maxwell looks as if he has not aged. Beyond that, he looks like he could still light it up as he did in some of the greatest moments of Rockets history.

That is undeniably true and someday Maxwell might have to reveal the picture of Dorian Gray he keeps in an attic somewhere. But how fit he still looks obscures the smile that should be obvious.

Maxwell, long estranged from the franchise that defined his career, is back in the good graces of the Rockets. How he left the team is no longer relevant. The trials of a life sometimes gone wrong are behind him.

Maxwell returned for the 20th anniversary reunion of the championship teams. He does some college scouting for the Rockets, mostly informally and occasionally. He had made his peace with the way his time with the Rockets ended, when he was so enraged that they brought Clyde Drexler in to play his position that he protested so vehemently that Rudy Tomjanovich sent him packing, allowing the memories of his triumphs to rise again.

He was once again celebrated as the unstoppable force that put up 31 second-half points in Phoenix to help deliver the Rockets from Choke to Clutch City. He was the guy with the finishing kick against the Knicks when he scored 21 points in Game 7 as the Rockets clinched their first title. He was the fearless defender that was eager to take on even Michael Jordan, a key to the Rockets' success when they won five of six meetings with the Bulls during Chicago's first three-peat.

"People always ask me, if you have to pick one guy you want to go on the court and battle with, I tell them Vernon," former Rockets forward Robert Horry told NBA.com at the reunion. "Forget Shaq [O'Neal], forget Dream [Hakeem Olajuwon], forget Kobe [Bryant], you know because I know Vernon is going to fight until the end. He's that type of guy if you cut half his leg off, he's still going to be dragging out there trying to give you his all. That's one of the things we respect about him, so that's why we said whatever happened between you and management happened. We are still going to want you on this team if you want to be here. Unfortunately, it didn't work out that way,"

Because he was so often itching for a fight, the Mad Max side of him, part of what made him so integral to the Rockets' success, often got in the way. He went into the stands to punch a heckler in Portland, earning a 10-game suspension and a $20,000 fine. His quick temper earned technical fouls and ejections, and more fines for the difficulty to get him off the court. Finally, when he could not accept that the Rockets traded for Drexler, Tomjanovich banished him, beginning the two decades in which Maxwell was separated from the franchise.

"I handled it the wrong way," Maxwell said. "I shouldn't have left the way I left. I got upset because they brought Clyde in and nobody ever said anything to me about the trade. I just felt like they disrespected me. Then we went to Utah and played in Utah the first game. I didn't really play and I felt disrespected again."

"I overreacted like I normally do. Bad decision. I wish it wouldn't have happened."

It was not his last bad decision. He declared bankruptcy, failed to make child support payments, faced assault charges, and spent some jail time. But he also turned things around. When he was back in Houston and honored in Toyota Center, he and the Rockets had returned Mad Max to the best of times, when that fire worked for him and for them. He had gone home again, and back to the embrace of those that could marvel at how much he had grown, even if he looked nearly the same as ever.

"It helps me out a little bit [coming back to Houston], you know what I mean, because of the way I left, and then I haven't been back here since," Maxwell said. "I closed that door on this chapter of my life as far as Houston, Texas. I said I would never go back to Houston, Texas, again, but I opened it back up again. I'm here. I'm cool. I'm good."

35 O.T.

Think of the Rockets' first championship team and let the images return as if in a pregame highlight video.

You will quickly picture Hakeem Olajuwon "Dream Shaking." You might see Vernon Maxwell destroying the Suns or throwing that air punch as the triumph against the Knicks became certain. You could see Kenny Smith or Sam Cassell knocking down threes, or Robert Horry finishing dunks, or Mario Elie snarling defensively.

Otis Thorpe? You won't hear his voice. There is no signature moment. You might picture the strength of a piano mover or hands large and strong enough to crush a bowling ball, but he remains the stoic bass player providing the beat while attention is drawn to the singer at the front of the stage.

If the Rockets of the first championship season were a flag dancing in the breeze, he was the flagpole—strong and straight and sturdy—that made it work. No one notices the flagpole, but where would the flag be without it?

"OT was the guy who had my back," Hakeem Olajuwon told the *Houston Chronicle* in 2006. "There were a couple of years after Ralph Sampson was traded that I felt one of our biggest needs was to have somebody strong at the power forward position. I felt like if I went to block shots or to do all that I could on defense, that I was leaving us open on the inside.

"But all of that changed when OT came to the team. He was the kind of guy who you could always depend on. He was there for us every night and would always do whatever it took."

The Rockets knew what Thorpe brought, an understanding that made the move a season later to acquire Clyde Drexler at the cost of Thorpe even more daring than many recall. But in that first championship season, Thorpe was the quiet backbone, setting screens for shooters and hitting the boards as Olajuwon challenged shots. He defended the outstanding power forwards of the time and provided a second force inside.

In seven seasons with the Rockets, Thorpe averaged 15.8 points and 9.7 rebounds, making 55.9 percent of his shots. In 1991–92, when he averaged 17.3 points and 10.3 rebounds, he joined Olajuwon on the Western Conference All-Star team in Orlando.

"I would say my role was to back up Hakeem and take care of the boards, just to try to free up my guards, just to give us second opportunities on the offensive end," Thorpe said.

He fulfilled that masterfully, yet was often overlooked. He was a part of the 1984 Draft class, still considered perhaps the greatest ever. His best seasons were spent next to Olajuwon, the greatest Rockets player ever. When he was traded, he was dealt for a future Hall of Famer returning to his hometown.

When Houston celebrated that night, Thorpe was stunned and Rudy Tomjanovich uneasy not just with the difficult task of telling him, but with reaching the conclusion that the Rockets had to make the deal that would move a player so important to a championship season.

"Whenever you make a trade, it's going to be tough," Tomjanovich said that night. "I wanted to keep this team together and give them a chance to do it again.

"It's tough when you build a family. Otis was a big part of our championship. Sometimes, it isn't fair. But I have to give my strongest loyalty to the good of the Rockets. We felt this was a deal that could make us better."

The trade did help make the Rockets champions again. It did not change Thorpe's place in Rockets history as a vital part of the first championship team.

"Just being part of that team, you're talking about Kenny and Cassell, you're talking about Horry, you're talking about myself and Olajuwon… it was just unbelievable, unforgettable," Thorpe said. "We made it happen."

36 Sam I Am

As with the championships that seemed to come as soon as Sam Cassell pulled on his Rockets uniform, it was an all-too-brief flash of greatness before it was gone. But like those titles, Cassell's seasons with the Rockets were glorious and are cherished still.

The Rockets could not have known how great an impact Cassell would have. He was taken with the 24th pick of the 1993 Draft. He spent much of his rookie season backing up Kenny Smith, with Scott Brooks often the closer. He played just 17 minutes per game that season, averaging 6.7 points, but the boundless confidence was clear from training camp.

Once Cassell had his role, he owned it, loudly, proudly, and ideally as one of the stars of the championship teams.

The energy and enthusiasm were as irrepressible as all those pump fakes. Cassell would talk. And then talk. And then talk some more. He would board the bus after road games with his voice booming, an alarm clock to the sleeping veterans. When then-commissioner David Stern announced that the Rockets were "the 1994 NBA world champions," it is Cassell's voice that roars first, "Yeaaaaaaah!"

He backed up all that talk with the boundless confidence that had drawn Rudy Tomjanovich to him in the first place. The Rockets veterans had tested Cassell in that first training camp, going at him, measuring his mettle. Cassell took on all challenges, from those first weeks to the NBA Finals in Madison Square Garden.

"As a rookie, I knew it was going to be hard," Cassell said. "I just fought and fought and fought until I got the opportunity to showcase my talent to the city of Houston and to my coaching staff. Once they got comfortable with me, the rest was history."

By the postseason, he had moved ahead of Brooks and was nearly splitting playing time with Smith. He had earned his coaches' and his teammates' confidence, as he would soon demonstrate on the sport's biggest stage.

Still carrying rookie duties, with Tomjanovich still calling him "Rook," Cassell was closing games and was there in Game 3, at the top of the key, when Hakeem Olajuwon made his moves on Patrick Ewing, drawing Derek Harper off Cassell just enough for Olajuwon to deliver his pass. Cassell never hesitated, nailing the game-winning three-pointer with 32.6 seconds remaining. He would add a pair of no-doubt free throws to ice the win and cement his reputation for unshakeable confidence.

"When we got to The Finals, I think older guys—Robert [Horry], Vernon [Maxwell], Otis [Thorpe], and Hakeem—they didn't consider me a rookie anymore," Cassell said. "I was seasoned.

I'd been through the Western Conference playoffs against Phoenix and Utah and Portland. They had great teams at that time. By the time The Finals came, when I got an open jump shot, they expected me to make them. It wasn't surprising when I made that shot in Game 3 in New York. I took it and I made it."

By his second season, those performances were routine. When Kenny Smith had a sensational performance in Game 1 of the 1995 Finals, it was almost expected that Cassell would take his turn in Game 2. He did, scoring 31 points in Orlando on the way to the Rockets' sweep for a second consecutive championship.

Cassell backed up Smith for one more season. The Rockets struggled with injuries, never recapturing the momentum or magic of the championship seasons. After the Rockets were swept in the second round by the Seattle SuperSonics, the Rockets traded Cassell and Horry to the Phoenix Suns to bring in Charles Barkley.

The Rockets did it to give Olajuwon more help inside, especially on the boards, but Cassell was stunned and "bitter."

"To this day, I don't know why they traded me," Cassell said, 15 seasons and seven teams later. "I'm not bitter about it. That's in the past. At the time I was bitter. To win two championships and be traded."

He got over it. He played for six teams after the Suns, won a championship with the Celtics, and rejoined his coach in Boston, Doc Rivers, as an assistant with the Clippers. But just as Rockets fans will always think of Cassell as the young, cocky guard off the bench with the championship teams, Cassell still thinks fondly of those years in Houston.

"We had probably the best chemistry in basketball for two years," Cassell said. "We knew that wasn't the most talented team, but we understood we had the best player… in Hakeem Olajuwon and one of the best shooting guards of all time in Clyde Drexler.

"This is where it all started. I think it was the best two years in this franchise's history, the years that we won it from '93 to '95.

Nothing can replace that. Being on top of the mountain... and then coming back the next year and standing on that mountain was tremendous."

It was all over quickly, after just three seasons. But as with the championships they brought, Cassell's seasons in Houston only seem to have gotten better, more cherished with time.

"At the time, I didn't realize how big it was," Cassell said. "Now, as the years go on, I definitely understand what that means to the city of Houston, to my former teammates, to the coaching staff, it was tremendous. The city needed that. Being a young player, I didn't understand what it meant to win an NBA championship. I do now, trust me."

37 Sir Charles

Of all the things Charles Barkley has said about the Rockets, from his disparagement of Rockets general manager Daryl Morey and the use of analytics to his spin on the origins of the grudge he's had over the years, he should have gotten one basic thing right.

He did not. He was not always awful when playing for the Rockets, despite his analysis of his time in Houston.

He finished his career as a very different player than he was through most of his NBA seasons, lacking the explosiveness to dominate as he once had, almost looking like a retired player making a comeback before he actually hung them up. When he describes his play with his last NBA team he generally seems to be talking about the player he became.

He was by then slow and heavy, "backing it in, backing it in," as Rockets broadcaster Gene Peterson so often described it.

But though Barkley does not admit it, he was actually pretty good after the stunning deal that delivered a postseason rival to Houston.

He had forced the deal to the Rockets, threatening to retire if he was not traded to a contender, and specifically citing the Rockets.

"I'm excited because I called the shots," he said at the time. "When push comes to shove I think you have to stand up to the system."

The stunning trade sent four Rockets regulars—Robert Horry, Sam Cassell, Chucky Brown, and Mark Bryant—to the Phoenix Suns to acquire Barkley, with him hopefully becoming the difference to overcome a powerful Sonics squad. The goal was to have him prop open Hakeem Olajuwon's window longer. Instead, Barkley's closed too soon.

Barkley did help deliver on the original goal. Eliminated by the SuperSonics in a second-round sweep in 1996, the Rockets knocked off Seattle in the second round in 1997, Barkley's first season in Houston.

The Rockets seemed headed to Salt Lake City for Game 7 in the Western Conference Finals, but Clyde Drexler missed in the closing seconds, Barkley was late to switch defensively, and John Stockton hit a three-pointer at the buzzer to eliminate the Rockets.

Barkley averaged 19.2 points and 13.5 rebounds that season, the second-most rebounds he would average in his 16-year career. His numbers fell off a bit the following season as he battled injuries. The Rockets slipped into the playoffs at 41–41, but led the Jazz 2–1 in their first-round series. The Rockets led by 10 early in Game 4 of the best-of-five series, but Barkley went out when a collision with Antoine Carr left him with a torn triceps muscle.

The Rockets collapsed, scoring just 71 points in the loss and 70 points in Game 5, with Barkley's value clear when he was out.

Things began to unravel from there. The 1998–99 season started late because of the NBA lockout. Drexler had retired, but

August 19, 1996: Charles Barkley answers a question during the news conference after his trade to the Rockets, as new teammate Clyde Drexler laughs at his comments. (AP Photo/Christobal Perez)

the Rockets brought in Scottie Pippen. They never seemed fully in sync. After Game 1 in that season's first round against the Lakers slipped away, the Rockets were blown out in Game 2 and lost the series in five games.

After Game 1, Pippen blamed Barkley for intentionally fouling Shaquille O'Neal. Barkley pointed out that Pippen turned the ball over in the final half-minute with the Rockets holding a lead. Barkley averaged 23.5 points and 13.8 rebounds in the series, but everything about Barkley's tenure with the Rockets had begun to spiral.

When the Rockets were deep in trade talks with the Trail Blazers to deal Pippen, Pippen blasted Barkley, saying Michael Jordan had warned him about joining a team with Barkley and his notoriously bad work ethic. That ended the trade talks. The Rockets had to take the Blazers' offer on the table. But Barkley felt betrayed, having taken a $1 million contract to create the cap space for the Rockets to sign Pippen.

When he signed for $9 million to return to the Rockets, Barkley felt he had been short-changed, starting the grudge that lasted through his star turn on TNT's *Inside the NBA*.

By that last season with the Rockets, he was terribly miscast. Olajuwon was hurt. The Rockets were transitioning to the back-court of Steve Francis and Cuttino Mobley. Early in the 19th game of the season, Barkley's career came to a crashing end, back in Philadelphia where it began, when he ruptured his left quadriceps.

He'd said in the preseason that the season would be his last and flew in his mother and grandmother for his final game in Philadelphia.

"I am a little sad," Barkley said. "I cried a little bit. I cried a lot. But it's ironic that it happened here in Philadelphia. But I guess that's the Big Fella's way of working it out for you."

He did come back for one more game, rehabbing enough after his surgery to make a cameo in a last game with the Rockets. He grabbed an offensive rebound, put in a layup, and left to hugs and cheers.

On TNT, he became a frequent and vocal critic of the Rockets, eventually saying he was bitter because he was given a $9 million contract for his final season when he expected the $14 million he had made the season before he took his paycut to accommodate Pippen.

Morey shot back after one of Barkley's on-air criticisms of the Rockets, tweeting "Best part of being at a TNT game live is it is easy to avoid Charles spewing misinformed biased vitriol disguised as entertainment."

That sent Barkley into a long, postgame rant about the use of analytics, which he labeled "crap" and said those that use them are "a bunch of guys who have never played the game, and they never got the girls in high school."

In the coming years, the critiques became so frequent, Barkley eventually acknowledged the contract dispute that helped fuel them, and, after a particularly harsh rebuke, offered an apology to Morey, CEO Tad Brown, and former Rockets owner Leslie Alexander.

The feud largely seemed to end there. Brown had mocked Barkley's play with the Rockets and Barkley agreed. But there was a brief time in which he was the force the Rockets envisioned when they made the deal. It just did not pan out and did not last.

38 Tilman Fertitta

Tilman Fertitta had finished second, which in the competition to own the Rockets was a tie for last.

He still went to games in the years that followed. He remained a fan. He struck up a friendship with Leslie Alexander, the investment banker from New York and Florida that had barely edged him out to buy his hometown team, the team he loved since he was a child and his favorite player, Elvin Hayes, was its star.

He would build his restaurant, hotel, and gaming empire. He became the chairman of the board of regents at the University of Houston, his beloved alma mater. He became a star of a cable television program, *Billion Dollar Buyer*. But there remained a void to fill.

Fertitta was just 36 years old when Alexander's offer topped his by just $4 million. When Alexander made his surprising decision to sell the Rockets 24 years later, Fertitta was determined he would not lose again, even if he had to pay more than anyone ever had for an NBA franchise.

"There were a lot of people after this team," Fertitta said. "I got this team because I outworked everybody, I out-passioned everybody and just decided I would do whatever it took to get it.

"I just could not picture somebody else owning this team but me. I just couldn't fathom it."

Fertitta paid $2.2 billion to own the Rockets and control the operating rights of Toyota Center, becoming the 10th primary owner in Rockets history.

Fertitta, the chairman and CEO of Landry's Inc., was an "advisory director" to Alexander after Alexander purchased the team. He had been a fan since the 1970–71 season when a group led by Wayne Duddleston and Billy Goldberg called "Texas Sports Investments" announced the purchase of the team with a plan to move it to Houston.

"They had announced they were moving to Houston the next year," Fertitta said. "As soon as they announced it, you turn on the radio, because in junior high, you're such a big sports fan. I started listening to the Rockets because I knew they were going to be here. Even when I was in elementary school I was an Elvin Hayes fan. I was a University of Houston fan growing up. The Big E played for the San Diego Rockets and they were moving to Houston.

"To look 40 years. It's a business now, and a hobby, and a dream."

After his failed first effort to become the Rockets owner, Fertitta was so determined to get the team when it went on the market again, he did not make his bid based on what he thought they were worth, but on what he thought it would take to win. He declined team president Tad Brown's offer to see some of the books other prospective buyers had examined. He did not include the customary contingencies.

"Now, that I think about it… I had to sit there for 24 years," Fertitta said. "Les has been a very nice man to me, but I still had to look at him and be very friendly to him. I had him at Thanksgiving at my house. But I lost. I just didn't want to lose this time and I wanted to own a team in my hometown. I wanted to own the Houston Rockets. I was just not going to lose again.

"Everybody puts in a lot of contingencies. I put in $100 million, non-refundable, and no contingencies. And I said, 'I want to close on the team before the season starts October 17.' Nobody else did that. I knew it was my last opportunity."

Fertitta brought his family together to ask if there were anything else they would rather he spend $2.2 billion to own. Nothing, he said, came in a close second. Fertitta has continued with his television program and other endeavors, as well as the opening of The Post project, including its new hotel. He has been a regular at games and said he stays well-informed on decision-making by Brown and general manager Daryl Morey, but does not plan to take over from the office above the Toyota Center practice court.

His sons, Michael and Patrick, will be more closely involved, describing themselves as "in training" for future roles in the team's management as part of the family's ownership. Their father, however, has remained thrilled to have finally landed his team, his indefatigable enthusiasm unmistakable from the owners' front row seats.

"Very few people in life get to have every dream come true," Fertitta said. "I can tell you Tilman Fertitta so far—and life is funny, you never know if good or bad is going to happen—has been one of the fortunate ones. I get to have my dream come true."

39 Leslie Alexander

Few saw Leslie Alexander coming. Fewer expected him to leave.

An avid poker player, Alexander knew better than to show his hand. There were no tells. He offered few signs, even with the advantage of retrospect, that he would sell the Rockets 24 years after he had arrived as a relative unknown investment banker, a move controversial at the time but which birthed the most successful stretch in Rockets history.

Alexander did as he pledged, and then was gone. The Rockets competed for championships, winning in each of his first two seasons as owner, and they gave back to the community.

Those were the missions Alexander had described in his first meeting with former Rockets general manager Carroll Dawson and coach Rudy Tomjanovich. In that regard, he left with his mission accomplished.

His legacy will go well beyond his characteristically brief mission statement, from ushering in the NBA's analytics movement with his surprise choice of Daryl Morey to succeed Dawson to several portions of the NBA's collective bargaining agreement he helped create and even to the day in Phoenix he labeled the Rockets "Clutch City."

In Alexander's 24 years as owner, the Rockets had the second-most winning seasons in the NBA and the fifth-best winning percentage. The Clutch City Foundation, the team's charitable wing, raised more than $35 million for local charities, including the $4 million Alexander donated in March. His final act as owner, other than coming to an agreement to sell the team to Tilman Fertitta, was a personal donation of $10 million to Mayor Sylvester Turner's Hurricane Harvey Relief fund.

It never got better, however, than the way it started.

"I'm the only owner in the history of sports who has bought a team that won the championship the first two years," Alexander said before the 2013–14 season, 20 years after his purchase of the team. "When I got to the Rockets, I realized it was really a golden opportunity because the team was so good. I thought I was buying a championship team when I bought it. I watched a lot of basketball. When they lost to Seattle the previous year, I said, 'Man, next year, they're probably going to win it all. They are really good and they have the best player in the league.' I thought I was buying a championship team."

He did, and to make it sweeter, they won by beating the Knicks, the team of his youth. But the years since the championships saw incredibly mixed results. The Rockets followed Alexander's penchant for headline stars, bringing in Charles Barkley, Scottie Pippen, Yao Ming, Tracy McGrady, and James Harden and Chris Paul. They also went through crushing injuries and spectacular postseason defeats.

The Rockets twice reached the Western Conference Finals in the seasons after the championships, but advanced past the first round in the playoffs just five times since Alexander held the championship trophy.

As an owner, he was far more involved than his reputation, insisting on being well-informed on every significant move and the logic behind it. Staffers learned that they could not say what they believed needed to be done, but rather had to be prepared to make a convincing argument. That made Daryl Morey an ideal fit, with his data-driven approach as a general manager well-suited for Alexander's pursuit of information as an owner and investor.

"He's a pioneer in all these industries, which is the way he made his money," Morey said. "You have to be forward-thinking, smarter than everyone else. He transferred that to basketball."

Alexander also played a role, generally behind the scenes, in the creation of some of the staples of the NBA's collective bargaining rules, including the use of a percentage of the salary cap to determine maximum contracts, veteran contracts in which the league contributes a portion of the salary, and the "one-and-done rule" for college players entering the league.

Though he appeared to study the games more than enjoy them, Alexander cared deeply, as any staffer on the phone after a win or loss clearly knew after hearing Alexander unashamedly giddy or angry.

In the end, however, that led Alexander to decide he was ready to give up the team. Had he cared less about the results, or were not as involved in the decision-making, there would not have been a grind to escape.

For all his interests and time spent far removed from Toyota Center, Alexander could not run the Rockets any other way. As if putting the Rockets' house in order, in his final months as owner, he signed CEO Tad Brown and Morey to long-term contracts, extended Harden's contract for $228 million over six years, and completed the trade for Paul.

He also, typically, sold high, selling the Rockets to Tilman Fertitta, whom he barely edged to buy the team 24 years earlier, for a record $2.2 billion.

There was a time, however, long after the championships had been won, after stars had come and gone, that Alexander still enjoyed owning the Rockets, almost as much as when he first came to town an unknown soon-to-be-a champion.

"I love owning the team," he said 20 years after the first title. "I love having the opportunity to give back to the city. I love a lot of the people I've met in the city, the players, some of the business people, the coaches, all the people involved in it."

Then, he decided he'd had enough, with his feelings just as unknown before the stunning announcement that he would leave as they'd been when he arrived.

40 Charlie Thomas

Had Charlie Thomas sold the Rockets sooner, he would have still had a hand in the success to come, having presided over the assembly of much of the talent that would win championships in each of the first two seasons with Leslie Alexander in the owner's corner office.

Thomas likely would have still taken his seats, part of the deal when he sold the team to Alexander, a few rows off the court next to the players' entrance in The Summit. He would have collected his cars and run his dealerships and been just fine.

It was better, however, the way things had worked out, with peace in his time.

Thomas, who had let Moses Malone go to the 76ers when the price of keeping the MVP became too steep for a new owner, had reached an impasse with Hakeem Olajuwon a decade later.

Olajuwon had cited a hamstring injury. The Rockets argued Olajuwon was angling for an extension of his contract. Olajuwon demanded an apology. The Rockets suspended him.

The atmosphere became toxic and the Rockets slumped badly, winning just one of their final six games to miss the playoffs. At next season's media day, Olajuwon and Thomas shook hands and then went to neutral corners to demonstrate little had changed.

Olajuwon called Thomas "a coward." Thomas, who had tried to trade the player that would become a franchise icon, said he was not trying to create a friendship.

"I'm not trying to build a personal relationship here," Thomas said. "If he wants a personal relationship then it's up to him to come to me. You know who makes people happy? Themselves. People make themselves happy."

Olajuwon had no interest in that.

"There is an old saying in my country, 'Silence is the best answer for a fool,'" Olajuwon said. "I don't want to get down in the mud with this organization. Everything will come out."

Had it ended there, 10 years after Thomas had purchased the team from the Maloof family for $11 million, two years after George Maloof died, Thomas would have likely moved on with no regrets. But he had trouble finding a buyer and remained the owner for the 1992–93 season. On the long flight to Tokyo to open the season against the SuperSonics, Thomas and Olajuwon finally sat together, spending enough of those 14 hours of travel to work out their differences.

"I'm a businessman," Thomas said. "He's a businessman."

Both were very good at it. Olajuwon had one of his best seasons, averaging 26.1 points and 13 rebounds. In March, he received that contract extension. The nucleus of the first championship team—Olajuwon, Otis Thorpe, Vernon Maxwell, Kenny Smith, Robert Horry, Sam Cassell, and Matt Bullard—was in place. Rudy Tomjanovich had become the head coach in 1992.

In July of 1993, Thomas sold the franchise to Alexander for $85 million. He had worked his way up from poverty, building a car dealership empire, at one point owning about two thirds of the Houston car marketplace. In the coming years, he would indulge in his hobby, collecting more than 160 antique cars. And he continued to be a fixture at Rockets games, able to revel in the championship teams he helped build.

41 Linsanty-ish

Not quite seven months earlier, Jeremy Lin was one of too many players rushing through a lockout-delayed training camp on the Toyota Center practice court.

The Rockets had liked what they saw. First-year Rockets coach Kevin McHale loved the attitude on display even in those few practices. The Rockets, however, cut Lin on Christmas Eve, knowing there would be little playing time for a third point guard behind future All-Stars Kyle Lowry and Goran Dragic, and believing the contract of Jonny Flynn could be more useful in a trade.

Now, Lin was back, with satellite trucks lining the street outside the practice court windows. The court, turned into an oversized press conference room, was packed with media. Requests poured in from ESPN, CNN, *Today*, *The Late Show with David Letterman*, *Late Night with Jimmy Fallon*, *HBO Real Sports*, *The Dan Patrick Show*, *The Jim Rome Show*, *Mike and Mike*, and *Pardon the Interruption*.

His departure from Houston had been barely noticed, more noteworthy as a move to clear a roster spot for center Samuel Dalembert than for the player that left.

His return was celebrated, a scene that vividly demonstrated the incredible sudden blast of success and celebrity of Lin's ascension from obscurity to sensation in New York.

In some ways, however, it also marked the final day of Linsanity.

Yet, as unique as Lin's rise with the Knicks had been, his time back with the Rockets was remarkable in its own way from start to finish.

It began with Lin signing an ingeniously crafted contract designed to keep the Knicks from signing the star of their previous season.

When Steve Nash agreed to sign with the Lakers, rather than the Raptors, the Rockets traded Lowry to Toronto to get the first-round pick they hoped would key a trade for Dwight Howard and eventually was used to land James Harden.

The Rockets lost Dragic as a free agent when they would not agree to give him a player option on the fourth season of his contract. They had been in talks with Lin, but with Lowry and Dragic gone, had increased urgency to land him, reaching agreement on a four-year, $28.8 million contract with the final season at the team's option.

Rockets owner Leslie Alexander, however, instructed general manager Daryl Morey to come up with a deal tougher for the Knicks to match, so the new deal was reworked to be $25 million over three years, with $15 million backloaded to the final season. That could have forced the Knicks to pay $35 million in salary and luxury taxes that season. New York owner James Dolan was offended that Lin reworked the deal with the Rockets. Just as the Rockets had in December, the Knicks let Lin go.

They did not stop there, however. In 2012, teams had to deliver the actual offer sheet to representatives of a player's previous team or team offices to begin a three-day clock to match and keep a restricted free agent. With the Knicks offices closed for the weekend, Glen Grunwald, then the Knicks general manager, refused to open the door in his Las Vegas hotel room or come to the front desk to pick up the offer sheet. Soon Rockets staffers fanned out from his hotel to the UNLV arenas to try to find him and hand him the signed offer sheet.

Once the offer sheet reached the offices in New York, the teams agreed on a time to consider the clock started, but Morey still did not believe he would land Lin. Even after reports surfaced that Dolan had signed off on letting Lin walk, Morey did not believe it. The night before the deadline, Grunwald told Lin of his decision and the Knicks signed Raymond Felton to replace him, allowing Morey to finally exhale.

The Rockets had always thought Lin had a chance to succeed on some level in the NBA. They had offered Lin a contract after he went undrafted out of Harvard, only to be beaten by the Warriors' larger guarantee. They picked him up on waivers to get a look at him in that brief camp. Days before Lin's run with the Knicks would begin, he had a long visit with Rockets coach Kevin McHale before a game in Toyota Center. At the height of Linsanity, when Lin stunned the Lakers, McHale had called around Phoenix in search of a sports bar showing the game.

By the next season, with Lin back in red, the Rockets seemed certain to be shorthanded, relying largely on a backcourt of Lin and Kevin Martin. Days before the season, however, the Rockets pulled off the trade for James Harden.

In New York, Lin had taken off when injuries and absences left the Knicks with little choice but to put the ball in his hands and let him attack in pick-and-roll. When Carmelo Anthony returned, Lin was no longer as featured or dominant. With Harden, Lin played well, but he was not ideally suited to playing off another star.

He played well, but did not repeat Linsanity. It was never fair to measure him by that standard and McHale often reminded people that he should not be expected to live up to that sensational level of play. Lin had averaged 24.6 points and 9.2 assists in that stunning 10-game run with the Knicks, going from a guest on Landry Fields' couch to an international sensation.

In his first season with the Rockets, Lin averaged 13.4 points and 6.1 assists, close to the numbers of his season in New York, though he battled knee issues through much of that season. He matched the 38 points he scored against the Lakers at the height of Linsanity with 38 against the Spurs. He had 22 points with nine assists in his return to New York. He had 28 against the Warriors and a solid 14 points with 10 assists in his first game back in Oakland. With Harden out, he had 34 in Philadelphia.

The playoffs, however, were a struggle. He made just 5 of 20 shots in the first three games, before going out with a chest injury. The Rockets were eliminated in six games, clearly missing him after his injury.

By the next season, Lin was moved to the bench, with McHale believing he could be more of an instant-offense focal point with the second unit and that Pat Beverley was a strong fit with Harden.

There were moments again, particularly with the preseason trip to Taipei, where Lin's appearance in Taiwan reminded of how immensely popular he remained in his parents' homeland. He rose to that occasion, scoring 17 points and throwing down a sensational dunk, as if a gift to those that yearned to relive the madness that made him such a sensation in the first place.

Lin averaged 12.5 points and 4.1 assists that season, starting 33 games. As with the Rockets as a whole, he was wildly inconsistent through the playoff series loss to the Trail Blazers. When Damian Lillard's three-pointer at the buzzer ended that season, it was clear that the Rockets that reconvened the following season would be very different.

Even that inspired outsized emotions and one last stunning turn of events. While recruiting Carmelo Anthony as a free agent, the Rockets produced images of him wearing No. 7, the number still assigned to Lin. Lin's fans were outraged. Lin was offended.

Days later, to create cap room for their near-miss pursuit of Chris Bosh, the Rockets shipped Lin to Los Angeles, adding a first- and second-round pick to get the Lakers to take the $15 million left on Lin's contract off their hands.

It was an ignominious end to Lin's two seasons in Houston. In many ways, however, Lin's initial two-week and subsequent two-season tenures in Houston were marked by issues of timing. He was let go the first time because the Rockets had Lowry and Dragic at the position. Had they kept him, he likely would not have had the opportunity that begat Linsanity. He was reduced to a role player the second time because the Rockets acquired Harden and eventually Dwight Howard.

Lin played well in Houston, but he was not a star and eventually, not a starter. His time with the Rockets came before and after his ascension to stardom unlike any other. It did not measure up to that, but it was an interesting ride.

42 The Franchise

The goal was as simple as the nickname and the nickname was about much more than a fortuitous pun.

Bestowed by Rockets play-by-play broadcaster Bill Worrell at the first chance he had, the nickname stuck. Steve Francis became "Stevie Franchise." His job was clear. His ambition was great enough to embrace the pressure of outsized expectations in a city and fan base still close enough to the championship years to yearn for a return to that glory and accept nothing less as satisfactory.

Rockets coach Rudy Tomjanovich and general manager Carroll Dawson had sought to rebuild without falling to the early picks. When Francis balked at playing in Vancouver, making no effort to hide his draft-night displeasure with being selected second by the woeful Grizzlies, the Rockets made their move.

The Rockets sent Michael Dickerson, Othella Harrington, Brent Price, Antoine Carr, and a first-round pick in a massive three-team, 11-player, three-pick deal to make Francis the hope of the future.

Francis would play two seasons with Hakeem Olajuwon. He would team in a backcourt with Cuttino Mobley, becoming "brothers" in Houston. He would duel Vince Carter in an unforgettable dunk contest in Oakland. He would even start three All-Star games, letting Michael Jordan goad him into taking a free throw with his eyes closed in one, scoring 20 points in another, and lobbing a perfect pass to Yao Ming in a third.

For all the ups and downs—and there were plenty—Francis played well in Houston, averaging 19 points and six rebounds over five seasons. Yet, Francis was always measured against the hopes that came with him as soon as he engineered his controversial move to Houston before ever playing a game in Canada. (He always said his reaction was in part from shock because Grizzlies general manager Stu Jackson had told him that the Grizzlies were not drafting him.)

The Rockets' hopes were not unfounded. Francis had been a sensation at Maryland, filling the evening sportscasts with highlights in the year the NBA lockout created a void. He averaged 18 points and 6.6 rebounds as a rookie and was named co-Rookie of the Year with Elton Brand, the player taken ahead of him in the draft.

He averaged 19.9 points in his second year and 21.6 the following season. But he also developed an inner ear condition, Menieres Disease, that caused blinding migraine headaches. The Rockets slumped to 28–54, but with Francis on the lottery podium, won the right to draft Yao Ming.

Steve Francis, following his draft-day trade from Vancouver to Houston, grins during a press conference with coach Rudy Tomjanovich. (AP Photo/Pat Sullivan)

The Rockets bounced back enough to go 43–39, but that late season, Rudy Tomjanovich had to take a leave of absence to treat bladder cancer. The Rockets faded late and missed the playoffs again. In many ways, though no one could have known, the clock began ticking toward the end of Francis' time as the Franchise.

When Tomjanovich stepped down as coach, Jeff Van Gundy was hired to bring the discipline former Rockets owner Leslie

Alexander believed the Rockets lacked. Francis and he clashed, most notably when Francis skipped a flight to Phoenix to attend the Super Bowl in Houston. Van Gundy suspended Francis for the game against the Suns. When the team returned to practice in Houston, Francis said he and Van Gundy worked things out over breakfast. Van Gundy later said he had no idea about any meal together.

With Van Gundy moving the Rockets' offense to the inside-out style he preferred, and that better suited the growing gifts of Yao Ming, Francis' numbers suffered. Francis went along with the changes, with the Rockets finally making the playoffs. They showed more promise than the 4–1 series loss to the Lakers might indicate, losing Game 1 by a point and another in overtime before the Game 5 blowout.

Van Gundy went into that off-season unsure if Francis could partner with Yao as the cornerstones of a champion, but he was not ready to rule it out. The Rockets had made undeniable progress. Francis had entered his prime, but Yao was not yet in his. The Rockets had not decided to move on from Francis, but he was clearly no longer the Franchise.

When Tracy McGrady balked at an insistence by former Magic general manager John Weisbrod that he pledge to remain in Orlando after the following season, rather than opt out of his contract to become a free agent, Dawson made his move. He engineered a seven-player trade that would send Francis along with Mobley and Kelvin Cato to the Magic for McGrady, Juwan Howard, Reece Gaines, and Tyronn Lue.

Francis would remain with his backcourt buddy Mobley, but again would be supplanted as the Franchise by a young star center, Dwight Howard. He put up good numbers that first season, but was traded by the next trade deadline. He never reprised the sort of excitement and promise of those initial seasons in Houston.

Francis was dealt from Orlando to New York and New York to Portland. The Trail Blazers bought out the remaining $34 million on the max contract Francis had signed in Houston before he ever played there. He did have a largely forgotten 10-game cameo in Houston in 2007–08, but soon retired after nine seasons at 30.

There was, however, that brief time when Francis shined.

"I can definitely say that my time here as a Rocket helped me become a better person and a better basketball player," he said. "I'll always be a Rocket."

43 The Cat

Cuttino Mobley could have considered himself cursed by timing, forced to win in a no-win situation. He never looked at it that way.

Mobley viewed himself as blessed, fortunate to be drafted to a team with three Hall of Famers, luckier still to be joined a year later by a like-minded young talent that would become his brother.

To others, it might have seemed that those six years in Houston were a time the Rockets could not realize their potential. In some ways, they were. To Mobley, they were a joy ride, the best times of his career.

Mobley was drafted in the second round in the season the Rockets had three first-round picks. But the Rockets decision-makers, Rudy Tomjanovich, Carroll Dawson, and Dennis Lindsey, had targeted him through that season at Rhode Island and spent much of that 1998 draft night with fingers crossed even as they sought to bolster the roster with players taken earlier.

Mobley had been overshadowed by the other moves, not just by Michael Dickerson, who was the lottery pick, or Bryce Drew, the NCAA Tournament hero taken next, but also by the decision to take Mirsad Turkcan with the next pick, with the team controversially passing on local high school star Rashard Lewis.

When the NBA lockout ended the next January, the Rockets signed Scottie Pippen to add him to a frontcourt with Hakeem Olajuwon and Charles Barkley, but the backcourt needed to be entirely rebuilt.

Clyde Drexler had retired after the 1997–98 season. Matt Maloney's brief tenure as the Rockets starting point guard ended with the first-round loss, reduced to 15 games in an injury-filled season and then a release.

That left the Rockets turning to their draft picks. Dickerson slid in easily at shooting guard, bringing athleticism and shooting range behind a frontcourt lacking both. With Drew not ready, Mobley took over at the point.

Mobley, however, was no point guard, as Pippen and Barkley repeatedly reminded him. Still, he overachieved that season, averaging 9.9 points for a 31–19 team and establishing himself as part of the core of the Rockets rebuilding to come.

"Coming to Houston and having Scottie Pippen, Charles Barkley, and Hakeem Olajuwon my first year was a dream come true, three of the top 50 players ever to play the game teaching me every single day," Mobley said. "I took that and figured if they believed in me I can believe in me."

Before the next season, Pippen was shipped to Portland, Barkley announced that the 1999–2000 season would be his last, and the Rockets traded for Steve Francis, the second pick of the draft. With Dickerson traded in the deal for Francis, Mobley could move to his natural shooting guard position. He and Francis would become the heart of the Rockets' hopes to rebuild without losing.

Mobley and Francis, both young talents from Northeast cities (Philadelphia and the Washington area, respectively,) immediately clicked, with Mobley calling them "brothers for life."

"Dream and Charles, when they left, it was more so Steve's and my team," Mobley said. "I just loved playing off him. Playing off of Steve and Steve playing off of me, after a while, it became natural."

They played five seasons together in Houston, with Mobley averaging 17.1 points and four rebounds with the Rockets. But just like his time at point guard after the primes of Barkley, Olajuwon, and Pippen, Mobley was caught between Rockets' eras.

He and Francis were traded for Tracy McGrady before Yao Ming reached his potential. Mobley remained a reliable scorer, far more accomplished than would have been expected of the 41st player taken in a draft. But he never had the success to match the hopes that came with playing with Hall of Famers or as one of the faces of the franchise when they left.

Still, he had no complaints, looking at his time in Houston as the best of his career.

"To be here," he said, "was a blessing."

44 Jeff Van Gundy

Jeff Van Gundy missed being miserable. If nothing else, his four seasons with the Rockets delivered that.

There were successes and disappointments. There were moments, from Tracy McGrady's 13 points in 33.3 seconds to Yao Ming's flashes of dominance, that demonstrated great promise. But there were the postseason disappointments, especially and ultimately the final series of his Rockets tenure, when the Rockets lost Game 7 at home to the Utah Jazz, that led to the messy breakup.

"The misery is part of what you miss, that pit in your stomach every day of the year about what could go wrong and trying to find solutions to problems," Van Gundy had said on the day he was introduced as Rockets coach. "The great thing about broadcasting is when you're done with the game you don't go back to the hotel and worry about the result.

"The problem is, you don't have the elation after you have a great win or a playoff series victory. I miss the competition and certainly you miss the camaraderie of the players and coaching staff. There are a lot of good reasons to get back into coaching."

The Rockets chose Van Gundy over such luminaries as Larry Brown, Paul Silas, and Mike Dunleavy to succeed Rudy Tomjanovich. He sought to instill discipline to a young, talented team led by Yao, Steve Francis, and Cuttino Mobley; ended a four-year playoff draught in his first season; and then pulled off the trade for McGrady.

As with many Rockets teams of the time, things went wrong when the injuries took over, but at first, it was not Yao and McGrady that broke down. McGrady did have back issues at the time, but he and Yao played throughout the first-round series against the Mavericks, taking a 2–0 series lead in Dallas. But the Rockets ran out of healthy bodies around them, with Juwan Howard out with a heart condition, Bob Sura going out during the series, and David Wesley struggling to play hurt.

With that, the injuries caught up to Yao and McGrady. By Van Gundy's fourth season, Yao did return for the first round, though clearly not at full strength. By Game 7 in Houston, Yao and McGrady both had 29 points, but the Rockets were unable to secure a defensive rebound on three consecutive missed Jazz jump-shots, as the Jazz took the win and the series.

New general manager Daryl Morey sought to talk to Van Gundy about returning, but Van Gundy, distraught after the loss, wasn't ready. They differ on Van Gundy's endorsement of starting a coaching search, with Morey saying Van Gundy thought Morey and former Rockets owner Leslie Alexander should consider their options, and Van Gundy calling that "revisionist history."

The following week, Van Gundy did speak highly of Rick Adelman, but as he got further removed from the loss, he did want to return.

By then, Alexander had come to view Adelman as his preference.

"At the end of the season, we were ready to sit down and discuss [Van Gundy coming back as Rockets coach]," Morey said. "But at that point, Jeff was unsure. We then went ahead and talked to alternative candidates and became positive about them.

"It really hadn't come to a head until Jeff came to us and said he wanted to coach. At that point, we were positive about alternative candidates."

There were talks about Van Gundy remaining in an advisory role, but they went nowhere. He was fired a day short of two weeks after the loss to the Jazz, with Adelman brought on to replace him.

In an unexpected turn, however, Morey and Van Gundy developed a strong relationship. Van Gundy remained in Houston while working as the lead game analyst for ABC/ESPN. When the Rockets were looking for a successor to Kevin McHale, Morey wanted Alexander to consider Van Gundy and Van Gundy was open to meeting with Alexander.

Nothing came of that. Alexander quickly decided that if he were to hire a veteran coach it would be Mike D'Antoni. Alexander wanted to play an up-tempo style and decided that even if Van Gundy was willing to adjust and play that way, it would not be as natural to him as it is to D'Antoni.

Van Gundy returned to coaching with the USA Basketball senior team for FIBA AmeriCup 2017, seeming much happier in the role, and often more comical on the air, than he was with the Rockets. Van Gundy was as he said he would be when he took the job, and nearly broke through before a few rebounds bounced away and he lost his job while deciding whether he was willing to fight for it.

"This is probably as good as it gets," Van Gundy said when introduced as Rockets coach. "I'm going to look as good as I can today and then it will be all downhill, the bags under the eyes, the worry, but I'll be fine. I never quite feel as bad as I look."

He just missed the misery, and in that respect, he found what he was missing only to learn he could live without it.

45 Rick Adelman

Leslie Alexander was sold nearly as soon as he met Rick Adelman. He liked Adelman's experience, loved the free-flowing offense, was happy to move from games played in the 80s to regularly topping 100.

As with so much about the Rockets in those years, all that was true, but it also did not pan out, with Adelman—as with Jeff Van Gundy before him and Kevin McHale after—exiting after four seasons.

Adelman might never had had a chance to achieve much more than he did as the Rockets coach during the years of Tracy McGrady's and Yao Ming's injury-filled decline. He left with the best winning percentage in Rockets coaching history, though that would be surpassed by each of his successors, Kevin McHale and Mike D'Antoni. But Adelman had to win with Yao often breaking down and McGrady succumbing to a rapid regression following microfracture surgery.

The Rockets at their best under Adelman, however, were unbeatable for one thrilling, remarkable, unforgettable stretch.

When Adelman's offense, with high-post and elbow-passing and constant movement, took hold, the Rockets could score reliably even without his stars. The defense was far better than most recall, ranking second in points allowed per possession in 2007–08. When the Rockets reached their peak, they ran off 22 consecutive wins, rolling from late January to mid-March before finally hitting a wall.

The Rockets lost Yao 10 games into the winning streak. They went through so many injuries, only Shane Battier, Chuck Hayes, and Rafer Alston avoided injuries that would cost extensive stretches. After the streak, the Rockets went 9–7 the rest of the season. They lost to the Utah Jazz in six games in the first round of the playoffs.

A year later, the Rockets finally broke through, beating the Portland Trail Blazers in the first round and taking the eventual-champion Lakers to seven games, even with Yao hurt again, this time going out in Game 3. The Rockets had gone from winning 55 games to winning 53, and were viewed very much as a team on the rise.

Then, they fell apart, in some ways literally.

Yao did not play at all in the 2009–10 season. McGrady played in just six games, at one point in Minneapolis declaring himself back before the team or doctors agreed, even digging his uniform out of a travel trunk and forcing a pregame conference with Adelman. Before long, McGrady was sent back to Houston to focus on his rehab while the Rockets worked to trade him. The team Adelman signed to coach was largely gone.

McGrady was traded for Kevin Martin. The Rockets slumped to 42–40 and missed the playoffs. The following season, the team moved to rebuild mode, dealing Shane Battier back to Memphis. Adelman and Rockets general manager Daryl Morey never seemed quite in concert again.

"You cannot succeed in this league unless everybody is on the same page," Adelman said as that season wound down. "You may not agree with everything together. But you have to be on the same page, and you have to have each other's back, or the players—they sense it. They know it when there is a disconnect. Frankly, I would say in the last month and a half, since the trade, people have gone their way, and we're here to fight the battle.

"When it's all good, it's pretty easy. When it's not all good, it's even more important that you have communication and an interchange that is pretty consistent day in, day out."

The Rockets finished strong that year, going 17–8 down the stretch. But they missed the playoffs again, becoming the first team since the Phoenix Suns in 1970–71 and 1971–72 to have consecutive winning seasons fall short of the postseason.

The Rockets had moved from the era built around Yao and McGrady—who played just 72 games together in Adelman's four seasons—to a team that was built around Adelman's motion-based offense. But when Adelman and Morey met after the season, the disconnect was clear.

They had met over the course of four days, with Adelman so encouraged by the way his rebuilt team came together down the stretch, he was certain he wanted to continue coaching but unsure he wanted to do it in Houston. He called Adelman "a Hall of Fame coach" when he showed him the door, with Adelman happy to take it.

As with so much in that era, Adelman's time was marked as much by what could have been as what was accomplished. But there were the flashes, from the postseason success to the regular-season streak, that endure.

46 Kevin McHale

Over his years as Rockets owner, when the subject of contract extensions came up, Leslie Alexander insisted he saw no point. A coach under contract did not need to supersize the contract. He would not be going anywhere.

Then, shortly before Christmas in 2014, Alexander announced a three-year extension for Kevin McHale.

Alexander believed he had such a coaching star, he wanted to take no chances on McHale becoming a free agent. When the Rockets reached that season's Conference Finals, Alexander once again seemed prescient. He had given McHale a rich deal, worth $4 million for each of the three seasons he had added to McHale's contract. But he had the coach he wanted locked up before the Rockets' best season since 1996–97 had ended.

Less than a year after breaking all of his precedent, Alexander did something else he never had before and always said he would not. He fired McHale just 11 games into the 2015–16 season.

McHale's four-plus sometimes-stormy seasons as Rockets coach had ended as stunningly as it began when he was the surprise choice to succeed Rick Adelman on the Rockets bench. Alexander had gone from selecting coaches that had taken teams to the NBA Finals—Jeff Van Gundy and Adelman—to a Hall of Fame player that had never coached a full NBA season.

The first season was rough, starting late after the NBA lockout with McHale determined to push his new team into shape rapidly in the abbreviated training camp. Accustomed to Adelman's low-key style, Rockets players balked at McHale's demands in the Bill Fitch mode. He clashed with Kyle Lowry, at one point grabbing his point guard in Denver and dragging him into a huddle. Lowry declared after that season, he would not play for McHale again.

He never did. Lowry was traded to the Raptors for the pick that would key the trade for James Harden. Chandler Parsons, in his second season, excelled. Jeremy Lin and Patrick Beverley gave McHale solid backcourt options next to Harden. The Rockets, by then very much in sync with McHale, won 45 games.

They repositioned their roster to have cap room to chase Dwight Howard, and landed the prized free agent of the summer of 2013 in large parts because he wanted to play for McHale.

The following season ended in the first round on Damian Lillard's buzzer-beater in Portland, but a year later, the Rockets broke through. Their comeback in Game 6 in Los Angeles led to a seven-game series win and their first appearance in the Conference Finals since 1997.

They were never the same. Harden sprained an ankle in the off-season, struggled through the preseason, and was inconsistent in the first few weeks of the 2015–16 season. Howard, who had missed half of the previous season with knee problems, struggled with his role and did not mesh with Harden. The more McHale warned of the issues he saw, the more his team tuned him out.

The Rockets lost each of the first three games of the 2015–16 season by 20 points. They won four straight, but seemed disinterested through four consecutive losses that led to the decision to fire McHale.

"The team was obviously not responding—on offense, on defense—they weren't playing hard," Alexander said. "It continued for a while. I considered four or five games losing by 20 points something we can't take here. I've never seen my team in the 23 years [as owner] play as poorly and with less effort.

"I'm not attributing it to the coach. I'm attributing it to circumstances. Who knows whose control it is? But I had to do something to make a change. It couldn't keep going on like this. Do I want to watch us lose over and over and over again?"

McHale did not dispute Alexander's evaluation of the first weeks of that season, but firmly believed he could turn things around.

"We just weren't playing with any juice, with any rhythm," McHale said after he was let go. "We haven't been able to get the problems solved. We probably had more meetings in the last six weeks than in my previous four years here. It wasn't working. We got off to a terrible start to the season. I would have obviously liked the opportunity to solve the problems."

Instead, J.B. Bickerstaff was made the interim coach, but the problems that cost McHale his job, and the need for team meetings, continued through a trying 41–41 season. The Rockets slipped into the playoffs on the regular season's last day, but left quietly with a first-round loss to the Warriors.

McHale's extension earned him $12 million over three seasons, including his 11 games in 2015–16. When he was fired, he had a 193–130 record, then the best winning percentage in Rockets history.

Alexander said he did not regret giving McHale the extension, saying McHale would have earned a new contract after the Conference Finals run, anyway.

McHale has said little about those years or the way they ended. But when he praised the Rockets' addition of Chris Paul, he said Harden is not a leader, criticism that led Harden to call his former coach "a clown."

"I did anything and everything he asked me to do. I tried to lead this team since I stepped foot here in Houston," Harden said. "To go out there and downplay my name, honestly, he's never taught me anything to be a leader."

McHale doubled down, citing the most frequent criticism of his former star, which he had often disputed when he was Harden's coach.

"Calling me names is not going to change my opinion as to what I saw when I was there," McHale said in his role as a TNT analyst. "It's hard to have credibility if you don't play defense."

Their comments about one another were largely uncharacteristic, though they seemed to reveal underlying issues that might have existed when things suddenly went sour, toward a stunning, premature end. But they were far from the only precedent set in McHale's tenure.

47 Mike D'Antoni

The shock that the selection of Mike D'Antoni inspired never made much sense when looking past the surface. The initial reaction was that the Rockets needed to upgrade defensively. D'Antoni's reputation was built on his cutting-edge and ultimately revolutionary offense. After an agonizing 41–41 season in 2015–16, the expectation was that the Rockets would go another way.

Pull back a bit to the big picture and the selection of D'Antoni made perfect sense. It could have even been predictable.

Leslie Alexander, then the Rockets owner, was making the selection and Alexander had long made no secret of his preference for fast pace and three-point shooting, the hallmarks of D'Antoni's offenses. He had tried a coach that had never led a team through a full season, Kevin McHale, before Alexander chose him to succeed Rick Adelman, and then had an interim coach, J.B. Bickerstaff, with no head coaching experience.

Prior to McHale and Bickerstaff, Alexander had never hired an inexperienced head coach, and rarely even interviewed anyone without a long track record.

After he selected D'Antoni, a coach with a shared vision of the optimal NBA style of play that he had long coveted, he was stunned by the backlash, and in the only surprising part of the process, called out the "naysayers."

"We felt we want to win all the time, every year, try for a championship at all times," Alexander said a week after his selection of D'Antoni. "We wanted somebody who really was a master of the craft. Who really knew what to do, how to win. Mike has won 60 games twice in his career. There are only three NBA coaches who have done that, Doc [Rivers], [Gregg] Popovich, and [Steve] Kerr.

"If you hire a young guy, you're going to have a learning experience. He is going to have to make mistakes learning his craft, learning what to do. We with the Rockets, with James Harden, who is a great, great player, didn't want to go through that experience. The NBA today is ball movement and speed. Mike is one of the real experts at that. He will be able to put guys in position to win and better their game."

Alexander was right. D'Antoni immediately clicked with Harden, making him his point guard and making the rebuilt Rockets offense into one of the best ever. He won Coach of the Year in his first season, and led the Rockets to the best regular season in franchise history in his second season.

The Rockets defense also improved, with D'Antoni empowering Jeff Bzdelik to install an aggressive, switching style and then prioritizing it with his rotation, relying on Luc Mbah a Moute and P.J. Tucker for consistent minutes.

Most of all, D'Antoni did what should have been considered the top priority, he meshed with Harden, the Rockets' best and most important player.

"He gives his players freedom to communicate and to go out there on the court and be who we are," Harden said. "Everybody is going to make mistakes, but if you are playing with that mindset that you can go out there and play free, you're going to be that much better. I needed that. I needed it."

By the second season, there were new doubts after the addition of Chris Paul. But that too helped reveal the errors in the narratives about D'Antoni and his style. It turned out, he was not devoted to the pace-and-space style of the Suns breakthrough, but to a pragmatism to fit the talents of his team.

The Rockets slowed down. They moved far from the ball and body movement of D'Antoni's Suns to an emphasis on forcing switches and exploiting mismatches one-on-one. It worked, with D'Antoni even more sure of his methods than when he was considered rebellious with the Suns. He doubted himself at times then, but now has the support of the front office, from general manager Daryl Morey to new owner Tilman Fertitta.

"You do have to have the players and the talent, but… everybody has to get in line—the management, the star players, the coaches, the owner," D'Antoni said. "Everybody wants to play a certain way. It is different, and it was weird. Now it's catching on."

It caught on to the point that most teams play at a faster pace and shoot more threes than D'Antoni's Suns ever did. D'Antoni had moved on from there to New York, where half his rotation was traded for a poor-fit star, Carmelo Anthony, and Los Angeles, where his stars, Kobe Bryant, Steve Nash, and Dwight Howard, either broke down or struggled with injuries. But Alexander had looked deeper, seeing a smart, seasoned coach, and a perfect fit for what he needed, even if others did not look long enough to see things the same way.

They do now.

"It makes you feel good," D'Antoni said. "You want to be successful in what you do. I think I'm old enough to know, if you get good players, there are a lot of coaches that can have good records. But at the same time, I'm not screwing it up. That's good to know."

Mike D'Antoni talks to James Harden in a 2018 game against the Timberwolves. (AP Photo/Andy Clayton-King)

48 Ray and Steve

There are Patterson fingerprints all over Rockets history, from The Finals teams of the '80s to the champions of the '90s. There is undisputable evidence of the role Ray Patterson and his son, and briefly, successor, Steve, had on the Rockets' success, and in Ray's case, their viability.

Yet, in many ways, the image of Ray Patterson, long the iconic chief executive who shepherded the Rockets from an experiment to a force, is about something far more nebulous than draft picks and roster moves.

It is impossible to think of the Patterson reign with the Rockets, and not think of his booming voice and equally large presence, likely to rip into a reporter one moment and buy him a beer the next.

More substantially, Patterson came to the Rockets in 1972 from Milwaukee, where he had won the coin flip to draft Kareem Abdul-Jabbar (then Lew Alcindor) and build a championship team, to run a franchise that was hoping just to establish that professional basketball could work in Texas. An audacious idea at the time, Patterson was so committed to it in the barnstorming days of the Rockets he once took out a second mortgage on the family home to make payroll.

Patterson dealt former University of Houston star Elvin Hayes, much to the opposition of fans who knew little else about the Rockets, but would bring in Moses Malone, who would become the MVP and the force that brought the Rockets to the 1981 Finals.

When owner George Maloof could not pay Malone, Patterson dealt his star and began rebuilding with Ralph Sampson, the prized target in his sights. He won another coin flip and drafted Sampson, then won another and picked Hakeem Olajuwon, leading the NBA to begin the draft lottery.

Patterson thrived as Rockets president and general manager through six owners and the early days of the Rockets playing home games around the state, from Waco to El Paso, in search of a crowd, winning NBA Executive of the Year honors in 1977 when the Rockets reached the Eastern Conference Finals, and building teams that would reach the NBA Finals in 1981 and 1986.

Finally, in 1989, Patterson stepped down as general manager, elevating his son Steve to the position. A year later, Ray Patterson retired as team president, while Steve brought in many of the players—Otis Thorpe, Kenny Smith, Vernon Maxwell—who would help Olajuwon take the Rockets to consecutive championships.

Then Rockets owner Leslie Alexander fired Patterson in 1993, before the first championship season began, to restructure the management of the team and put more control of the basketball side in the hands of Rudy Tomjanovich. Patterson was succeeded by Tod Leiweke, then a PGA executive and now the NHL Seattle CEO, who would replace Steve Patterson again in 2007 with the Trail Blazers.

But when the Rockets finally broke through for that title, it was a triumph of the roster that the Pattersons had largely built and the vision that Ray Patterson had when he came to Texas.

"Ray Patterson is the Rockets' franchise," Jim Foley, who had accompanied Patterson to Houston from Milwaukee as media relations director and who would become their longtime radio commentator, said when Patterson died of heart and lung complications in 2011 at 89. "There would not be a Houston Rockets franchise today had not Ray Patterson come to Houston."

 **CD**

There in the Toyota Center rafters, across from the championship banners and next to the uniform numbers worn by Hall of Famers Hakeem Olajuwon, Moses Malone, Clyde Drexler, Calvin Murphy, and Yao Ming, a banner contains just two initials: CD.

No other words are necessary. The impact Carroll Dawson, known simply as CD before initials became a trendy way to identify the sport's stars from KD to CP3, had long been clear. The honor given to an individual who never scored a point or grabbed a rebound was a no-brainer.

If those banners could talk, Olajuwon's could thank Dawson's for teaching him his unstoppable jump hook and the counter moves off it that had NBA players from Kobe Bryant to LeBron James flocking to Houston to learn. Drexler's could cite Dawson's impact on the championship Drexler won when he joined the Rockets. Yao's could share laughs, as Yao and Dawson so often did, about how Dawson brought Yao to the United States not just by choosing him with the first pick of the draft but leading to the complicated negotiations in his easy, endearing way.

The stories Dawson's and Rudy Tomjanovich's banners could share would last a lifetime, as has the relationship that changed the franchise forever when Tomjanovich and Dawson became more "brothers," as Tomjanovich often put it, than friends or even partners on the Rockets bench.

"He's been a Red Auerbach–like figure for the Rockets, but without the publicity," his successor, Daryl Morey, told the team's website when Dawson retired in 2007. "He's been navigating the Rockets for the past 27 years. And it's been a pretty good run."

Dawson's low-key manner and dry sense of humor, coupled with the humility he said came from growing up in tiny Alba, Texas, had always been among his greatest assets. When he left the Army at 24 years old, it was why his college assistant coach at Baylor Bill Menefee, hired him to be his assistant and then watched him relax and charm recruits with everything from jokes to card tricks. It made him a successful scout for the Dallas Cowboys and briefly a salesman for Converse.

That style was definitely why Del Harris brought him back to basketball, making him a Rockets assistant though he had no experience in the NBA as a player or in any coaching or front office position.

Dawson spent 16 years as a Rockets assistant, with every coach that took the job over the years keeping him on his staff. He taught big men, from Elvin Hayes to Ralph Sampson, with Olajuwon and Yao his prized pupils.

When it was his time to become the head coach, however, he could not do it, instead pulling off the most important recruiting job of his career.

In 1989, when Dawson and Tomjanovich were on the course at Houston's Southwick Golf Club, Tomjanovich felt a jolt, and Dawson felt a strike on his right hand, burning him through his glove. Dawson had been hit by lightning, causing a detached retina in his left eye and periodic vision loss in his right.

When the Rockets head coach, Don Chaney, was fired midway through the 1992 season, Dawson, Chaney's lead assistant, was to be his successor, but his vision would not allow him to take the job. It fell to him to convince Tomjanovich to step in, knowing, as always, just what to say.

Dawson told Tomjanovich that if he did not agree, the entire staff could be out of a job, then he pledged to be his right hand every step of the way. Two seasons later, they celebrated the first of back-to-back championships.

"I'm very proud of the fact that, being in a so-called football state, I was a part of a team that brought the first NBA championship to Texas," Dawson said. "If I ever wear a ring, it would probably be that '94 championship. That was the first one in the state. I'm very proud of that."

By 1997, however, Dawson's vision had worsened, making it impossible to continue coaching. By then, he and Tomjanovich had been empowered to make the team's personnel decisions. Rockets owner Leslie Alexander made Dawson his general manager, with a shared sense of daring and taste for big deals.

Dawson engineered the acquisition of Scottie Pippen, the trades for Steve Francis and then Tracy McGrady. When an agent with no clients called, Dawson called back and forged a relationship. Years later, when that agent, Jeff Fried, had a client, Steve Francis, he remembered the general manager that had befriended him with nothing to gain and called again, leading to trade from Vancouver.

Dawson scouted Yao since he was a teen, and when others thought Duke's Jay Williams should be the first pick or Rockets players believed the Rockets should trade the pick for veterans, Dawson convinced his players that Yao was too special and was steadfast in his own belief.

As the difficult negotiations with the Chinese government and the China Basketball Association dragged on, Dawson's manner again won, bringing Yao to Houston in time for his rookie season with none of the controversies and complications that had been predicted.

Yao and McGrady were unable to stay healthy long enough for the Rockets to reach their potential, though Dawson did build the four Comets championship teams in the first WNBA dynasty. Dawson spent one season preparing Morey for the position and then stepped down. His legacy, however, was set in the relationships that endured.

"It's obviously a great honor when you're able to stay in one place, [27] years in one spot. Usually, the posse gets you before that," Jeff Van Gundy, the first head coach Dawson hired, said when Dawson retired. "It's a great accomplishment. It doesn't happen very often; that's for sure. Everybody that comes into contact with him enjoys him and trusts him. As a general manager, that goes a long way."

In the end, that was why Alexander put a CD in the rafters. Dawson never wanted attention, much less praise. Though he had a policy that he would return every phone call, he asked the media to never cite his work, never credit him for Rockets successes.

The relationships, however, meant everything, and they are why there is a CD next to the numbers high above the Toyota Center floor.

"It wasn't my idea [to be honored for my work], but I appreciate it," Dawson said. "It's been my living and breathing existence. I'll always be a Rocket."

50 Daryl Morey

Leslie Alexander just wanted to win. He had made the most unconventional hire of his tenure as Rockets owner for the most conventional of reasons. He wanted an edge, an advantage he could exploit. As always, he trusted his gut.

Alexander grabbed Daryl Morey out of the Celtics' front office to become the Rockets general manager, accepting the disbelief and derision his choice would inspire in the conviction that Morey's approach, then considered everything from cutting-edge to nonsense and at the time wildly misunderstood, would bring him information others lacked.

"With the high level of competition in this league," Alexander's statement that stunning April day in 2006 announced simply, "you can never have too much information."

Rockets owner Tilman Fertitta (left) and general manager Daryl Morey (right) talk during a 2017 game against the Memphis Grizzlies at Toyota Center. (Troy Taormina/USA TODAY Sports)

That was it. He was not trying to change the way the world watched and discussed basketball. He was not trying to revolutionize anything. As much as Alexander had made his fortune by seeing the future, he could not have imagined that Morey would become something of a sports celebrity, the face of the next generation of the analytics movement, and foe of dinosaurs determined to resist change that threatened them.

Alexander just wanted to win. He saw something different, liked what he saw, and trusted his instincts.

A decade later, Alexander gave Morey a contract extension, assuring that Morey would remain the Rockets general manager when Alexander put the team up for sale. In between, Morey had gone from a polarizing lightning rod for debate on analytics to an established general manager building a championship contender in a business that had changed in ways he heavily influenced.

When Morey was hired to succeed Carroll Dawson as general manager, after a one-season apprenticeship under Dawson, he was generally unknown. Dawson's road to the front office had been largely conventional. A longtime coach who was Rudy Tomjanovich's right hand in the championship years, Dawson was as respected as he was well-liked. He knew everyone and anyone could get along with "CD."

Morey was behind the scenes in Boston. He had studied computer science with an emphasis on statistics at Northwestern and received an MBA from the MIT Sloan School of Management.

He never played, coached, or scouted professional basketball, as many rapidly pointed out when he was thrust into the NBA spotlight and for years to come. But he had closely followed Bill James' work with Baseball Abstracts and, while still at Northwestern, took an entry level job with STATS, Inc., a Chicago-based firm that provided statistical analysis to teams and media, hoping to work his way on to a professional sports staff.

No one returned his calls, however, so Morey decided he would become wealthy enough to buy his own team. He joined a firm, Parthenon, that was giving out shares of internet companies during the internet bubble. That did not bring him the fortune he hoped, but it did bring him in contact with Wyc Grousbeck, the head of the ownership group working to buy the Celtics.

Morey ran the point of the valuation process and when Grousbeck and his group purchased the Celtics in 2002, Morey was brought in as a senior vice president of operations and information, splitting his time between management and the basketball side, headed by Danny Ainge.

The Rockets offered a chance to be entirely on the basketball side, allowing Morey to use his data-driven analysis as the foundation of decision-making.

Morey formulated a team of analysts, but his work was immediately misunderstood. The analytics were not to replace traditional scouting. It is certainly not to get by without talent, as Charles Barkley so often charged in the common inaccurate harangues about analytics, but to provide more information to find better talent and access greater logic than if just driven by tradition.

Morey and the Rockets' front office still scout as much as any general manager and staff in the league, but seek to marry the observation with the analysis, and when the numbers don't match with the scouting, to keep digging to find the truth. Data strategy is a part of all decision-making, supported by a large staff of analysts with backgrounds similar to Morey's when he could not get teams to give him a second look. But when staffers with more traditional training and functions have moved on, Morey has replaced them with others with playing or coaching perspectives.

Analysis drives the way the Rockets play, though with the hiring of Mike D'Antoni, the determination to shoot three-pointers rather than long twos or mid-range shots did not need data reports in the coach's office.

Along the way, the use of analytics has become universal around the NBA. Data is mined to varying degrees, but Alexander's once-stunning choice can only be viewed as ahead of its time, rather than peculiar and even misguided as it was at the time.

The Sloan Sports Analytics Conference Morey co-founded at MIT has become an enormous annual event. Morey has become one of the NBA's most recognizable general managers, far beyond the "Dork Elvis" as Bill Simmons once dubbed him as the leader of the analytics nerds.

Over the years, he has had smashing successes, highlighted by the trade for James Harden, and enormous misses, most notably cutting Jeremy Lin. Other moves, such as landing Dwight Howard when he was the NBA's most coveted free agent or finding Chandler Parsons in the second round, were viewed as triumphs, but did not pan out.

He has excelled with late first- and second-round picks, including Aaron Brooks, Carl Landry, Parsons, and Clint Capela. But he has not gotten more from his mid-first-round picks, including Patrick Patterson and Marcus Morris, than the pick used to get them.

He guided the Rockets from the injury-hastened end of the Tracy McGrady and Yao Ming era to the promise of the team built around Harden and Chris Paul.

Along the way, he has become known for his interests, from Broadway musicals to chess and table tennis, and he has been perhaps the most active and visible general manager on social media.

Yet, the measure of Morey's impact and how much has changed from the day Alexander chose a nearly anonymous executive in Boston to be a general manager is that he will be evaluated the way all general managers are judged.

Morey's reputation, methods, background, and influence won't matter as much as the results on the floor, a measure he welcomes and shares. With that, the unconventional choice will be viewed in the most traditional of ways.

51 Dwight Howard

When Dwight Howard left the Rockets, departing as a free agent with little of the fanfare of his arrival, he had been the Rockets center for roughly the amount of time that it took to get him.

He had been general manager Daryl Morey's white whale for years, from the trade that never quite came through to the off-season deal made to position the Rockets to get him. The Rockets saw Howard and considered him to be the latest in their line of dominant centers, stretching from Elvin Hayes to Moses Malone, Ralph Sampson, Hakeem Olajuwon, and Yao Ming.

Finally, they got a chance to see if he could be. He wasn't.

After the Rockets' first season with James Harden, they viewed Howard as the ideal partner, the inside force to go with Harden's perimeter brilliance. They pulled out every stop to get him. Chandler Parsons called or texted nearly every day. He and Harden joined the free agent pitch team in Beverley Hills. Clyde Drexler and Olajuwon flew in. Yao sent a video message. At the end of the meeting, Howard and former Rockets owner Leslie Alexander talked it over alone. By the end of the week, Howard chose the Rockets over the Lakers, Warriors, Mavericks, and Hawks.

His arrival was celebrated with throngs of fans outside Toyota Center in downtown Houston beneath a five-story poster placing him among the Rockets' "Legacy of Bigs."

It all served to demonstrate the enormous hopes the Rockets had for him.

His time in Houston lasted three seasons, marked by one stunning playoff loss, one surprising playoff run in an injury-filled season, and one dissatisfying, anxiety-filled slide to an unhappy 41–41.

Through it all, the Rockets could not escape the thoughts of what could have been, of the potential they saw when Howard was their target and a free agent addition Alexander called "the biggest free agent acquisition in the history of the Rockets,"

No one disputed that declaration at the time. The Rockets had tried to get Howard in a trade at the 2011 deadline when Howard vacillated about his free agency plans. They were on the phone with the Magic up until the deadline in case Howard forced Orlando's hands.

After that season, the Rockets traded Kyle Lowry to the Raptors to get the first-round pick they believed could key a deal with the Magic. Instead, the Magic chose a three-team trade that sent Howard to Los Angeles for the final season of his contract. The Rockets used the pick to land Harden.

Finally, after that unhappy season in Los Angeles, the Rockets got him and reveled in the expectations.

"The biggest thing was a championship potential," Howard said. "I watched the team after we got out of the playoffs. I looked at their team. I looked at a couple teams. Their team just stood out. I think this is the best fit for me as far as playing basketball. I'm looking forward to it."

The Rockets never came close to that championship potential. Howard excelled in his first postseason with the Rockets, averaging 26 points and 13.7 rebounds, but the Rockets were eliminated by the Portland Trail Blazers when Damian Lillard hit his series-ending buzzer-beater.

Things began to go downhill in his second season, with a knee condition limiting Howard to 41 regular-season games. The Rockets reached the Western Conference Finals after their stunning comeback against the Clippers. But with Howard in a diminished role offensively and limited by a Game 1 injury after a collision with Josh Smith, the Rockets were eliminated in five games.

By his final season in Houston, the mix of Howard and Harden began to fracture. The Rockets got off to a terrible start, losing each of their first three games by 20 points. Kevin McHale, among the reasons Harden signed with the Rockets, was fired after 11 games. As he had been with the Lakers, Howard was reluctant to be used primarily in pick-and-roll with Harden, though he was far more effective in that role than when posting up.

Howard averaged 16 points and 11.7 rebounds in his three seasons with the Rockets, and just 13.7 points on 8.5 shots per game in his final season, his fewest points and attempts per game since his rookie season as a Magic teenager.

Through it all, Howard had become a target of criticism, a subject of widespread debate. That had begun with his awkward final season with the Magic and accelerated with his one season in the Lakers' spotlight.

By the time he made an appearance on TNT's *Inside the NBA*, where Charles Barkley and Shaquille O'Neal had been sharp critics, the session was treated as an intervention.

"I would say people see me and see the success I had in Orlando and see me now and are like, 'What's the difference?'" Howard said. "I think I was very likeable in Orlando. The way that situation ended, I think people thought I was a bad guy. I'm all about myself. I'm a diva. I'm stuck on me, Dwight Howard, this famous basketball player.

"People say, 'We don't like this guy.' I hear that a lot. It really hurts me because my heart and my attitude have always been the same. My drive has always been there."

Howard was no diva in Houston. After he returned with the Atlanta Hawks, he was celebrated for the charity work he had never let slide even if his play did. He had become a poor fit with a team increasingly built around Harden. The locker room became fractious as the Rockets set records for team meetings but with stars that were too non-confrontational to ease the tension.

Howard opted out of the final season of his contract. The Rockets never publicly ruled out bringing him back, but three seasons after they signed him, made no real effort to sign him again.

His tenure in Houston never came close to the hopes. He left far more quietly than he arrived. Howard and the Rockets had entered their marriage with intensions as great as the expectations. Neither fought to stay together, but with few regrets.

"I've always been at peace with who I am," Howard said. "I'm blessed. The stuff I've done in the NBA has been great.

"I can't control how people feel, what they say about me. I'm happy with who I am. I'm always humble. I laugh and joke and have a good time, but when I get on the court, I'm as serious as I can be. I smile because it's a great life."

52 The Big E

As Elvin Hayes makes his way to his front row Toyota Center seat, soon to be introduced to the crowd, joining Hakeem Olajuwon in the treatment reserved for Rockets royalty, many images of his many roles could come to mind. His importance to Rockets history, undeniable if perhaps accidental, rarely comes to mind, though in many ways it could be viewed as the most essential part he played of all.

Hayes had been a legend before he began his NBA career. He and Don Chaney had broken the color barrier at the University of Houston. He would take the Cougars to the Final Four. He starred in the ground-breaking spectacle of the "Game of the Century" when the University of Houston stunned UCLA in the showdown of Hayes and Kareem Abdul-Jabbar (then Lew Alcindor), which demonstrated the power of college basketball to fill stadiums and capture the imagination of viewers nationwide.

"Even when the NCAA comes back here, that arena [the Astrodome] sitting over there quietly, silently, will never be outdone," Hayes told the *Houston Chronicle* with the Final Four returning to Houston. "What has been built now [NRG Stadium] may be the top of the tree. But the root of it all [the Astrodome] is sitting right there next to it."

Hayes would be the first pick of the 1968 NBA and ABA Drafts, choosing the San Diego Rockets over the Houston Mavericks. As a rookie, he averaged 28.4 points per game and remains the last rookie to lead the NBA in scoring. The next season, he became the first player since 1957 other than Wilt Chamberlain or Bill Russell to lead the league in rebounding. He was well on his way to a Hall of Fame career, a no-brainer choice as one of the NBA's 50 greatest players ever.

Yet, all of that might have laid the groundwork for his most permanent contribution to Rockets history.

Back in Texas, real estate developer Wayne Duddleston was looking for an NFL franchise. He and *Houston Post* columnist Mickey Herskowitz checked in with the NFL, but were told the league was not considering expansion for five years at the soonest. Herskowitz suggested that Duddleston check out the NBA, where commissioner Walter Kennedy said the Milwaukee Bucks, Cincinnati Royals, and San Diego Rockets could be for sale.

The Rockets were pricier, but they had the Big E, the sort of attraction in Houston that Duddleston believed would make the experiment work.

"I was very happy to be back where I played my college basketball," Hayes said. "I was very excited... that was some really good days. I really enjoyed it."

Hayes averaged 25.2 points and 14.6 rebounds in the 1971–72 season in Houston. But the barnstorming Rockets, playing home games not just in three Houston arenas, but in San Antonio, Waco, and El Paso, struggled to draw crowds. Hayes did not fit well in coach Tex Winter's triple-post offense, the forerunner of his "triangle" that Phil Jackson used in Chicago and Los Angeles. The Rockets could not afford the contract Hayes had signed in San Diego, worth $1 million over 10 years.

When Ray Patterson was brought in from Milwaukee, he dealt Hayes to Washington, where he played 12 seasons, winning the 1977–78 championship.

Hayes, however, did return home one last time, when the Rockets sent a pair of second-round picks to Washington to bring Hayes back to Houston for the final three seasons of his career. The Rockets were stunned in the first round of the 1981–82 playoffs. Moses Malone was traded. The Rockets began their spiral toward the first pick of the draft in consecutive seasons as Hayes' career finished where it had begun, at the University of Houston.

Hayes did attempt to return one more time, but without quite pulling it off, and there was a reminder of his importance in Rockets history.

Hayes had put together a group to bid on purchasing the Rockets when Leslie Alexander put the team up for sale in 2017. He met with Rockets president Tad Brown, but knew his chances were a longshot, even sounding as if he were endorsing fellow Cougar Tillman Fertitta soon after.

After Fertitta bought the team for a record $2.2 billion he said he had been a Rockets fan nearly all his life and happily talked about how he had, as a child, adopted the San Diego Rockets as his team.

The Rockets, Fertitta said, had Elvin Hayes, and that was all he needed to know. Decades later, the team that moved to Houston because it had Hayes was thriving, and Hayes was happily taking his place in the front row.

53 Shane Battier

From the start, the Rockets' trade for Shane Battier underwhelmed, a damper on a draft party, though in many ways, that too was fitting. The qualities that would eventually be appreciated were also a tough sell on draft night.

Battier understood. He knew what he was. The Rockets knew what he would bring. Battier would eventually be celebrated as the sort of player that helps make great players into champions. He just never got a chance to do that with Yao Ming and Tracy McGrady and the Rockets, instead serving that role with the Miami Heat.

Before Battier would be labeled by a *New York Times Magazine* piece as the "No Stats All-Star," the epitome of a player with qualities that Rockets general manager Daryl Morey's advanced analytics can appreciate in ways traditional numbers fail to capture, he was the Rockets' 2006 Draft night acquisition, sent from Memphis to the Rockets for Stromile Swift and the draft rights to Rudy Gay. The draft party immediately ended.

"I understand the reaction of fans because draft night is all about the potential of your draft pick," Battier said. "So I wasn't really upset about the reaction. I'm just going to work hard, play the right way, and help this team win some basketball games. If I do that, fans will come around."

He was right, and not just because Gay, who had the talent of a player taken with the first pick of the draft, would coincidentally become in his All-Star and Olympics seasons the antithesis of an analytics-world star.

Battier was not brought in to be a star. He was to be little more than a defensive specialist, keeping McGrady from those toughest assignments. He would be the glue on a team that had its superstars. As with his time in Memphis, which inspired Carroll Dawson to make the move and for Morey to push for the deal in his one season as the general manager in waiting, the Rockets' numbers went up dramatically when Battier was on the floor, even if his didn't. Though dealing a talent as obvious as Gay for a screen-setter and a ball mover would always have detractors, the Rockets believed Battier would help McGrady and Yao win at the highest level.

"Coming here with a great coach like Jeff Van Gundy, I knew it was an amazing opportunity for me to win and win big," Battier said.

There would be a reason the Heat saw him the same way in the final seasons of Battier's career. The Rockets, however, had only acquired the eighth pick of the draft that year because the injuries to Yao and McGrady had so derailed the 2005–06 season, with McGrady playing 47 games, Yao 57. They would never simultaneously stay healthy long enough for the Rockets to reach the heights planned when they traded for Battier to be a perfect puzzle piece between them.

There were highlights along the way, from the 22-game winning streak in 2008 to the 2009 playoff run when the Rockets finally broke through in the first round and took the eventual-champion Lakers to seven games in the second round, even while losing Yao after three games. In five seasons with the Rockets, Battier averaged 8.8 points and 4.7 rebounds and was twice an All-Defensive Team selection.

Still, it took a season with McGrady and Yao getting hurt to get Battier. Injuries to Yao and McGrady kept that era from ever reaching its potential. Battier was sent back to Memphis in 2011, largely so the Rockets could get a draft pick to begin rebuilding again before Battier would become a free agent.

There might have been no more fitting end to his time in Houston. As with the deal to bring him from Memphis, fans detested the trade that sent him back. Battier's ways to contribute, relatively inconspicuous at first, had become widely appreciated.

There was, as with much of that time, a sense of what could have been. But in many ways, Battier's five seasons with the Rockets were celebrated.

"Houston is as special as any place I played," Battier said. "First of all, both my babies were born in Houston. They are proud Texans, as they like to remind me.

"For me, I came into my own as a professional basketball player in Houston. I sort of grew up. I thought I had my prime years playing for Van Gundy and [Rick] Adelman. I look back at those years, and though I'm sad we missed opportunities because we didn't go further in the playoffs, I was proud to be part of those teams."

54 Luis Scola

As the Rockets' bus made its way through Washington, D.C., Luis Scola kept his focus out the window to his right, determined to see the sights like a tourist that won a trip of a lifetime. His helpful new teammates, hazing the rookie forward, told him to be patient, that the White House would be right outside that window any moment, as the bus pulled past 1400 Pennsylvania Avenue to the left.

Scola laughed harder than anyone each time he retold the story, knowing he had seen more of the world than most ever would. But more than just see every sight, he experienced everything he could find through five seasons with the Rockets. From Miami's South Beach to Seattle's Pike Place Market, Scola was determined to take it all in.

When he returned from the 2008 Olympics in Beijing, finding himself with a few hours to fill, he did not even leave the airport before he made calls to line up U.S. Open tickets, becoming a tennis fan that day. At the end of each season, he would take his young family to destinations the NBA did not travel before their return to Argentina, determined to pass his love of life and learning to his boys.

Scola maintained that enthusiasm throughout his career, and happily moved on to China when the NBA opportunities were gone. But it was not just a gusto for touring the world that so endeared him to Rockets fans.

Scola played that way. He practiced that way. He worked every day that way, refusing to skip a day even when the team was given time off, hating to miss anything. He played every summer for Argentina, cherishing each opportunity. He revelled in living in the

Olympic Village every four years, loving that he could walk across the dining room and see the stars, sometimes even sit with them, and lamenting that his fellow NBA players on the USA Basketball teams had security needs keeping them in luxury hotels, rather than the veritable dorm rooms that suited him just fine.

The enthusiasm came through, making him more of a fan favorite with every head fake, scoop, or mid-range jumper.

"It means a lot to me to be a part of the Rockets," Scola said. "Especially in that kind of case, that I came from another country. I am happy I was finally able to achieve that."

The term "finally" was appropriate. The Spurs had drafted Scola in 2002, but with Tim Duncan at power forward and a powerhouse of a roster, they had little need to make him the sort of offer to bring him over from Spain, where he won a Spanish League championship and was an All Euroleague First Team selection.

The Spurs won three championships in the years after Scola was selected and before the summer of 2007 when they were finally ready to deal his rights to a team willing to take on Jackie Butler's contract. When a deal with the Cavaliers fell through, Daryl Morey jumped in, sending the rights to Vassilis Spanoulis to San Antonio in his first trade as Rockets general manager.

Spanoulis, who had vowed 10 days earlier never to play for the Rockets again after a frustrating rookie season, never played for the Spurs. Scola, who had the attitude ideal for the Spurs and his close friend Manu Ginobili, became the one that got away in San Antonio.

He had five strong seasons with the Rockets, topped by 2008–09, when the Rockets finally broke through in the postseason, beating the Trail Blazers before taking the eventual-champion Lakers to seven games, and in 2010–11 when he averaged 18.3 points and 8.2 rebounds.

Scola's final season in Houston was 2011–12, the trying lockout season. Needing cap room to retool, Scola was released in an amnesty waiver, sending Scola to seasons in Phoenix, Indiana, Toronto, and Brooklyn. He won a silver medal in the World Championships in Indianapolis, a gold in the Athens Olympics, a bronze in Beijing. He happily moved to China after the NBA, viewing it as another experience to embrace.

Hornets forward Carl Landry (24) gets caught between Luis Scola (4) and Patrick Patterson (54) during a 2012 game in New Orleans. (AP Photo/ Gerald Herbert)

All along, Scola never lost his appreciation for his place in the NBA, or his enthusiasm for every bit of the journey, with a special place for his time with the Rockets.

"I always dreamed about playing in the NBA," Scola said. "For four or five years, which in my career playing basketball is a lot of years, I saw a lot of players go to the NBA. I thought maybe I would never make it. When I came to the Rockets, it was like a dream come true."

55 Pat Beverley

From the day he first stepped into a Rockets locker room, fittingly in his hometown of Chicago, Pat Beverley knew who he was, from where he came and the long road he traveled to the NBA.

Love him or hate him, and he inspired plenty of both around the NBA, Beverley would be true to himself, all with fearless passion that he called on to drive him far beyond the expectations so many had for him.

He would eventually compile awards and accomplishments. He would win the Skills Challenge in New York. He was a First-Team All-Defensive Team selection in 2017, a second-team pick in 2015. He won the NBA's Initial Hustle Award in 2017, based on an aggregate score of the league's hustle stats. In five seasons with the Rockets, he made 37.5 percent of his threes, making him an ideal backcourt partner for James Harden.

Yet the snapshots of Beverley's time with the Rockets are all about his fire and determination, in a combination of the nicknames "Wolverine" (for his tendency to return rapidly from injuries) and "Mr. 94 Feet" (for the determination to value every inch of the floor) that sought to describe the fire that forged an unlikely success story.

He would become reviled in Oklahoma City for trying to get a steal as Russell Westbrook called time out, leaving Westbrook with a torn meniscus that would eventually put him out for the playoffs, to the point that Beverley received death threats and extra security at his home and at return trips to Oklahoma City.

He would be celebrated in Houston when he took a jack-hammer screen set by Oklahoma City center Steven Adams, only to pop up as if he loved it, much to the delight of Texans star J.J. Watt, sitting a few feet away. He eventually helped seal that Game 1 win in 2017 with a corner three, showcasing how he had grown into a three-and-D guard. He made 38.2 percent of his three-pointers that season, his last with the Rockets, after sinking 40 percent the season before.

Beverley, a Marshall High star in Chicago featured in the documentary *Hoop Reality*, had left Arkansas after acknowledging a paper had been written for him, and was a last (and controversial) cut by the Miami Heat, leading him to seasons in Greece, Ukraine, and Russia. He signed with the Rockets in January 2013, and by the next preseason he supplanted Jeremy Lin as the Rockets' starting point guard.

By the end of his tenure in the Rockets' backcourt, he had gone from a relatively unknown midseason pickup, to a lightning rod, celebrated for his style and strengths. In his final season with the Rockets, before he had become dissatisfied with his contract and was a part of the deal to acquire Chris Paul, he had become the seventh player in league history 6'1" or shorter to average at least 5.5 rebounds while playing in at least 40 games.

Beverley moved on, becoming a chief antagonist from the bench in the January 2018 game between the Rockets and Clippers, when emotions became so heated that Rockets players entered the Clippers' locker room after the game. He had been out with an injury, an issue in three of his four full seasons with the Rockets. He had hoped the move to the Clippers would offer a chance to expand his game, to go beyond his role defending from baseline to baseline and running to the corners to shoot threes.

That role, and his boundless determination, had made Beverley a celebrated force. When he returned, he was featured in Toyota Center in a tribute video that left him characteristically emotional.

"This is my second home," Beverley said. "My home is here. My mom is here. My fiancé, she's from here. There's nothing but love since I've been here and going forward.

"Houston will have a special place in my heart."

56 Dikembe Mutombo

The images come back quickly and easily. Dikembe Mutombo wagging one long, scolding finger. The 1,000-watt smile. The impossibly deep voice of distant thunder.

Picture Mutombo celebrating the Rockets' 22-game win streak with the iconic image of two fingers on each hand high above the crowd around him, or in the back of the Capitol as an honored guest at the 2007 State of the Union address. Imagine him on all those charter flights laughing with Yao Ming, giants who shared a humanity and humility as much as a need to duck under doorways.

Consider Mutombo, always proudly impeccably dressed, from the starched collar to the shined canoe-sized shoes, and it is impossible to not smile.

Viewing Mutombo's career just for his years with the Rockets would be as narrow and incomplete as looking at his impact for just what was done on the court.

Yet, it does say something about Mutombo and his legacy that he can be celebrated for every step along the way, including the final long strides of five seasons with the Rockets.

Mutombo had an undeniable impact on the court with the Rockets, most demonstrably when he emerged to replace an injured Yao for the final 10 games of the Rockets' 22-game winning streak. A season later, he sat out until he was needed, signing at midseason to play in just nine games before he was hurt in the playoffs, ending his career.

Beyond the court, however, Mutombo had reached the point in his career and life that every road trip represented a chance to set up meetings around the country, raising the funds for the Dikembe Mutombo Foundation to build the Biamba Marie Mutombo hospital in Kinshasa of the Democratic Republic of Congo.

The seventh of Samuel and Biamba Mutombo's 10 children, Dikembe Mpolondo Mukamba Jean-Jacques Wamutombo arrived at Georgetown on an academic scholarship, only to be discovered and mentored by John Thompson, realizing he could make a greater impact as a basketball player than a doctor.

He was right, though he likely could not have imagined how far his works would reach. In 2007, he opened the $29 million, 300-bed hospital, initially donating $3.5 million to the project and then $15 million to complete it.

His work with the Mutombo Foundation and Special Olympics earned him the Kennedy Citizenship award in 2001 and 2009. He was the winner of a Presidential Service Award in 1999. He serves on the United States' Board of Directors to UNICEF; in 2009, Mutombo was made an NBA Global Ambassador; and in 2015 was inducted into the Naismith Basketball Hall of Fame.

Yet, with all that, even as a four-time Defensive Player of the Year and six-time All-Defensive Team selection, it is impossible not to think of the final stop of Mutombo's career and not picture the joy he brought to the game and to the locker room.

The feeling was mutual.

"The Rockets did a lot for me and the foundation," Mutombo said in his Hall of Fame acceptance speech. "I could not get the hospital going without their help and the wonderful people there."

57 Toyota Center

The battle began when the Rockets were still celebrated champions and Houston was bracing for the then-impending departure of the Oilers.

Still-new Rockets owner Leslie Alexander suggested his team would need a new arena to remain competitive. The process began. Battle lines were drawn. The long struggle to get the Rockets from Compaq Center to Toyota Center threatened the future of the Rockets in Houston before ultimate victory.

Chuck Watson, who owned the minor-league hockey Aeros and controlled Compaq Center, pushed back. Politicians lined up on either side. The Rockets began traveling the long, tough road to the Toyota Center.

There were lawsuits as the Rockets tried to leave the Compaq Center lease after a $30 million buyout offer was rejected. There were forced compromises with Alexander, and Watson put in joint control of the arena until the Rockets' departure. There was a referendum defeat that threatened the future of the franchise in Houston in 1999. There were even negotiations with Louisville, Kentucky, about funding for an arena there.

Finally, there was a landslide referendum win in 2000. Groundbreaking was in July 2001 with the ribbon cutting in September 2003.

Toyota Center was built for $235 million, with the city paying $182 million and the Rockets picking up the costs for the enhancements and other additions. Toyota won the naming rights, for $100 million over 20 years with options to extend the deal, in February 2003, with Gulf States Toyota paying richly to have the Toyota name, logo, and even vehicles throughout the arena and on the roof.

Alexander sought to have the largest percentage of lower-bowl seats in the NBA in an effort, ultimately unsuccessful, to create an intense home-court advantage. But with Morris Architects, he did design a large lower bowl built 32 feet into the ground so customers would walk down to their seats from the street level entrance.

That also gave Toyota Center a low-profile appearance, fitting in downtown near the George R. Brown Convention Center, rather than towering over the neighborhood as most arenas do.

The arena was outfitted with clubs and restaurants, with more added in the event level over the years. The original 40'x32' center video boards, with the rocket that simulated takeoff before the opening tip, was replaced by the massive 59'x25' video screens, then the largest and most high-definition in the NBA.

Over the years, changes were made that were visible to fans; others far off limits. The Rockets' training facilities received an extensive upgrade in 2013, with a massive, high-tech home locker room along with coaches' facilities and new video, weight, training, and family rooms stretching to the section of the arena that had previously housed the WNBA Comets.

The practice court on the street level, however, remains small, with room enough for just one court. In Mike D'Antoni's second season, the Rockets have come to practice on the main court whenever available.

The arena, however, has been an enormous success. It has hosted a pair of All-Star games, and with the upgrades since the October 6, 2003, opening night (for a Fleetwood Mac concert) and the October 30 Rockets debut in their new home (against the Nuggets), it has remained remarkably current. While other arenas of its generation have rushed toward premature obsolescence or at least show their age, Toyota Center has held up.

It is far from the sort of intense homecourt Alexander envisioned. For the 2017–18 season, the Rockets added the power to dim the lights over the crowd, theatre-style, making the arena feel more elegant than like a gym.

More than that, it was from the beginning, a triumph. Toyota Center was birthed as a victory over the political infighting and severe stadium fatigue (after construction of new stadiums for baseball and football franchises). It grew up into a major reason the Rockets were sold for $2.2 billion.

Most remarkably, it remains—with a few facelifts along the way—a looker. Toyota Center might have saved the Rockets for Houston. In the years since, and more than two decades since Alexander first brought up the idea, it still works.

58 The Summit

Anachronistic as it became, The Summit was never antiquated. Insufficient as the Rockets home ultimately might have been, a monument to what the NBA was rather than what it would become, it never lost its charm or importance.

To the Rockets, The Summit was more than home. It was a statement. It was a monument to the growth of a franchise from an experiment to a champion.

It was sleek, gleaming along the Southwest Freeway about three miles west of downtown, sitting among mid-rise office buildings, including Greenway Plaza where the Rockets' headquarters were housed, with residential neighborhoods to the south across the freeway. It had the single-concourse design style of the era, shared by arenas in Miami, Dallas, Philadelphia, and Uniondale.

It felt intimate compared to the next generation's towering arenas, with stacks of suites and filled with clubs and restaurants, that would soon be considered essential.

The Summit, opened in 1975, did not have all that. It had a food court. It had end zone video boards, rather than the customary center-hung, four-sided scoreboards that became more typical. It had multi-colored seats, later replaced by Kelly green, that helped make it appear that they were filled with large crowds in the day before the Rockets drew well.

Mostly, The Summit held champions.

The Rockets won their two championships in The Summit. The minor league Aeros won hockey titles, the Avco, and Turner Cups. The Comets won the first four WNBA championships.

Built for $27 million, The Summit opened on November 20, 1975, for a concert by The Who and held its final concert, ZZ Top, on November 22, 2003, in the final of their Thanksgiving shows there. In between, it was home to circuses and ice shows and, briefly, the indoor football of the Texas Terror and Thunderbears. When the name was changed in 1998 to Compaq Center, it became the first Houston sports facility to sell naming rights.

The most extreme change, however, was its last. In 2005, after the Rockets had decamped for Toyota Center, The Summit was reworked and reborn, as the headquarters for Lakewood Church.

The Summit had been transformed, but inside the megachurch at 3700 Southwest Freeway, it is easy to see the once-groundbreaking arena that was the Rockets home, and even the championships won there.

59 Barnstorming

When the Rockets moved to Houston, they moved out. And back. And out. And back.

After four seasons in San Diego, the Rockets called Houston home beginning with the 1971–72 season opener, but they would spend those early seasons barnstorming Texas, more of the Houston Statetrotters than Houston's home team.

After that home opener, a loss to the 76ers before 4,771 in Astrohall (according to the newspaper box score the next day, though another report listed the attendance at the much more modest 1,467), their next "home" games were in San Antonio and Waco.

By the time the Rockets played a second game in Houston, it was also in their second Houston venue, moving from the Astrohall to a section of the Astrodome.

They would go back and forth for the first two months of the season, but by December, they had a new home court, playing games in Hofheinz Pavilion on the University of Houston campus where they played 14 of their next 15 games in what was then considered a modern, comfortable arena, though it seemed built for theater in the round.

They would play two more games in San Antonio and returned to Waco. But by March 1, the Rockets went as far across the state as possible, playing a home game in El Paso, roughly 750 miles away.

That first season, the Rockets played 35 games in Houston, split among three arenas.

"You never knew if you were coming or going," Rudy Tomjanovich said, "because half the time, even when you were home, you weren't."

In the second season, when the Rockets established Hofheinz as their Houston home, the Rockets played 13 games in San Antonio. This was not entirely uncommon in the early 1970s in the NBA. The Rockets played the 76ers in Hershey, Pennsylvania, the Bucks in Madison, Wisconsin, the SuperSonics in Portland, Oregon, and even played the Celtics in Providence, Rhode Island. But with the Rockets, there was a sense that the idea of professional basketball in Texas was an experiment, its potential uncertain.

The Rockets were barely noticed in their first few seasons in Houston, less so as they made the rounds like a band of traveling salesman. One of the games in Waco drew just 458 fans. They were said to average just less than 5,000 that first season, though many tickets were given away in an effort to market the team.

"Most of the fans were there to see other teams," Tomjanovich said. "They rooted for the Celtics or Knicks or Lakers, whoever they knew."

Eventually, they would grow to know Tomjanovich, Calvin Murphy, and the Rockets. Home games were played in Houston.

On November 2, 1975, the Rockets moved into The Summit, topping the Milwaukee Bucks before 7,142 fans in what was then a state-of-the-art arena.

But if anything demonstrated how uncertain the NBA experiment was, it was those first years for the first NBA team to play in Texas, when they traveled far and wide to spread the word.

60 E.G.

Eric Gordon had always been a starter and usually a star. He had been Mr. Basketball in Indiana, the object of a celebrated recruiting battle. He was a college All-American. He was of course a lottery pick, a talent so undeniable he was traded to New Orleans for his future Rockets teammate Chris Paul.

Mike D'Antoni had another idea. It might have always been viewed as a possibility when Gordon signed as a free agent with the Rockets in the summer of 2016 that he could come off the Rockets bench. The Rockets had James Harden and Pat Beverley in their backcourt. Even coming off a dreadfully disappointing season, it was not a shock that they might want to keep that mix together.

Still, a conversation seemed in order. Gordon had been drawn to the Rockets' potential and D'Antoni's offense, but before the season would begin, D'Antoni told Gordon he would be coming off the bench.

Gordon kept his response brief. He said, "Okay."

That was it. He had other thoughts. He kept them to himself.

"I explained that he's a sixth man, and he accepted it immediately," D'Antoni said. "I didn't have to talk to him."

The conversation continued. D'Antoni did not think of Gordon as demoted. He had been an assistant coach with USA Basketball when he saw Gordon fit easily with the best players in the game. He was putting in an offense that would greenlight any open three-pointer, knowing Gordon still had that remarkable and fundamentally sound shooting stroke his father had taught him, and which Gordon perfected all those years in the JCC across the street from his home in Indianapolis. D'Antoni wanted Gordon to star, but at different times in the game.

"One thing Coach told me, 'If you're going to come off the bench, you better win Sixth Man of the Year,'" Gordon said. "I'm going to take advantage of that. It's always good to hear how the coach pushes you to that edge of being really good."

Gordon averaged 16.2 points, 2.7 rebounds, and 2.5 assists in his first season coming off the Rockets bench. He was the Sixth Man of the Year. He won the All-Star weekend three-point shooting contest, shooting his way past the boos in New Orleans a day after he said the Pelicans he encountered for five seasons were "dysfunctional."

By his second season in Houston, he more often filled in as a starter with Chris Paul missing 24 games and James Harden missing another seven, bumping his scoring average up to 18 points per game, his most since 2011–12, his first season in New Orleans.

More important than the accolades or statistics, though, Gordon helped the Rockets win.

Most of all, he won. The Rockets won 55 games in his first season, 65 in his second, both career highs for Gordon.

"That's really always my top priority—doing whatever I can to help my team win," Gordon said.

After seasons derailed by injuries in New Orleans, Gordon arrived in Houston slimmer and stronger. By his second season, he seemed even more explosive off the dribble, getting to the rim more regularly. He improved defensively, becoming one of the keys to the Rockets' switch-everything style, which made him an option to close games with Harden and Paul.

"The thing is, I think we forget how good he is defensively, and everything he does, the ball handling he does, setting up things, and driving to the basket, and then hitting threes—ridiculous threes," D'Antoni said. "His game is really good."

That did not change when Gordon became a sixth man. If anything, Gordon elevated his game, becoming more than a scorer, even if he was no longer a starter. He became more of a winner.

"It's all about me being ready whenever I come off the bench… really be productive," Gordon said. "Every time I step on that court I want to bring it offensively and defensively.

"You've got to do whatever it takes to win. I just want to make a major impact any time I'm on the floor."

61 Clint Capela

Most of the time, on the best Clint Capela slams, opponents never saw him coming. Plays began with a screen, usually set for James Harden. They knew that with a pick comes a roll, with Capela dashing through the lane as rapidly as any guard heading to the rim.

Somewhere between that screen and the airspace above the bucket they lost sight, as if he could not close the remaining distance in the time that passes from Harden's decision to the flight of the ball reaching its apex.

Capela had mastered his part of those pick-and-roll slams with chemistry between he and Harden that neither fully explains other than by citing the trust they developed since late in Capela's rookie season, and especially the following season when Capela was still Dwight Howard's understudy. But Harden appreciated Capela's sure hands and determination to fit the role the Rockets had for him.

Yet, Capela's ascent to the ball on all those no-look Harden flips over the defense was nothing compared to Capela's rise from the 25th player taken in the 2014 NBA Draft, who the Rockets thought might be better served with one more season in France, to a legitimate member of a Rockets Big Three with Harden and Chris Paul.

Much of that comes from aspirations to take his role and wring everything possible out of it, chasing greatness from morning workouts with Rockets development coach John Lucas to afternoon skull sessions with assistant coach Roy Rogers.

"You've got guys who are just comfortable being in the NBA, and you've got guys who actually want to have a legacy," Harden said. "Clint is one of those guys."

Clint Capela celebrates after scoring over Kevin Durant in the 2018 Western Conference Finals. (AP Photo/David Phillip)

He has a long way to go to leave a legacy, but he quickly won the respect and encouragement from the player with the greatest impact in Rockets history. Hakeem Olajuwon worked with Capela in his first two seasons, with Capela taking more affirmation and inspiration from the sessions than the actual moves Olajuwon taught him.

"He makes me want to go harder," Capela said of Olajuwon's comments. "Whenever I hear stuff like that, it makes me want to work even harder, get earlier [to] practice and do what I do."

That work ethic drove Capela's success from Geneva, Switzerland, to Elan Chalon in the French league, from the Rockets G League affiliate to a key to the Rockets plans under Mike D'Antoni.

With Howard leaving nearly as soon as the ink dried on D'Antoni's contract, Capela had been elevated to the starting center. With Harden moved to point guard, Capela's ability to cut hard to the rim and catch anything Harden tossed in his general direction forced defenses to sag to the middle, helping to create the open shots the Rockets used to set three-point records.

Capela grew as a defensive force, not only swatting shots, but changing them and dissuading many others, all while moving quickly enough to play in the Rockets' switching schemes.

By his second season under D'Antoni, Capela's fourth in the league, he had his fingerprints on everything the Rockets do.

"He's just really good," D'Antoni said. "Clint is guarding the rim. Blocked shots and… missed shots with people going in for layups gets us running. When we can run and we get a good pace to us, we're really good offensively. That starts a lot with Clint.

"What he does for us in Houston and for me as a coach is invaluable. When I took the job, I didn't know if he could make the leap from part-time player to a starting center on a team that wants to win a title. He's done that and more. He's been terrific."

More than terrific at what he does, with a determination to fill the role assigned him, D'Antoni often said Capela became the ideal center for his time. The Rockets did not call plays for him. They ran pick-and-roll and ran the floor. Those abilities became coveted enough for Lucas to go from telling an incredulous Capela in their initial 2016 workouts together that he would one day be a max player to calling him "the Swiss Bank."

"I know where I came from, I know how much work and focus that I've put into this," Capela said. "I've wanted to make myself important to the team. I'm just glad that now everybody sees it. It just gives me more motivation and confidence to continue what I'm doing."

62 Bill Worrell, the On-air Point Guard

So much had changed over nearly 40 years as the television voice of the Rockets, but for Bill Worrell, there was always a constant.

He would change on-air partners and broadcasting styles. He would change stations and networks, calling games with six different mic flags in his hands. There would be ever-changing rosters and coaches and management, even four different owners.

Yet, after all the years and all the changes, Worrell said one thing remains that is most obvious on the broadcasts.

"I still love it," he said. "I love the action. Baseball is totally different. You have a lot of time to kill and have to tell a lot of stories. Not being a professional baseball player, I didn't have a lot of insights into my playing time in the Major Leagues. All these guys use that. That's one of the reasons when [Jim Deshaies] came along I decided to do one sport and that I'm going to do basketball."

A college baseball player at his beloved University of Houston, Worrell became an on-air anchor at KPRC, moved to sports and then left to broadcast Rockets games. After three seasons broadcasting Rockets games, first on Channel 39 and then on Channel 20 in Houston, Worrell called Astros and Rockets games on HSE beginning in 1983. Over the years, whatever entity had the rights to broadcast Rockets games—beginning with HSE, then Prime Sports, Fox Sports Southwest, Comcast, Root Sports, and now AT&T SportsNet—it made sure to have Worrell call the games with his usual mix of polish and passion.

Perhaps most impressive, however, was how he was always the perfect setup man for his broadcast partner, with his time working with Calvin Murphy still nearly as cherished by Rockets fans as Hakeem Olajuwon's with Rudy Tomjanovich's.

"I still get stopped once, twice a week with people talking about the years with Calvin," Worrell said of the mix of his professionalism with Murphy's over-the-top exuberance.

Worrell, 70, had started working with John Egan before McCoy McLemore, Mike Newlin, Murphy, Matt Bullard, and finally Bullard with Clyde Drexler at home games. In the 2016–17 season, Worrell stopped traveling, calling only the games from Toyota Center with Craig Ackerman (the radio play-by-play broadcaster for home games) working the road games with Bullard. But the great many on-air partners and his easy rapport with all of them demonstrated Worrell's gifts as the point guard that makes those around him better.

"I think to be a good play-by-play you have to adapt to who you're working with," Worrell said. "It's become more and more of a color game. When I first started, it was all play-by-play because the guys doing color didn't have as much to add as they do now. Now, with all the bells and whistles we have, all the instant replay, there is so much they can load into a broadcast, it's become more of an analyst game, so you learn how to back off.

"I've always been a distributing point guard. I think that's one of my strengths. But it's been fun working with the Rockets and all the different management. It's the same. You still have to have the players."

Worrell was referring to the stars on the floor. But even if he never seemed to notice, he had been a star, too. In all the years, that never changed.

63 Gene and Jim

A decade since Gene Peterson and Jim Foley called their last game together, it's easy for Rockets fans to hear not just the iconic calls that marked their three decades on the air, but also Peterson's perfect smooth baritone and Foley's cheerful exuberance.

It is as if they are still on the air.

"How sweet it is!" Peterson cried out after each win, but never more enthusiastically than when he counted down the final seconds of the 1994 Finals.

"Oh Mother! Houston, the Eagle has landed," Foley followed with his customary gusto. "Your team is on top of the basketball world!"

It is still difficult to picture Ralph Sampson's game-winner to beat the Lakers and not hear Peterson's, "Yes! Yes!" followed by Foley's "We're on our way! We're on our way!"

They had timing. They had camaraderie. They had chemistry, with Peterson's "pipes" bringing the action from a time when radio was so important to fans and Foley adding the benefits of his inde-fatigable research.

"They have been doing the games for so long and their voices are so familiar, it's going to be like walking into your house and calling, 'Hi, Mom! Hi, Dad!' and have somebody else answer," former Rockets guard and TNT analyst Kenny Smith told the *Houston Chronicle* in 2008, shortly before they signed off.

In Houston, you could go into any rec center, play pickup on any outdoor court, and before long, someone would say a player was "backing it in, backing it in, backing it in," as Peterson would, or make a shot and shout "Bingo!"

Foley had been with the Rockets for 39 years, first as the media relations director brought in from the Milwaukee Bucks, then as the radio analyst. Peterson had been the voice of the Rockets for 33 of his 45 years as a broadcaster.

Peterson had started as many of his time did, moving from station to station, team to team, from the South Dakota State Jackrabbits and on to Eau Claire, Wisconsin; Albuquerque, New Mexico; and Kansas City, Missouri, before landing a spot as the sports director at KPRC in Houston. A year later, former Rockets general manager Ray Patterson called and offered the last job Peterson would hold.

Foley had done public relations work for the New York Central Railroad after getting out of the Navy before moving to Milwaukee to do media relations for Al McGuire at Marquette. He moved across town to the Bucks under Patterson before joining him in Houston in 1972 when the NBA was still considered something of an experiment in Texas.

Foley's affability helped spread the word, building media atten-tion as the Rockets put in roots. He would sit in on occasional broadcasts with Peterson until the move was made to pair Peterson and Foley full-time in 1987.

"Gene was one of the best ever play-by play guys," Foley said. "Working with him," Peterson, "was an absolute pleasure."

They were traveling companions through three decades of NBA seasons, bringing the rapport from their time off air to the broadcasts.

When they retired, the media dining and work rooms at Toyota Center were named the Peterson-Foley Media Center, featuring two wall-length photo collages from their careers.

"It was a real fun time to work as many years as we did for the same franchise," Foley said.

How sweet it was.

64 From Clutch to Turbo and Back

When the Rockets were at their best, so was the show when they were not on the court.

It is not that Clutch the Bear, the mascot that roamed the stands and sidelines, was a better entertainer in the mid-'90s. He was not even a different comic inside that bear suit. But when Robert Boudwin created Clutch and Jerry Burrell flew as Turbo, it was all new and ground-breaking, with the timing coinciding with the second championship season to make every gag, every flying dunk captivating.

They were far from the original sports mascots, though Burrell, as Turbo, was something of a trend-setter and then a mentor for other NBA mascot fliers. But they were idiosyncratic and iconic.

Boudwin created Clutch to be an easy-to-embrace (often literally), comic, and cartoonish mascot. He was a student of the

Phillie Phanatic style and of its creator, Dave Raymond, a fellow University of Delaware graduate, and with that in mind began a 21-year tenure as Clutch, beginning in March of 1995. The Rockets Power Dancers debuted the same season.

In the early years, Clutch would be a part of skits during time outs and often halftime. Over the years, however, greater emphasis was placed on Boudwin's outsized improvisational talents, dancing, pranking, cake smashing, and doing just about anything for a laugh.

He was named the NBA Mascot of the Year in 2005 and 2013 and was in the inaugural class of the Mascot Hall of Fame in 2006. Over the years, he high-dived, skydived, and ran a half marathon for organ donation awareness, all in full costume.

Turbo had a much shorter run, but also influenced many that followed.

Burrell had been a gymnast at Arizona State and brought that athletic talent to his performances, filled with flips and twists, with and without the trampoline.

In a red-and-yellow spandex leotard and shorts, with a super hero mask, Turbo was almost entirely about his athleticism. He had a pose after dunks, but other than that, there was no act. That was up to Clutch.

That made them a strong combination. Burrell moved on with a touring band of dunkers. Boudwin left the character after 21 years. But his more than two decades in the role was a triumph.

65 The Clipper Comeback

For two decades, Clutch City stood alone as the standard to which all Rockets teams aspire. It still does. But it has company.

In Game 6 of the 2015 Western Conference Semifinals, the Clippers led the Rockets by 19. Blake Griffin had put in a spinning layup. The celebration in Staples Center had begun.

The comeback from a 19-point deficit was the Rockets' largest in the postseason since the championship-era Rockets climbed out of a 20-point hole against the Orlando Magic in the 1995 NBA Finals. But that was not all that made the rally so inexplicable, so unforgettable. The 13-point Clippers lead heading into the fourth quarter was the largest the Rockets had ever escaped in a playoff game. But there was even more that made the turnaround stunning.

Dwight Howard had 20 points and 21 rebounds that night, the first 20/20 game in an elimination game since Shawn Kemp in 1997. But he went the entire fourth quarter without a field goal.

James Harden, who had driven the Rockets through the second quarter but made just 1 of 7 second-half shots, took a seat with the Rockets down 17 in the third quarter and never played again.

More than anything, the Rockets blitzed the Clippers—outscoring them 40–15 in the fourth quarter—with a trio of players with famously unreliable shooting driving them. Four players that were key to the comeback—Corey Brewer, Josh Smith, Terrence Jones, and Jason Terry—and former Rockets coach Kevin McHale, would be gone within two seasons. But on that night, they were unstoppable.

Jones helped keep the Rockets in the game late in the third quarter, putting in a reverse off an offensive rebound, hitting a three-pointer, and sinking a pair of free throws. Brewer took off to start the fourth quarter, finishing a pair of drives and hitting a three. Smith knocked down a pair of threes, then drove to the rim. Finally, Brewer and Smith each hit another three and Brewer took a Smith pass to a dunk. Between them, Brewer and Jones combined for 29 fourth-quarter points.

While the Rockets soared, the Clippers collapsed. Griffin had made 12 of 15 shots for 28 points through three quarters. He missed all five of his attempts in the fourth. The Clippers missed 15 consecutive shots in the quarter, most coming at the rim or on open shots they nervously missed. The Clippers made just 4 of 22 shots in the fourth quarter, including the three Chris Paul put in on the way off the court when the Rockets were too giddy to notice.

"What happened 20 years ago was great for the city and great for that team," Howard said after the comeback was complete, reminding of the Clutch City rallies, "but we have to make our own history."

The Clippers never entirely recovered. The teams had the same regular-season record, 56–26. They split their four regular-season games. They were tied in their playoff series 3–3. But after the specular comeback (or collapse), the Rockets were soaring, the Clippers reeling, battered far more for how they blew a 19-point lead than encouraged by their ability to build it in the first place.

The Rockets rolled in Game 7, advancing to the Conference Finals for the first time since 1997. They flamed out there, losing to the Warriors in five games. But on that night in Los Angeles, they had channeled Clutch City.

"If we win this game right now," Brewer said of the mindset heading into the fourth quarter, "that's how you become a champion."

They did not accomplish all that, but they took a comeback triumph worthy of the legacy left them by the champions of the Rockets celebrated past.

66 0.9

The Rockets knew far more than just their first-round playoff series and the hopes that came with it had ended. No one said it. They knew.

They will never know how things might have changed the other way if not for those 0.9 seconds, if a series of events had gone another way, with each step leading to the next up to Damian Lillard's three-pointer to take the Trail Blazers to a 99–98 win, clinching the 2014 first-round playoff series in six games. But as the Rockets sat, with the visitors' locker room in Moda Center as quiet as a graveyard, they knew the team that should have accomplished much more would never be together again.

They could not have predicted the exact changes to come. In the weeks that followed, Chandler Parsons would jump to the Mavericks, while Jeremy Lin and Omer Asik, starters through most of that series, would be traded. The roster would be dramatically rebuilt. But for just a moment, before the Rockets knew how much was over, they believed far more was just beginning.

That all changed not just in the sudden lightning strike of Lillard's dagger, but in the series of events that led up to it.

Even the basket that preceded it, with Chandler Parsons putting in an offensive rebound to give the Rockets a two-point lead, had to fall the way it did for the Rockets to lose that Game 6 and the series. Had Parsons missed, or if there would have been a battle for the rebound, the final ticks of the clock would have slipped past and the game would have gone to overtime.

"I was like, 'Oh, we won, the game is over,'" Lin said. "I didn't even know there was 0.9 left until the timeout. Worst-case scenario was overtime because we said no threes."

The Blazers used their last 20-second timeout. Rockets coaches worked to quickly calm their players for the final possession, instructing that they switch on all screens to prevent a three-pointer, then calling a timeout after they saw the Blazers line up. With Howard on the ball, James Harden was on Aldridge. The Rockets used their 20-second timeout to change that, putting Harden on Wesley Matthews and substituting Terrence Jones for Lin to defend the inbounds pass.

At the last moment, Harden instructed Parsons to pick up Lillard instead of Pat Beverley. Beverley took Mo Williams. Dwight Howard, who was originally assigned to defend the inbounds pass, was shifted to LaMarcus Aldridge. Blazers coach Terry Stotts had drawn up a play in which Lillard cuts to the corner and Nicolas Batum lobs a pass to Aldridge rolling to the basket.

As the Blazers took the court, they saw an opening. Williams shouted to Lillard, "Go to the ball, go to the ball." Jones, defending the inbounds pass, was positioned to challenge a lob inside and Howard sniffed out Aldridge's cut and took it away. But Lillard saw a clear sprint toward Batum.

Lillard took off, immediately getting a step on Parsons, but Batum wasn't looking. Still planning a pass inside to Aldridge, he heard Lillard clapping and shouting "Nico, Nico!"

With no screen set, the Rockets did not switch as planned. Parsons could not catch up to Lillard. Harden, looking for the screen to signal he should pick up Parsons' man, did not see Lillard spring open until it was too late.

At that moment, 0.9 seconds moved in slow motion. Batum turned to see Lillard and delivered his pass. Lillard caught and shot in one smooth motion. The shot looked good as soon as it left his hands.

"It was a great shot," Harden said. "He had a good look, and he knocked it down."

Had Parsons not made his go-ahead basket, had Howard not defended Aldridge so well, had Batum not heard Lillard, had Lillard not caught the pass cleanly, had he shot more slowly, had he missed, the game either would have gone to overtime or the series would have headed back to Houston for a Game 7 that the Rockets were convinced they would have won. Even the Blazers wondered if Lillard's shot would have been their last shot had he missed.

"Momentum is on their side," Batum said of the potential of facing the Rockets in a Game 7. "It's going to be a tough one. I was like, *Please make it. Please make it.* When he made it, I was surprised at first. Then everything went crazy. It took me like five, 10 seconds to realize, *We did it.*"

The Rockets never played that Game 7. If they won, they would have faced the Spurs, having swept the season series against the team that would win the NBA championship.

They were certain they would have won a Game 7, and were confident about a series against the Spurs. But they'll never know for sure what would have happened had 0.9 not happened.

"It was an elimination game," Parsons said. "It allowed them to advance and ended our season. I think the best game-winners are the ones with the biggest stakes, and The Finals or a playoff makes it bigger than ever. This was up there with any I have ever seen, just with what was at stake. They eliminated us and moved on."

More than that, Lillard and the Blazers ended that Rockets team's time together, as they seemed to know that night in Portland.

67 Game 6

The whole thing is still difficult to comprehend, made no clearer by the score or the rumors it spawned.

Spurs 114, Rockets 75, still does not seem possible.

It was not just the blowout that seemed and still seems inexplicable, though the Spurs were within one point of the biggest rout of the Rockets ever in the postseason.

It was not even that they did it with Tony Parker and Kawhi Leonard out, or that the Rockets had seemed in command of the second-round series in 2017 when Leonard was still playing two days earlier and the Rockets held a fourth-quarter, Game 5 lead in San Antonio.

James Harden had been unstoppable to start that 2017 second-round series. The Rockets won in a rout. The Spurs had turned things around, then rallied to force overtime in Game 5, clinching the win when Manu Ginobili stuffed Harden's unlikely heave.

In Game 6, Harden had nothing left. He didn't look to shoot. He didn't look to drive and kick. He seemed in a fog, prompting speculation of everything from a fight with teammates to a concussion.

None were true. In some ways, that was more troubling. Instead, he had hit a wall, as he had by Game 5 of the 2015 Western Conference Finals when he had 12 turnovers against the Warriors.

That, however, was an undermanned Rockets team playing the eventual NBA champions. Against the Spurs, with one of the league's preeminent defenders on the bench, Harden was reduced to a slow-moving spectator.

Harden took just 11 shots, but most came after the blowout was irretrievable. He made two. He did not even attempt a shot in the first quarter. By halftime, he had as many turnovers [five] as points.

"It's frustrating," he said. "It's frustrating the way we were resilient all year long, playing through adversity, bouncing back. It hurts. It stings."

Resilience had been the Rockets' primary emphasis throughout the season, the improvement they wanted most after the disappointment of 41–41 in 2016. In that regard, they failed in Game 6, with the Spurs playing with energy that was off the charts and freedom that came from knowing they would have Game 7 at home with Leonard likely back.

The Rockets never could match the Spurs' energy, and never shot well enough to keep pace anyway. Eric Gordon made just 2 of 9 shots. Ryan Anderson went 0 for 6. The Rockets made just 28.6 percent of their shots, just 9 of 33 in the lane. The Rockets' only lead lasted 38 seconds. After failing to score 100 points just five times in the regular season, the Rockets fell short of 100 three times in the six-game series against the NBA's best defense.

"For whatever reason, this game we didn't have the juice and the stuff, and it was right across the board," Rockets coach Mike D'Antoni said. "I told them, one, it was a pleasure to coach them. They tried to do everything they could to make it a great year. And I'm proud to be their coach.

"I know they feel as bad as I do. This is going to hurt and linger, but hopefully it will spur us on to… where we got to go."

It spurred change. The Rockets have insisted they were not driven through the 2017–18 season to make up for Game 6. They had a mix of camaraderie and success that made it impossible to look back on their worst loss for motivation. It did, however, bring a retooling of the roster.

The Rockets concluded that Harden, rather than a victim of the conspiracy-theory conclusions, had not bounced back from the demands on him in the series. He had carried the Rockets offense as its leading scoring and primary playmaker, leading the league in assists. The load was heavy enough to bring in help.

Help came in the form of Chris Paul, who could handle some playmaking duties, but would also be a tough-love leader when necessary and a mid-range scorer if the teams defended as the Spurs had, by contesting at the three-point line and backing a center to the rim.

They added defenders, signing P.J. Tucker and Luc Mbah a Moute as free agents, and then emphasized defensive toughness, moving to an aggressive switching defense that could better match up with the Spurs' motion and the league's increasing emphasis on three-point shooting.

They built camaraderie and then put together the best regular season in franchise history to help leave Game 6 in their past. It was not forgotten. It was too stunning, too complete a breakdown for that, with the Rockets needing a triumph of comparable magnitude to relegate it forever to a part of their past.

68 Van Gundy vs the Commissioner

Jeff Van Gundy intentionally made his accusation sound worse, more conspiratorial than it was. David Stern, having issued the largest punishment for a comment in NBA history, intentionally made his threat sound more ominous than he likely ever intended.

With that, the battle lines were drawn, Van Gundy on the playoff stage with his power to use it to shape public opinion; Stern with his unquestioned power over the league he ruled.

Both lost.

The issue began after Rockets centers Yao Ming and Dikembe Mutombo were called for moving screens set against the Mavericks in Game 4 of their 2005 playoff series. At a Dallas hotel the next day, with only a few media members present and a question directed to Van Gundy unrelated to the fouls that were called, Van Gundy said he had been warned by an unnamed league "official" that the NBA would watch Yao more closely while he set screens.

Van Gundy said that because Mavericks owner Mark Cuban "has been hard on" the NBA and its officiating and officials, "he's gotten the benefit.

"I didn't think that really worked in the NBA, but in this case it has," Van Gundy said.

That sent shock waves, with Van Gundy seeming to have a secret informer inside the NBA revealing a conspiracy against his star center. Van Gundy even let those assumptions continue, saying later that he chose the word "official" to be intentionally vague and protect his friend's identity.

The "official" was actually a league employee, and not a referee as many assumed. Stern likely could have guessed who tipped the Rockets coach. But Stern was livid.

Stern hit Van Gundy with a $100,000 fine but threatened to go far beyond that. Before Game 5 of that series in Dallas, Stern said that the fine was merely an "intermediary step" and implied that Van Gundy could be banned from the NBA.

"If he's going to say things like that, he's not going to continue in this league," Stern said. "If the attitude reflected in those comments continues to be public, he's going to have a big problem with me as long as I'm commissioner.

"This is the first case I can remember when an allegation has been made and the perpetrator hasn't cooperated. At this time of year, there usually is a craziness in the land that has to do with referees as coaches jockey for position. This one, in our view, set a new low for that. That's why the fine is what it was and that's why the investigation is continuing."

Van Gundy called those comments "interesting" but did not back down, refusing to publicly name his friend in the NBA office.

"I didn't see anything wrong with what I said," Van Gundy said after Stern's comments. "But certainly, obviously, for a statement like that to come out, he obviously differs. That's all right."

Van Gundy was cheered as he never had been before in Toyota Center. Local furniture-store owner and Houston celebrity Jim McIngvale offered to pay the fine. Yao offered to pick up the tab himself.

Van Gundy paid the fine, but did not seem disturbed by the threat. He joked that his wife would make him sleep on the porch. He laughed at the fine being levied by Stu Jackson, who hired Van Gundy as an assistant when Jackson was the coach of the Knicks before becoming a longtime league official. Cuban cracked, "It's nice to see someone else buying the coffee and danish for the NBA."

After the Rockets lost the series in seven games, the league dropped its investigation with no further penalty.

"I may have been purposely vague, but I made sure I was telling the truth," Van Gundy said. "The implication from the start, that I might have fabricated the call, was disturbing and I'm glad the NBA confirmed that there were talks with league personnel."

Van Gundy kept his job and remains in good standing with the league as one of the lead broadcasters for ABC and ESPN.

He also received a form of vindication. Cuban had acknowledged that the Mavericks had given the league examples of screens they believed should have been fouls on Yao and that the NBA agreed, basically confirming Van Gundy's charge that the league officials would watch Yao closely (assuming they did not wish to continue to miss fouls.)

In the years that followed, the NBA even added a rule that would prevent the entire incident from ever occurring again.

If the league office communicates with one team about officiating in a series, the other team is given the same communication. It just would not need Van Gundy's unnamed NBA "official."

69 Nene's Night

The Rockets were in trouble, unable to soar past the Thunder, their three-point shooting betraying them in one of those postseason games that turn hard and ugly.

The Thunder lead swelled to 14, matching the number of shots Oklahoma City blocked in the first half. James Harden, slowed by a sore ankle, was bottled up. Bodies were crashing into one another, with the Oklahoma City frontline of piano movers—Steven Adams, Taj Gibson, and Enes Kanter—moving close to pulling even in the 2017 first-round series.

With that, the Rockets turned to an old-school veteran with dashes of gray in his beard and a body-builder's physique, as if he were cast for the occasion.

Nene not only hit back, he hit every shot he took. The Rockets not only emerged with a 3–1 series lead, Nene took a place in the record books for making the most shots without a miss in an NBA playoff game.

"It was kind of a man's game and he's a man," Rockets coach Mike D'Antoni said. "He was unbelievable in all facets. That's Nene. It doesn't surprise me. He was able to gather up a lot of stuff and just dunk it."

He matched the record set in 1975 by D'Antoni's long-ago Kansas City–Omaha teammate Larry McNeil, but Nene and the rail-thin, high-flying McNeil could not have been more different. Nene achieved his triumph with brute strength around the rim that could not be stopped.

"This game is a lot of physicality," Nene said. "We try and stick with it. This game we came and played physical. We made shots. We exploited their weakness. That is why we won."

Nene did not realize he was perfect that afternoon until he saw the stat sheet in the Chesapeake Energy Arena visitor's locker room and checked his phone, blowing up with text messages. Still, he said he was just doing his job, filling in for slender, young center Clint Capela during a series, and especially a tough road game, that called for his muscle.

"When I step on the court, I just try to do my job, help my team, make the right decision," Nene said. "When I received a lot of texts, I realized a little bit.

"I didn't realize. I didn't think. I just do what a coach asks me to do and try to be in the right spot, the right moment, and when I have a chance, catch and finish the best way possible. Like I say, I was focused. I was nervous. Everybody was nervous. But when you're focused, you don't let any noise, any bad calls, nothing get in your way.

"After the game, yes, I realized a little bit. But that kind of stuff don't change me."

Nene scored 28 points that day and finished the series shooting 84.8 percent. He had given the Rockets just what they needed that season, remaining healthy through much of the season as D'Antoni carefully monitored his workload by holding him out of games in back-to-backs and limiting his minutes, all with the postseason in mind.

"I'm one of the first to get here and the last to leave the arena," Nene said the day after his record performance. "I do a lot of things to take care of myself, take care of my body, to feel fresh when I can. That's what the young fellas look [to], these actions.

"To be playing for 15 years on that kind of level, that kind of intensity, I have to take care of myself. I have a little extra motivation. I've been through a lot of adversity. When you get a little older, you have to take better care of yourself."

Nene played 67 games that regular season. In Game 4 of the second round, however, Nene went out with a torn adductor muscle, ending his first season with the Rockets. When he was injured, the series with the Spurs was tied 2–2. The Rockets did not win another game.

Nene, however, will always have that day in Oklahoma City when, in a physical, old-school game, he could not be stopped.

"You have to have guys on your team like that, who know how to take care of themselves on and off the court, how to respond to big games, how to respond to physical games," D'Antoni said. "It's all cute and fun when you are dancing around, but when you get down to mud-slinging, it's nice to have a guy like that in the back alley with you. That's where he's been really good."

70 Eddie Johnson and the Shot

Just the mention of his name brings back that image. Both names are not required. Just tell a Rockets fan the first name—as in "Eddie! Eddie! Eddie!'—and the picture of the shot and the celebration that followed comes quickly to mind.

Eddie Johnson was in his first of three seasons with the Rockets to complete his career. The Rockets were locked in another of their epic playoff series with the Utah Jazz, down two games to one, but tied in Game 4 with 6.7 seconds left. Johnson had been the star of Game 3, scoring 31 points off the bench, but had made just 1 of 4 three-pointers in Game 4.

The play was not necessarily designed to go to Johnson, but Matt Maloney knew where he would be. Johnson inbounded to Maloney, who quickly got the ball to Clyde Drexler. Drexler looked inside to Hakeem Olajuwon, but the Jazz double-teamed Drexler, forcing him to give the ball back to Maloney. Johnson, who had started to set a screen for Maloney, popped to the top of the key, and Maloney swung the ball to a wide-open Johnson.

Johnson never hesitated. There was not time, but even if there were, he had the shot he wanted. When he swished his three-pointer at the buzzer, he set off a wild celebration, first with his own high-stepping dash to the other end of the floor with his arms held high. Charles Barkley reached Johnson first, lifting him from the floor as, for the second consecutive game, The Summit crowd serenaded him with, "Eddie! Eddie!"

On the radio broadcast that would become nearly as iconic as the shot, Gene Peterson and Jim Foley simultaneously shouted, "Yeeeeeeessssss!" Foley then added a characteristically delightful,

"Oh Mother! Eddie Johnson!" Finally, Peterson said, "Eddie Johnson does it again. Unbelievable!"

"I always thought about playing in Houston, the team that they had," Johnson said. "They had three Hall of Famers: Charles Barkley, Clyde Drexler, and Hakeem Olajuwon. I knew that I would perform. I knew given the right opportunity… I would flourish in Houston. Unfortunately, after the first two games in Houston, they pretty much handled us. So, we came back to Houston down 0–2.

"I came out in Game 3 very aggressive. I ended up with 31 points. That was a special game because it got us back in the series. There's nothing better than hearing a sold-out arena chanting your name."

That turned out to be a warmup for the theater of Game 4.

The Rockets did not win another game in that Western Conference Finals series. They lost Game 5 in Utah and were eliminated in Game 6 when John Stockton hit his buzzer-beater.

Johnson had signed with the Rockets in March at 37 years old, after he was dealt by the Pacers to Denver, who immediately released him. He averaged 11.5 points in his 24 games with the Rockets that season, 8.4 the next. He played in just three games in 1998–99 before he retired. But though he played in just 102 games in those odd, striped Rockets uniforms, he will be forever remembered for that shot, and the jubilation that it brought.

"When your teammates are excited for you, that's the best feeling in the world," Johnson said. "It was the most exciting time I've ever had in my life, how the fans reacted, how my teammates reacted."

71 Stockton's Dagger

The words still hang in the air of memory, warning of what was to come in those next few moments, slowed down as if witnessing a car crash in slow motion as it moves from possible to inevitable.

Bill Walton, broadcasting Game 6 between the Rockets and Utah Jazz in 1997, said, "Uh oh." Hearts of Rockets fans sank as if he were warning them again.

"The Shot," as it has come to be celebrated in Jazz history, as the greatest moment ever for that franchise, clinched the Western Conference Finals and in many ways, ended the Rockets' run as championship contenders, despite the star power that remained and would come and go.

With the game tied, Bryon Russell inbounded, Karl Malone engulfed Clyde Drexler, and John Stockton nailed the three-pointer at the buzzer to send the Jazz to The Finals.

In that blur of 2.8 seconds, a chain reaction of events made The Shot possible, but it took more than that for the Jazz to finally vanquish the Rockets, as the Rockets had beaten the Jazz on their way to consecutive championships.

The Jazz had won 64 games that season, had the league's MVP (Malone), and led the Rockets 3–2 in the series. But with less than seven minutes remaining, the Rockets led by 13, and though the series would have returned to Salt Lake City had the Rockets held on, they believed they would have taken a Game 7.

The Rockets still held a 10-point lead with less than three minutes left, but the Jazz made a run that changed everything. Russell hit a three. Greg Ostertag blocked a Hakeem Olajuwon shot. Stockton put in a pair of free throws. After Barkley made a pair of free throws, Russell sank another three-pointer and Stockton finished a layup, cutting the lead to two. Stockton then turned a steal into a game-tying layup with 63 seconds remaining.

After two more Barkley free throws, Stockton put in a runner in the lane. The Rockets had a final possession, or so they thought, with just 22.4 seconds left on the clock. Though Drexler had few touches in those closing minutes, he had scored 33 points when the Rockets went back to him. The plan was to hit the game-winner or go to overtime.

Drexler made his move through the lane early, put a spin move on Russell and clanged his shot off the rim too early, leaving the Jazz time to shoot for the win when Malone simultaneously snagged the rebound and called timeout.

The Jazz set up a play Jerry Sloan had used for years, but switched it to have Stockton catch the pass from Russell. Barkley laid off Malone, rather than stay up tight on the screener. Jeff Hornacek darted to the corner. Stockton began to curl. Drexler moved to cut it off. Malone set the screen on Drexler, wrapping his forklift arms around him and taking him out of the play.

"I was bear-hugged," Drexler said, as so many Rockets fans have throughout the years since.

Stockton, after one step toward his usual move around the pack, instead backed away to the three-point line. Barkley stepped toward Malone and Drexler, then switched too late, dashing toward Stockton with his arms raised but unable to interfere with the shot.

Russell saw Stockton begin his move toward the mid-court logo and delivered his pass perfectly. Stockton took one dribble to his left and nailed his three-pointer over Barkley.

Stockton began leaping and spinning. Sloan and Jazz players charged on to the floor. Compaq Center fell so quiet, the only noise came from the screaming visitors. Rockets coach Rudy Tomjanovich, having tried desperately to force a miss using will and body english, waved his right hand toward the other end of the floor, as if bidding farewell to the team the Rockets had been.

"We exorcised some demons when we beat Houston down there," Stockton, who scored 13 points in the final 3:13 of that game, told the *Salt Lake City Tribune* on the anniversary of The Shot. "Houston had beaten us in the playoffs a number of times on last-second shots or whatever. Or Portland.... They had beaten us. Phoenix, Charles had beaten us. We exorcised our own demons and we got over a couple huge, huge hurdles that had eluded us before."

The Rockets needed 12 years to win another playoff series. "Uh oh," indeed.

72 The Game 7 Loss That Changed Everything

There were near opportunities along the way. There were missed calls, including one in the final regular-season game weeks earlier. There was one bizarre sixth-man moment barely noticed for two decades. But the Rockets, facing the SuperSonics in Game 7 of the 1993 playoffs, second round, had their chances to win.

They had a long Kenny Smith jumper in regulation. They had a Vernon Maxwell fadeaway on the baseline in overtime. If either went in, the Rockets would have won Game 7 and advanced to the 1993 Western Conference Finals. Rockets history would have been forever changed.

It might not, however, have been changed for the better.

The series itself pitted two teams on the rise, stepping toward their prime and the three NBA Finals appearances to come between them. There were Hall of Famers on both sides, with Hakeem

Olajuwon at his peak as a dominant defensive force and Gary Payton and Shawn Kemp powering the SuperSonics. For six games, there were nothing but home-court blowouts, sending the series back to Seattle for Game 7.

The series also offered some intriguing contrasts, with the Rockets, preferring to play in the halfcourt when not counter-punching with breaks, and the Sonics looking to push pace. The Rockets in Rudy Tomjanovich's first full season as coach, were built around Olajuwon in the low post. The Sonics countered with George Karl's double- and triple-teams of Olajuwon to help Sam Perkins inside and a scrambling defense.

Vernon Maxwell got off to a good start and the Rockets built a 10-point first-quarter lead. Ricky Pierce, the former Rice star, helped keep the Sonics in the game until the fast break could get up to speed. After a Matt Bullard three-pointer, the Rockets led by 10 at halftime, holding the Sonics to 38 first-half points.

By the second half, the Sonics began finishing the shots inside they had missed earlier. With Otis Thorpe in foul trouble, Seattle got second shots when Olajuwon looked to block shots. The Sonics' threes started falling and they took a three-point lead into the fourth quarter.

Olajuwon tied the game with 70 seconds left and, with 32.7 remaining, he found Robert Horry for a 20-footer that put the Rockets up two and offered a hint of Horry's big-shot mastery to come. The Sonics posted up Pierce, whose jumper over Vernon Maxwell tied the game. The Rockets held for a final shot, with Smith missing at the buzzer. Overtime.

With the game tied, Olajuwon was called for a phantom foul and Pierce hit both free throws. Moments later, Perkins threw the ball away, but it was mistakenly called off Horry, just as another loose ball in the final minutes of regulation was wrongly called off Olajuwon. Kemp dropped in a jump hook for a four-point lead.

The Rockets, however, rallied one more time. Olajuwon beat a double-team to cut the lead to one. Derrick McKey missed a pair of free throws and the Rockets went to Olajuwon again. Triple-teamed, Olajuwon passed to Maxwell for a 15-footer, fading to the baseline. Maxwell missed and the Sonics took the series.

In a game and series that tight, there were many turns that could have changed everything. Before Maxwell's final shot, Horry cut toward the basket in position to finish, had Olajuwon found him. Bullard was open for a three. The Rockets could have lamented a pair of missed calls when the ball was incorrectly ruled off the Rockets. Pierce's final free throws were a gift.

The strangest missed call, however, went the other way, with ESPN.com reporting nearly 20 years later that on the final possession in regulation, Rockets reserve guard Winston Garland wandered onto the floor as an unnoticed sixth player, with SuperSonics coaches not noticing until days later when preparing for the series against the Suns. Had a technical foul been called, the Sonics could have won before the overtime.

Rockets fans, however, think of a different call they still believe might have been decisive, a call not in Houston or Seattle and long before Game 7.

In the regular-season finale, the Rockets led 109–107 when the Spurs' apparent final shot missed. David Robinson tipped in the rebound, but it came clearly after the buzzer. As official Hugh Evans ruled the shot good, sending the game into overtime, Rockets radio announcer Gene Peterson shouted, "That's bullshit!" The Spurs won in overtime, 119–117, sending the Rockets and SuperSonics to the postseason with identical 55–27 records, with the Sonics holding the tie-breaker for home-court advantage.

In a series in which the home team won all seven games, that advantage seemed significant. But the Rockets also believed something good had come from the defeat.

When the Rockets reconvened in Galveston for training camp, they were more determined than ever. They won their first 15 games the following season and the first of consecutive championships.

"I think it started… when we lost to Seattle in Game 7, overtime," Olajuwon said. "Coming back from Seattle, you could see the disappointment of all the players and all the coaches. The plane was so quiet coming back. I think that carried over that summer.

"Coming back in the preseason and the training camp, there was a bitter taste. You could see that determination from all the players for that season. We felt that in training camp. I know in the summer when I was training I felt very focused, knowing we lost a game we felt we should have won to go all the way."

73 See It, Three It

The minds that Rockets general manager Daryl Morey had assembled to fuel the data-driven decision-making of the organization could have taken the day off. The assorted coaches that worked for Morey did not need Morey's math club to know the first rule of Rockets' offenses: three-pointers are worth more than twos.

The data gets more detailed than that. It involves the shooting percentages of post-up players that normally take contested shots compared to three-point shooters that, if the offense is executed well, are open when they launch. It reports that mid-range shots rarely go in regularly enough to merit giving up the extra point that would come if the shooter just backed up a few steps. It proves that an open three, particularly from the corners, is a very good shot that richly rewards the shooter.

It all has added up to a basic philosophy that, for all the changes over the years, has become the Rockets identity: "See it, three it."

In truth, the Rockets general manager does not oppose mid-range shots. He spent years trying to land masters of the mid-range in Chris Bosh, Dirk Nowitzki, Carmelo Anthony, LaMarcus Aldridge, and Chris Paul, finally getting Paul in a trade in June 2017. But that also clarified the thinking that for a mid-range shot to be a good choice it should come from elite practitioners.

"I like scoring more points than the other team," Morey said. "You get more if you shoot threes or layups. It doesn't mean we're going to keep Chris, one of the best midrange shooters ever, from shooting them."

Before joining the Rockets, Paul had averaged nearly as many mid-range shots per game with the Clippers as the entire Rockets team.

He still takes them, but with the Rockets, nothing beats an open three.

"It's been a really fun way to play, getting off the ball, catch-and-shoot, stuff like that," Paul said. "I've always been capable of shooting the three."

This all pre-dates Paul's time with the Rockets. But by the time they added D'Antoni's green light there seemed to be no limit to the number of threes the Rockets would shoot. That impression might be because D'Antoni often said there will be no limit to the number of threes they would shoot. An open three taken by a three-point shooter is always a good shot, no matter how many had been taken before.

When the Rockets edged past averaging 40 three-pointers per game midway through D'Antoni's first season, he said why not average 50. Late in the season, he said he didn't even care if they go in. If the Rockets shoot enough three-pointers, D'Antoni said, they will eventually make enough to have the fire-away style work for them.

"It's [about] getting good shots," Rockets guard Eric Gordon said. "The other team, they can take as many twos as they want. They're not going to accumulate that to the amount of threes we make in a game. We get a lot of threes and a lot of layups.... It's a great philosophy."

In the 2015–16 season, the Warriors put up a record 2,592 three-pointers, 59 more than the Rockets, who were still giving Dwight Howard touches in the post. A season later, with James Harden moving to point guard to run D'Antoni's offense, the Rockets put up 3,306 three-pointers, more than 700 more than the Warriors had taken. In D'Antoni's second season, they broke the record again, taking 3,470 three-pointers, launching 42.3 per game and hitting 15.3 per game.

D'Antoni's offense had evolved since his days in Phoenix, and even since his first season with the Rockets. The Rockets don't play at the same pace, with Harden and Paul preferring to look things over and find preferable matchups when the quick-strike pass is not there.

The Rockets go one-on-one far more often than D'Antoni ever thought he would. There are relatively few cuts, with Paul and Harden working in the middle of the floor while shooters spread out to give them room to operate. But from their G-League affiliate to the possessions run by Harden and Paul, the Rockets love nothing more than layups, free throws, and especially three-pointers.

"We need to embrace who we are and do it well," D'Antoni said. "Some teams will try to take that away. Hopefully, that just means more layups. If they give us threes, we'll take them."

And take them. And take them.

74 The Chuck Wagon

The first signs were easy to overlook. Rockets coaches might have noticed Chuck Hayes that summer. But five summer games in Minneapolis, of all places, were not about to move the needle.

There was, however, something there, something that even with hindsight could be understandably missed when evaluating a 6'6", wide-bodied center that could not shoot. There was one thing Hayes did that summer, and it was not insignificant. He won.

With Tom Thibodeau coaching the Rockets' summer league team, each game he would return Hayes to the floor midway through the fourth quarter, along with veterans Lonny Baxter and Dion Glover, and the Rockets won, going 5–0. Hayes set bone-rattling screens, played the sort of defense the kids of summer leagues rarely play, and rebounded. Mostly, though, he won, leaving an impression the Rockets could not forget.

Hayes was brought to camp and released. He was to be brought back from the NBA Development League, but had a sprained ankle. Finally, in January, Hayes signed a 10-day contract, added with a roster exemption because of injuries. Few knew at the time, but with that, the legend of the Chuckwagon was born.

"That was a moment," Hayes said, "I was waiting for my whole life."

Hayes set no records, other than being the shortest starting center in Rockets history and doing it as a fill-in for the tallest (Yao Ming). But there were all those moments that he used his immovable strength in the low blocks combined with his studious approach to defense to make him so valuable.

There were games in Portland when LaMarcus Aldridge torched the Rockets only to have Hayes switch assignments and

Chuck Hayes (44) goes up for a basket during the first quarter of a game against the Miami Heat on Wednesday, December 29, 2010, in Houston.
(AP Photo/David J. Phillip)

turn off Aldridge's dominance as if shutting a water spigot. There was a game in Toyota Center when he frustrated Kevin Garnett as the Celtics star went at him, shouting and challenging him, only to have Hayes shut him down. There was the charge he drew on Utah's Derek Fisher to clinch Game 5 in the 2007 playoffs.

"I had to find my niche," Hayes said. "This was my dream. I had to find a way. Even though I was undersized, I did it with heart and I did it with effort."

Even his famously broken free throw shooting form, with a hitch along the lines of Charles Barkley's golf swing, worked out, with Hayes hitting an acceptable 62 percent in 11 NBA seasons. But Hayes was never about the numbers. He did produce a double-double in his second game on that first 10-day contract. He had a triple-double against his hometown Warriors.

Mostly, however, Hayes left a mark by doing what he had done when Kentucky tried to promote him as an All-American, with a slogan, "All he does is win." (He was all-SEC and SEC Defensive Player of the Year, but never All-American.)

A guy barely noticed when he first played for the Rockets, despite a college career in which he started 110 college games, matching the school record unlikely to ever be topped at One-and-Done U, Hayes was honored in the team's nightly 50th anniversary celebration and returned to the Rockets as a pro personnel scout in 2017.

From the arc of the 22-game winning streak to all the little effort plays to dive after loose balls, Hayes went from forgotten to a fan favorite. He locked down stars in Jeff Van Gundy's defense. He ran Rick Adelman's high-post passing offense. Mostly, though, he did what he had for Thibodeau in that forgotten summer—whatever was necessary to succeed despite the limitations that made him easy to overlook.

75 The First All-Star

In the first 50 years of Rockets basketball, 16 players were named to 58 All-Star teams. They have had All-Stars with the East and West. They have had Hall of Famers who were All-Star staples. They have hosted three All-Star games.

Yet, no matter how many All-Stars they have had or will have, no matter what they do in that spotlight, Don Kojis will forever be first.

In 1968, the inaugural season of the San Diego Rockets, Kojis became the first star of the franchise. He was, however, much more than a trivia answer.

Kojis was in his fifth season when the Rockets debuted. He had been a bit of a journeyman player, in both senses of the word.

Drafted in the second round out of Marquette by the Chicago Packers (one spot before longtime Nuggets coach Doug Moe would be picked), Kojis weighed his options. He had an offer from the Harlem Globetrotters to play for an opposing team of college All-Stars, but was concerned he would play only limited games in the Midwest and would stall his career.

He had played well in a pair of games against the ABL Pittsburgh Rens and was invited to what would amount to a job interview with another team, the Cleveland Pipers. Kojis flew to Cleveland, where he was taken to a restaurant meeting and offered a two-year contract worth $15,000 per season, twice what the Packers were offering. Kojis was ready to make the move and asked to see the contract when the young owner of the team complained that college kids ask too many questions.

Kojis never heard back from the team, but years later saw a picture of that young owner, immediately recognizing George Steinbrenner.

With that option gone, Kojis opted to postpone his professional career entirely to maintain his eligibility for the Olympics or World Championships, choosing to play AAU ball for Phillips Petroleum in Bartlesville, Oklahoma.

Kojis played two seasons of AAU basketball and in the 1963 Pan Am Games and World Championships in Brazil before he made the jump to the NBA in 1963, crossing paths with a variety of future NBA dignitaries and Hall of Famers like a high-jumping Forest Gump with a degree in philosophy from Marquette.

He played for one season in Baltimore before he was traded, along with future Bulls executive Rod Thorn, to Detroit for a package that included Bob Ferry and Wali Jones. He played two seasons in Detroit, behind and with player-coach Dave DeBusshere. He played one season in Chicago with the expansion Bulls, where he began to establish himself as a reliable starter for a playoff team. But according to an interview Kojis did with the National Basketball Retired Players Association, at the time of the expansion draft, a Bulls staffer crossed off the wrong name, making Kojis available.

That made Kojis a player taken in an expansion draft in consecutive seasons. But it also brought Kojis his breakthrough. He had a greater role than in his previous stops, even while sharing a frontcourt with a gifted rookie, Elvin Hayes. He roomed with another rookie, Pat Riley, who was the first pick in franchise history. And he averaged 19.7 points and 10.3 rebounds that first season in San Diego, earning his trip to Madison Square Garden for the All-Star Game.

"I felt like I had finally arrived in the NBA," Kojis told the *Houston Chronicle.* "I remember coming down the floor with Elgin Baylor at the top of the key and I'm in the corner. He passed me the ball, I hit the shot, and Elgin said, 'Hey, I think we might have a player here.'

"The experience was a validation for the work that I'd put in. After going from team to team in those early years, I wasn't sure I would ever get a chance to show what I could do. Coming to the Rockets was the break I needed. Coming to San Diego, I found a home."

Quick and remarkably bouncy as a 6'6" forward, Kojis had become an outstanding, aggressive offensive player that Wilt Chamberlain called "the jumpingest white boy I've ever seen."

The season after Kojis became the Rockets' first All-Star, he averaged 22.5 points per game and went again, this time starting along with Hayes. He played one more season with the Rockets before his contract was sold to the Seattle SuperSonics, never making it to Houston.

Kojis played five more seasons, including three with the Kansas City–Omaha Kings, where he would be teammates with Nate Archibald when Archibald led the NBA in scoring and assists, and a year later with future Rockets coach Mike D'Antoni.

When he retired, he founded Whispering Winds, a Catholic Camp and Conference Center in the Cuyamaca Mountains, about an hour from the city where he became an All-Star.

Kojis was more than just an All-Star. He will forever be the Rockets' first.

"It's something, you look back on your life," Kojis said, "and say, 'You know, I finally made it.'"

76 Sleepy Floyd

In any listing of the most celebrated and unforgettable eras of Rockets basketball, the era of the Twin Towers and the twin championships would rush to mind near the top of any list. They can be summed another way: before and after Sleepy Floyd.

Yet, Floyd did plenty to distinguish himself in 5½ seasons in the Rockets backcourt. He was swift and graceful at the point, with a mix of abilities to get to the rim and shoot from the three-point line ahead of his time. He could be explosive, taking over games with bursts of scoring, most celebrated in the 1988 playoff game when Floyd had 42 points, Olajuwon 41.

The Rockets never quite broke through in those seasons after the Rockets dealt Ralph Sampson to Golden State to get Floyd at the point.

"I heard the news that I was getting traded to the Houston Rockets, who were a much better team than we were at Golden State at the time, so I knew it would be an amazing opportunity to play alongside Rodney McCray and Hakeem Olajuwon and Robert Reid and Allen Leavell," Floyd said. "Their foundation was pretty set at that time. They were looking for a guard with my abilities to kind of give them something they didn't have at that time.

"The potential of coming to the Rockets and just going to the next level was eye opening. It was a great opportunity."

Floyd, a first-round pick of the Nets after starring at Georgetown, flourished with the Warriors. He was an All-Star in his final full season with Golden State, averaging 18.8 points and 10.3 assists. He averaged 11.5 points and 5.4 assists with the Rockets, who were built around Olajuwon's talents inside. But Floyd gave them what they needed after the fall of the 1986 Finals team: a reliable point guard.

"I think my greatest strength that I brought to the Rockets was getting to the basket, penetrating, getting easy baskets for my teammates, but also being able to score, being able to shoot the three-pointer," Floyd said. "It just made us a much more versatile team."

By the 1992–93 season, his final season in Houston, the Rockets had moved to a backcourt starting Kenny Smith and Vernon Maxwell. They had not advanced in the postseason in Floyd's first five seasons in Houston, but seemed on their way to something greater when they took the Seattle SuperSonics to overtime in Game 7 of the Western Conference Semifinals.

Floyd signed with the Spurs as a free agent and the Rockets became back-to-back NBA champions. But for the stretch between Finals teams, Floyd gave the Rockets just what they sought when they got him, reliability, making him far more than a footnote between eras.

77 Del Harris

Del Harris did not really want to play slowly. He was a product of the ABA, brought from Earlham College in Richmond, Indiana, to the ABA's Utah Stars to be an assistant for Tom Nissalke in 1975. He had joined Nissalke with the Rockets and succeeded him as head coach in 1979. The style that marked his greatest success as Rockets coach was a matter of pragmatism, not preference.

Harris might have preferred to coach an up-tempo style, but more than that, he wanted to win. He famously hit the brakes, downshifted to bully ball, and led the Rockets to one of the most improbable runs to the NBA Finals in league history.

Building his team around the brutish talents of Most Valuable Player Moses Malone, and often playing Malone with Billy Paultz on a team with Calvin Murphy, Tom Henderson, Mike Dunleavey, and Bill Willoughby, Harris led the 40–42 Rockets to the 1981 NBA Finals.

Along the way, the Rockets knocked off the Kings, Spurs, and defending champion Lakers. They took the Celtics to six games before finally falling. But Harris' team had made its mark.

"I am just proud to have been a Rocket in that pivotal time and made whatever contribution I may have made," Harris said. "The Rockets have become one of the key franchises in the NBA. We here in Houston, the people, can be proud."

The first conference title in franchise history did not immediately lead to bigger and better things. The Rockets went 46–36 in the next season, but were knocked out in the first round by the Seattle SuperSonics. The Rockets were sold to Charlie Thomas. Malone was deemed too expensive to keep as a free agent and was dealt to the 76ers to begin the rebuilding. The Rockets let their free agents go and sacrificed the 1982–83 season to get in the coin toss for the right to draft Ralph Sampson.

Harris stepped down as coach after a 14-win season, but in his first three seasons, the Rockets went 127–119.

"I have the satisfaction of knowing I did my job with dignity," Harris said when he stepped down. No one could argue.

Harris' talents and some good fortune took him to all sorts of stops, from coaching Kobe Bryant as a rookie to coaching Yao Ming as the star of the Chinese National team. With deep roots in Indiana high school basketball, he was there when Milan won the state championship, the underdog story that became the movie *Hoosiers*.

Harris' 1981 Rockets nearly matched them, going from a rocky, up-and-down season to the NBA Finals. For all his stops since, there are still many who remember him most for that season when a style fit a team and nearly pulled off an upset for the ages.

"I, believe it or not, run into people every month in my life… that will ask me about those days," Harris said. "They were here. They saw us play. Not a month goes by that I don't see a Houstonian in Dallas or in airports or wherever."

78 Bill Fitch

The Rockets knew what they had and what they needed. They had won the coin toss to draft Ralph Sampson, the 7'4" tower of talent that would be the foundation of their rebuilding from a 14-win season. They wanted a coach that would demand everything possible from someone so gifted.

The Rockets had lost the 1981 NBA Finals to Bill Fitch and the Boston Celtics. They knew how demanding Fitch could be. By 1983, the entire NBA knew. Fitch had resigned from the Celtics after four seasons, following a change in ownership. One week later, with Sampson as a draw, Fitch joined the team he had defeated.

"I'm looking forward to coaching someone of Sampson's ability," Fitch characteristically said, "but he's got an awful lot to live up to."

As with all rookies, and especially a rookie with the pressure of outsized expectations that Sampson faced, he had a lot to learn, too. Fitch would be his hard-driving teacher. Fitch would spend his career guiding reclamation projects and, after going 14–68, the Rockets were that.

The proud son of a Marine drill instructor, Fitch laid down rules. He had a "put up" list, things the team would put up with and would not.

"There can be no learning if you don't have discipline," Fitch said. "That's No. 1 in my book."

Sampson was rookie of the year, but the Rockets cleaned house around him, playing what was left of Elvin Hayes in his last season, and collapsing down the stretch. The Rockets went 29–53 in Fitch's first season and drafted Hakeem Olajuwon in 1984. The Rockets had the pieces and the coach to take a young, ambitious team with Sampson, Olajuwon, and Rodney McCray in the front-court and push hard.

Fitch had wanted Sampson to become a more traditional center, but with Olajuwon, he embraced the idea of Sampson facing the basket with Olajuwon in the paint. By Olajuwon's rookie season, Fitch's third in Houston, the Rockets were on the move. They went 48–34 before losing to the Jazz in the playoff's first round.

By 1985–86, the Rockets went 51–31 and kept on improving through the postseason. They upset the defending champion Lakers, clinching the series on Sampson's redirected jump shot, heading to The NBA Finals for a rematch with the Celtics.

The Rockets lost in six games, but seemed clearly on the upswing. Instead, it all began to unravel. Mitchell Wiggins and Lewis Lloyd were banned from the league after testing positive for cocaine. The previous season, Fitch had released John Lucas, a decision Lucas credits for saving his life.

By December of 1987, just months after Sampson had signed a six-year deal, the Twin Towers were broken up, with Houston bringing in Joe Barry Carroll and Sleepy Floyd. The end of Fitch's era was closing in. The Rockets went 42–40 that season and improved to 46–36 the following season. But the style the

Rockets needed, and that helped rapidly bring the Rockets back to The Finals, wore thin.

Fitch had become known as "Captain Video" for the long video sessions that would follow long, grueling practices. Players rushed to the flights because whoever arrived last had to sit next to Fitch and have his ears filled. When Sampson complained, first to Fitch and then to the media, Fitch made him read the newspaper coverage of his comments to the team the next day.

Still, just as he had driven the Celtics, Fitch had pushed the Rockets into a force. It did not last. The demands had worked, but the team Fitch built was gone. Much of his backcourt was out of the league. Sampson was sent to Golden State and then Sacramento. Robert Reid, who had stepped in so effectively in 1986, was traded to Charlotte. McCray and Jim Peterson were traded to Sacramento, with Peterson eventually going to Golden State in the deal for Sampson, the player he backed up in Houston.

When even Olajuwon complained about Fitch's demands, time was running out. The Rockets lost in the first round of the 1988 players and Don Chaney replaced Fitch as head coach.

Fitch, however, had given the Rockets what they wanted, building a championship-caliber team. It came apart before it could realize that potential. But when his teams are remembered for what they briefly became and what could have been, Fitch's strong hand is all over everything that had been built.

79 The I-45 Rivalry

The rivalry did not last. It had the ingredients, if only a limited history, to fuel it. But the Rockets were ascendant, the Mavericks in decline. The outbreak of hostilities whether real, imagined, or artificial, were entertaining, but gone quickly.

As always, the results on the court matter most. The Rockets stomped the Mavericks in a five-game, first-round series. The Mavericks faded. The rivalry might eventually flare up again, with some embers perhaps still burning, but it is not what it seemed to be building to when the Rockets beat the Mavericks for Dwight Howard, the Mavericks pilfered Chandler Parsons off the Rockets' roster, and Mark Cuban and Daryl Morey traded verbal shots.

On the floor, there never was as much of a rivalry between the teams. The Mavericks beat the Rockets in seven games in 2005, winning Game 7 by 40 points, and the Rockets, after all the tension, rolled through the 2015 first round. Rarely were the teams good, much less contenders, at the same time. But things got interesting in consecutive off-seasons when the front offices one-upped each other and had plenty to say about it.

Things heated up when Howard chose the Rockets over the Mavericks, Hawks, Warriors, and Lakers. Cuban said Morey reached out to talk about a trade for Dirk Nowitzki, an entreaty the Mavericks' high-profile owner initially thought was taunting.

"That's fine," Cuban told ESPN, "but payback is a bitch."

Cuban later said he made his comment just to stoke the rivalry, but needled that he might have helped the Rockets sell tickets.

"I think they need a little help," he said.

In a radio interview the following summer, his comments were more pointed.

"I was like, 'Are you kidding me?'" Cuban said. "He asked if we'd trade Dirk. At first I thought it was taunting, but now, knowing more about Daryl, I don't think it was in hindsight. That's just not his style.

"It says a lot about their approach more than anything else. They just have a different understanding and approach to chemistry than we do. Some teams, and that's not just the Rockets, just put together talent and the talent takes care of itself. We think chemistry matters. When Carmelo [Anthony] came to visit us, there was no chance that we were going to put him in someone else's jersey number and put it on the outside of the arena. That's not our style."

With that, it was on. Cuban had taken a shot at the Rockets' efforts to sign Anthony that famously included a picture of Anthony in a Rockets uniform No. 7, the number (at the time) worn by Jeremy Lin. The Rockets were days from trading Lin to the Lakers when the picture surfaced, but he was offended by the pitch to Anthony.

Morey, however, reacted to Cuban's comment about Morey's emphasis on chemistry and shot back.

"Our teams have had great chemistry, and it's something we believe in," Morey said. "Hey, if Mark believed so much in chemistry, he wouldn't have busted up a title team for cap room."

He did not stop there. The comment that drew more attention at the time was the comparison between the Rockets and Mavericks.

"Let's be clear: if the money's equal between the Rockets and Mavericks, I think players are picking Houston," Morey told *Yahoo Sports*. "Every time. For Dwight [Howard], I just don't think it was a hard choice between us and Dallas. If you want to win, you're going to want to join our organization. We have a First-Team All-NBA player in his prime."

With James Harden, Morey was proved correct, though not because he had landed Howard.

Cuban, however, might have seemed to have won the last laugh when he signed Parsons, inking him in, of all places, an Orlando nightclub.

Morey explained that the way the Parsons contract was structured made it "literally one of the most untradeable structures I've ever seen."

Morey was entirely accurate with that. The Mavericks intentionally structured the offer sheet that way to make it more difficult for the Rockets to match, especially if they had landed Chris Bosh, their primary target that week. Still, Cuban predictably shot back.

"That just says so much about the difference," Cuban told the *Dallas Morning News*. "They looked at every player as an asset. That asset was a step toward getting another asset. We look towards how do you build a team. Chemistry matters to us. Culture matters to us. We made it a difficult contract to trade because we have no intentions of trading him."

As it turned out, Parsons opted out of his Mavericks' contract after two seasons, the first ended by that short series against the Rockets. The Mavericks happily let him walk, with Parsons taking a max contract to sign with the Grizzlies. The Rockets swept the eight games against the Mavericks since. The rivalry lost its heat.

With that, it had become clear it was always about competition. When the rivalry lost that, there wasn't much left to the rivalry. But it was fun while it lasted.

Bull

After all these years, all the seasons spent describing far more Rockets games than Matt Bullard played, he still thinks of himself as a player. He likely will for as long as he can knock down three-pointers, and the threes still fall for him when he lets them come out to play.

That much won't change any time soon.

"I've been a broadcaster longer than I was an NBA player," Bullard, the television analyst on Rockets broadcasts for the past 13 years, said. "It's pretty surreal. I still think of myself as a player. I think as a player. I still shoot a lot. I still enjoy playing. But now that I'm a broadcaster longer than I was an NBA player, it kind of blows my mind—one, that I'm that old, but two, that's it's two different careers. Even though they are both based on basketball knowledge, they are two different skills.

"To be able to be good at two different things, I take a lot of pride in that. I work hard at it."

Bullard's place in Rockets history has long been assured as a member of the 1994 championship team. His place in the evolution of Rudy Tomjanovich's offense, despite modest stats, was significant, as a range-shooting power forward that helped lead to the move of Robert Horry to that spot late in games the following season and the spread of the style throughout the NBA.

Yet, he has become better known for his second career, even if he will still identify himself for his work describing the play of others. Much of that could be from the emotion that comes through on air with the clear affection he has for the team that bookended his career.

Bullard played four seasons with the Rockets to start his career and five more near the end. He had briefer stops with the Hawks, Hornets, and Greek power PAOK.

In his second stint with the Rockets, with the leaping ability he had at Iowa and Colorado long gone, sacrificed to five knee operations and back problems, he became known as "Air Bull." He laughed along with the moniker, as anyone that had heard the comedy he sprinkles into his analysis on broadcasts would expect.

When he stopped playing, Bullard moved quickly toward broadcasting, starting with a stint with Comets WNBA games and then with a runner-up stint on the ESPN show *Dream Job*. He has been a fixture on Rockets broadcasts ever since, to the point he is more recognized for that than his years as a player, even if he thinks of himself as he had when he was paid to hit three-pointers as a forerunner to the current style of range-shooting fours.

Either way, he remains most identified with the Rockets.

"I feel like I bleed Rockets red," Bullard said. "Even though I played for a couple different teams, I still feel like I'm a Houston Rocket. When I walk into the arena and I see the '94 championship banner, that's kind of the pride I have of being a Rocket. And now, being able to be in the organization for 22 years, nine as a player and 13 as an announcer, I've been around Bill Worrell and Clyde Drexler and Calvin Murphy so much as broadcasters, we have all gotten older, but all have Rockets red in our veins."

81 Ketchup and Mustard, Jet Streams and Stripes

For the most part, the Rockets uniforms were forgettable, which was a great improvement over the mess that came in between the ketchup-and-mustard attire and the current outfits.

Had the Rockets stayed in the championship-era uniforms, no one would have complained, as they have ever since. They were nothing special. They were not so beloved before the Rockets won consecutive championships in them. But once they became associated with the greatest era in franchise history, they were elevated to iconic.

Leslie Alexander, then the new owner of the Rockets, could not be faulted for seeking a change. He had begun the process before the championship seasons. NBA procedures dictated that once the revisions were in the works, there was no turning back.

Alexander did base the change on logic.

"Did you ever walk into a store and ask for a mustard-and-red shirt?" Alexander said. "Those colors are passé. The new uniforms are fantastic."

Those duds have been described in ways since, but "fantastic" is not among them.

The new colors, midnight blue and silver, were trendy. They just were not the Rockets' colors. The Rockets had worn green and gold in San Diego, but changed to red with the move to Houston. In 1972, the lettering was changed to white, with yellow on the uniforms' trim and the new logo on the right leg. The "e" and "t" in Rockets were in lower case, for reasons only described as a '70s thing.

Charles Barkley in the infamous "jet stream" Rockets jersey. (SMI/Newscom)

There was not a great deal that could be considered memorable about the look, but no one complained, either.

Then the new uniforms arrived. Players and coaches were torn. Some thought they were hideous. Others thought they were a well-executed practical joke.

For eight seasons, fans hated them.

They included the oxymoronic notion of thick pinstripes meant to evoke jet streams. The logo was an angry, cartoonish rocket circling a basketball. To keep red in there somewhere, a thick stripe went down the legs fading into white, as if the goal was to make anyone look clunky. The logo was placed low, across the belly, with the uniform number in the upper right corner.

They did not last long. If it was not clear enough that the hot-mess era of Rockets duds was a mistake, the next generation seemed entirely about going the opposite direction. In contrast to the previous get-ups, the uniforms were kept simple and very red.

Red returned as the primary color with Rockets president Tad Brown explaining that it remained in the Rockets' DNA. A New York–based agency, Alfafa Studio, worked with Japanese designer Eiko Ishioka to come up with a new logo in the shape of a stylized "R" meant to evoke a rocket during takeoff.

There have been complaints over the years, as has become tradition with uniforms, especially with the wide stripes around the arms, with the slashing font of the lettering and that the primary road uniforms used the name Rockets rather than Houston. When Nike took over the NBA account in 2017, the multiple wide arm stripes were removed, with double stripes on the shorts.

Over the years, a "Clutch City" alternate has been used to revisit the ketchup and mustard look. The black alternates have been popular. The gray short sleeves were not.

Generally, the current uniforms could be described in some of the same terms as the beloved championship-era duds. The choices on the lettering is a bit odd. The current toned-down version is generally simple and straight-forward. And it will be viewed over time largely by whatever is accomplished by the players wearing them.

82 The China Games

The crowds still turn out in waves of bodies that stun even the worldliest, most wildly popular NBA players. The fans, donning authentic NBA gear beyond even the outsized imagination of David Stern when he dreamed of sports-world domination, are as well-informed on every trend as any daily fantasy sports junkie.

The world has grown small. Chinese arenas, large and spectacular, have grown as well since Yao Ming first returned to Shanghai for the first China Games. NBA stars make their annual shoe company–sponsored pilgrimages east. Former NBA players fill China Basketball Association rosters. Chinese fans are as likely to fill closets with the latest uniforms worn by Stephen Curry or Kristaps Porzingis as they are the familiar Rockets uniforms of Yao or Zhou Qi.

In 2014, it was all new and exciting and in some ways even innocent when the NBA brought the cherished jewel of China sports home. Like Elvis Presley swiveling hips or The Beatles showing off mop tops on *The Ed Sullivan Show*, a week in Shanghai and Beijing, coupled with the grand Yao Ming experiment with the Rockets, triggered explosive change far beyond the screams of the moment.

Just four years later, China would have its shining moment, as Yao would carry his nation's flag at the Beijing Olympics and then drop in the three-pointer to open the Games and inspire roars that all but shook the planet. But in 2004, he was Shanghai's Yao Ming, the former star of the Sharks, back in his hometown with the Rockets and inspiring the sort of thrills that would indicate how much was possible.

Yao would become the personification of China's still-new economic and cultural outreach to the rest of the world, the 7'6" symbol of how removed it had become from the isolation of the Cultural Revolution. Yet, as he made his way through Shanghai, visiting his old school, taking his teammates to a welcome feast, and most of all, arriving at the old, long-since replaced arenas, the feelings he inspired were never more vivid.

Fans not only flooded the streets, chasing after Rockets busses like extras in *A Hard Day's Night*, many threw themselves at Yao's van, unconcerned with personal safety, in the hopes that for that moment they might get a glimpse of him.

"I was looking for the exit," Yao said the night of the game in Shanghai. "I was suffocating."

When the Rockets arrived in their locker room, fans had found a way through the walls to wait in the showers. When they boarded the busses, security lined up with arms locked, desperately trying to hold back the masses for the few seconds it would take Yao to run through.

"People here look at us like a rock band," Rockets star Tracy McGrady said at the time. "I love the international atmosphere. It's much different than in the States. They're constantly up, rowdy, cheering. It's fun. It's a great feeling playing in an atmosphere like this.

"It was amazing. I had to sit back and take it all in. I couldn't believe how people react to him, the true support he gets, the love they have for him. He's international. He's an icon. He's huge."

The Rockets rushed from the madness of Shanghai to the splendor and serenity of The Great Wall. They attended more receptions, gathered in the Great Hall of the People in Tiananmen Square. The crowds in Beijing, while still enormous, were as orderly as they were crazed in Shanghai, owing to the far different personalities of the cities, especially then. When the Rockets boarded their charter for Houston, they were weighed down with enough souvenirs to fill one of those old arenas, unaware that they would return often with their teams, on their own, or, even in a few cases, to play in the CBA.

The NBA returned in 2008 and has held China Games every year since. The Rockets were back in 2010 and 2016 with a trip to the Philippines and Taiwan in 2013.

Over the years, fans at the China Games would become incredibly knowledgeable, but no longer as giddy. In 2017, fans recognized and stopped James Harden's mother to pose for pictures. A buzz filled the arena in Beijing when rookie Chinanu Onuaku was fouled, with fans knowing he would take his free throws underhand, though he never had yet in an NBA game.

In 2004, they roared or groaned over every possession, laughed uproariously at every mascot skit, cheered heartily over every dance team routine. By the second half of that first game, fans sang, "Yao Ming, Jia Yo, Yao Ming, Jia Yo," or "Yao Ming, add fuel."

He did, and China's love for the NBA burned rapidly, with no sign that it could be extinguished. The NBA returns each preseason, no longer needing Yao to thrill fans. More NBA games are broadcast live in China than ever, with Chinese media stationed in the United States to cover the league.

"I think it's fair to say Yao Ming is the most important thing in the world for the development of the NBA in China that has ever occurred," Stern said at the first China Games. "With Yao Ming, this is even more extraordinary. But it would be historic with any NBA team. These games represent to us, the NBA, a historic occasion."

A pair of meaningless games never meant so much to so many.

83 Zhou Qi

The immediate assumption, as with all things related to the Rockets and a basketball player from China, was that the Rockets' selection of Zhou Qi with a 2016 second-round pick was about their history with Yao Ming and the marketing potential that would come in the world's most populous nation.

There was not much at stake with the investment of just the 43rd pick of the draft. But the Rockets saw potential that had nothing to do with selling sponsorships or t-shirts.

His size was undeniable and immediately recognizable. At 7'1" with a nearly 7'8" wingspan, his remarkably slender frame makes him seem even taller. There is a soft shooting touch with three-point range. But if there were still thoughts that Zhou's value would be tied to his fame back home, Mike D'Antoni watched him work with the Rockets between G League stints and saw nothing but a player with potential to unlock.

"He can be really, really good," D'Antoni said. "I don't think I'm exaggerating. Worse comes to worse, he's going to be a good player."

As far as Zhou has come literally and figuratively and still has to go, he stands out not just because of his size, but as an athlete, moving smoothly and easily from end to end. He shows promise as a shot-blocker that goes beyond his 9'4" standing reach. There is shooting range with potential to develop into a more reliable threat.

With that, D'Antoni—with no interest in marketing potential—saw qualities he'd want to develop in any young player.

"He has a chance. He has a real solid chance," D'Antoni said. "He's 7'2". He can shoot threes, run the floor, knows how to play. There's no reason other than strength and bulk and things that come naturally. I'm looking forward to having him up here all year and working with him. We'll play him when we can. We're not going to rush him. But everybody keeps going, 'Wow, he can be pretty good.'

"What's surprising is he's 7'2" and can shoot like he can, pass, and do all that running. He's very coordinated."

When the Rockets were in New York, D'Antoni even made a comparison, though at least partially inadvertent, to Knicks All-Star Kristaps Porzingis.

"I told [Zhou], 'Go get your tapes on him,'" D'Antoni said. "'That's who you need to be right there.' He shoots threes, runs the floor, long, thin. Everything, that guy's got it."

Zhou spent the bulk of his rookie season in the G League. In his cameos with the Rockets, he has generally misfired from deep. Even with the Rio Grande Valley Vipers, he has not shot or rebounded as reliably as the Rockets expect.

His time in the G League was always part of the plan when the Rockets used part of their mid-level exception to give him a four-year contract with more to experience than NBA-caliber talent.

"It definitely helped me a lot, especially adapting to a new life and new experiences," Zhou said through an interpreter. "Before, I never had been involved with a lot of Americans so they've definitely helped me find a new lifestyle and adapt being involved in the game."

When he has played with the Rockets, almost entirely in bench-clearing duty, the crowd reaction has been unmistakable. That, too, is a reminder of what could come in a career as a player from China on Yao's team.

"This kind of attention stuff, this kind of stuff [is] more of a challenge because a lot of Chinese people are behind [me]," Zhou said. "Yao achieved a lot here, stayed here for a long time. This is a new country, new lifestyle, new culture here. There's some difficulty there, but it's also a challenge to be... a better player.

"It's a challenge, but also a pressure, a little bit. [I'm] ready for the challenge and to go up one more step here."

Still, there will be the weight of expectations for a Chinese player on Yao's team. He might not have been chosen because of that connection, but the Rockets are never far removed from Yao, to the point that when Zhou was selected and the Rockets needed a translator for the call to tell him, they brought in Yao to play the role as interpreter.

"We feel," general manager Daryl Morey said, "that Zhou Qi has the potential to be the best Chinese player since Yao Ming."

84 Basketball Reasons

The Rockets had six months to put a plan in place. They were rebuilding, but impatient. They had good parts, but needed to be retooled.

As the 2011 NBA lockout dragged on into December, the Rockets made their way into the three-team deal that would rock the NBA, until it disappeared with little left, other than the expression "basketball reasons."

Chris Paul was the headliner of the deal. Heading into a lockout-abbreviated 66-game schedule, Paul was to be a free agent after the season and was certain to leave New Orleans. The Hornets were for sale and owned by the league, but with their previous management in place and negotiating.

As NBA commissioner David Stern completed the collective bargaining agreement with the NBA Players Association, the Hornets reached agreement on a deal to send Paul to the Lakers with Pau Gasol going from Los Angeles to the Rockets, Lamar

Odom going from the Lakers to New Orleans and the Rockets sending Kevin Martin, Goran Dragic, Luis Scola, and the Knicks' first-round pick to New Orleans.

For the Rockets, the move would have brought in Gasol to be a star in the frontcourt while clearing the cap room to sign Nene as a free agent.

Stern, however, had been empowered to act as Hornets owner. Bombarded by complaints from other owners, who had been similarly busy with the new CBA, he refused to sign off on the deal, with the NBA announcing he objected "for basketball reasons."

Stern insisted that he was not acting as NBA commissioner but in his temporary role with the Hornets, and that his objection was with the return in a deal giving up Paul. The other teams in the trade, however, were outraged, having been assured that New Orleans general manager Del Demps had sent updates on the trade negotiations throughout the process.

Stern repeatedly insisted that he was acting only in his role as the owner's representative of the Hornets, but that should have been clear from the start. He argued with those who said he blocked or negated the trade that, until he signed off, there was no trade. But that was a debate about the semantics.

Had the trade been completed, the Hornets would have had a haul of talent—Martin, Scola, Odom, and Dragic—along with the 16th pick of the draft. When they found a deal Stern would accept, they sent Paul to the Clippers for Eric Gordon, Chris Kaman, Al-Farouq Aminu, and a pick that would be the 10th pick of the draft.

Stern had said that he would not allow the first deal because it would not have brought enough return. He did, however, sign off on a deal that brought less.

In the interim, Martin returned to Houston clearly unhappy, a sentiment shared by Gasol and Odom in Los Angeles. Nene and

Chuck Hayes (who would have returned to Houston with the cap room created) signed elsewhere. The Rockets' rebuilding plans following the departures of Tracy McGrady and Yao Ming were cut adrift.

The Lakers had two more winning seasons, but in the six seasons following "basketball reasons," have won just one playoff series.

The Hornets, with Paul gone and the talent Demps tried to acquire remaining in Los Angeles and Houston, finished tied for the third-worst record in the NBA, but won the next draft lottery and selected All-Star Anthony Davis.

The Rockets might have been better off with the way things turned out. The subsequent season did not go well, with Kyle Lowry developing a dangerous infection and the Rockets fading badly down the stretch to miss the playoffs. But before the next season, Martin's contract allowed the Rockets to complete the trade for James Harden.

Rockets general manager Daryl Morey has said he likely could have found a way to make the salaries work in that deal even without Martin's contract.

Instead, the Rockets made it through one more up-and-down season before Morey used the player he tried to trade away to pull off the biggest trade of his career. And he did it for basketball reasons.

85 Ariza, Parts I and II

There are plenty of second acts in sports, many players that reinvent themselves to defeat time or those that time changes whether they wish it or not. Then, there is Trevor Ariza, who came to Houston to find out who he was and could be, and then returned because he knew.

Ariza had just celebrated the Lakers' 2009 NBA championship. He was a key part of the rotation in his hometown, coming off his best season in his fifth year in the NBA. He was happy.

He was also ready for a larger role. The Lakers, however, considered the Rockets free agent forward Metta World Peace, then still known as Ron Artest, to be an upgrade and signed him as a free agent, allowing Ariza to play the field.

Ariza mulled over a hard sell from LeBron James to join him with the Cavaliers. He thought about Portland and Toronto. But the Rockets had just taken the Lakers to seven games, the last four played without Yao Ming. They were a team on the rise and had offered something the Trail Blazers, Raptors, and especially the Cavaliers could not.

Ariza would get a chance to play the role of a star. He would be given the ball and an opportunity to shine as much as his abilities would allow.

"Every player wants to grow," Ariza said at the time. "Every player has goals. Every player wants to be the best player he can be. In L.A., they have so many great, great players. Kobe is the best player in the NBA, arguably ever. Pau Gasol. Lamar Odom. Andrew Bynum is coming into his own. I think I would have been stuck into one role there. Here, everybody said, 'We want you to work on your game. You have to do more. We believe you have the skill and the talent to do it. Come do it.'"

Had the Lakers not signed Artest, they likely would have matched any offer sheet Ariza received and he would have been fine with that. When they moved on, he made his choice based on the chance to expand his game.

"I chose to come [to Houston] because I thought in Cleveland I would be the same type of player," Ariza said. "I thought if I would leave a place, I might as well get better and try to find a role.

"I'm not a greedy person by any means. Fair is fair. I helped your team win. I'm not asking for the bank. I'm not asking for the house and the farm. I need something fair. At first, I felt hurt. It's my home. I was a little upset. But you get over it. I have great memories there. I had my first real opportunity to play there, won a championship. It was a great experience.... But you know, things happen."

Ariza had a solid season. His 14.9 points per game are the top scoring average of his career. But his shooting percentages dipped badly. The Rockets went 42–40 and missed the playoffs. Ariza was dealt to New Orleans and then to Washington to complete the five-year, $33 million contract he had signed with the Rockets.

When he became a free agent again, he did just what he had the previous time—signing with the Rockets—but for a very different reason.

Rather than joining the Rockets to explore the potential in his game, he signed on to play next to a star again, as he had in Los Angeles with Kobe Bryant. He had come to know his game well, playing off the ball again in Washington next to John Wall. He had become content with his role. And just as he had when he signed with the Rockets to replace Artest, he signed with the Rockets to replace another small forward, stepping into the void when Chandler Parsons left for the Mavericks.

A player that had signed with the Rockets five years earlier to expand his role signed again to play a role well-defined as the epitome of a three-and-D small forward.

No mere consolation prize after the decision, controversial at the time, to not match Parsons' Mavericks contract, Ariza exceled, seeming more comfortable with his role than when he tried to expand it.

"I don't get caught up in reputations or what people say," Ariza said. "I love to win. I love to compete. That's why I'm here."

86 Chandler Parsons, Here and Gone

Chandler Parsons sat on the right of the presumed stars of his draft class, barely noticed. Rockets general manager Daryl Morey predicted great things for his lottery pick, Marcus Morris, comparing his offensive skills to Carmelo Anthony. Kevin McHale traded quips with Donatas Motiejunas, enjoying Motiejunas' precocious confidence.

Parsons barely spoke and was generally overlooked.

Parsons, however, never thought of himself as an afterthought, never would accept a role as the other member of the 2011 Draft haul, and never would forget that every team with a first-round pick, the Rockets included twice, chose someone else.

By the third game of his rookie season, he was in the Rockets' rotation, and was a starter a week later, charged with defending opponents' top wing scorer. By his second season, he was a key to a team on the rise, already considered Morey's best draft choice and in the forefront of the Rockets' recruitment of Dwight Howard.

By the time his third season was over, he was a coveted free agent and gone.

Few could have imagined how rapidly Parsons would go from the background on draft night to the spotlight. Even in Parsons' second season, after Parsons hit the Knicks for 31 points in Houston, ESPN's Stephen A. Smith ripped the Knicks by doubting Parsons with a shout of "Some dude named Chandler Parsons, who I never heard of in my life, dropped about 34 on them."

Parsons, however, never doubted. Even as a rookie, when he slammed a put-back dunk over buddy Blake Griffin, he stared him down as if to announce he believed he belonged in that select company. He embraced all that came with his celebrity, living comfortably in TMZ's sights. After his second season, he was recruiting Howard like a college football coach after a top prospect.

Parsons' rapid rise was clear as he went from a guy who had the number 38 sewn into his shoes as a reminder of where he was taken in the draft to the player Dallas signed to a three-year, $46 million contract that Mark Cuban was certain the Rockets would match. More telling, however, might have been the outrage that came when the Rockets chose not to match the offer.

The Rockets could have kept Parsons under contract before, instead allowing him to become a restricted free agent, a move many thought was payback for his work in luring Howard to Houston, but also driven by the belief he would not receive an offer the Rockets would not match.

Morey believed the contract, with Parsons holding the power to opt out after two seasons, would tie his hands and that the Rockets were enough of a fully formed contender for him to rely on the roster he had. Had he signed Chris Bosh days earlier, with Bosh choosing at the last moment to stay in Miami, Morey said he would have matched the Mavericks' offer and kept Parsons. Instead, he signed Trevor Ariza as a free agent, later working out a sign-and-trade deal with the Wizards and Pelicans, and moved on.

"Is it better with Ariza plus the hundreds of moves that might be able to upgrade us?" Morey said. "That core was going to have to be the core we were going to have. If we were ever going to go after the other stars, it wouldn't be possible. We feel strongly turning down Chandler's option gives us a better chance to win the title than picking up the option.

"If you want to win the title, you have to be the team that finds the Chandler Parsons, not the team that gives Chandler Parsons the max contract."

Parsons said he was both "offended" by the process and understood it. He posed with Cuban in an Orlando club to sign the offer sheet and was celebrated in Dallas. A visible fan of Houston teams, he instead cheered for the Cowboys and Rangers. A fan favorite in Houston, he said Dallas was "cleaner," earning boos every time he touched the ball in Toyota Center.

"That's part of the game," Parsons said. "When you're passionate about a team and you're from that city and one of your favorite players leaves that city, you're not going to be a fan of them. You're going to let them know when they come back.

"[Houston] was home for me for three years, so I have no hard feelings toward them. It obviously got a little ugly during free agency, but Daryl told me it was going to, so it didn't surprise anyone."

By the time that first season in Dallas reached the playoffs, the Mavericks faced the Rockets. Parsons, who had exceled in a pair of first-round exits with the Rockets, tried to come back from the first of his knee injuries, struggled badly in one game and then was through for the season as the Mavericks were eliminated in five games. He was hurt the next season, too.

As Morey feared when he chose not to match the contract, Parsons opted out of the deal and moved on again, signing a $94 million contract with the Grizzlies, with Dallas fans booing him as Houston fans had been, even though the Mavericks, like the Rockets, had no interest in giving him the kind of deal he received elsewhere.

As Parsons continued to battle knee issues, Memphis fans have had their issues, too. But back when Parsons was relatively unknown, overshadowed by players taken in the first round, he exceled, going from nearly anonymous to stardom and all that came with it.

87 Visit the Dream "Statue"

The first thing most notice when checking out the Hakeem Olajuwon statue is that it is not a statue at all.

The monument is impressive, the centerpiece of a circular plaza that fits with the semi-circle main entrance to Toyota Center on the corner of Polk and LaBranch in Downtown Houston. But it does not in any way depict Olajuwon.

This was a fitting tribute to the man and what matters to him most.

"I am so grateful for their thoughtfulness to honor me," Olajuwon said before the unveiling in 2008. "It can't be any higher than that. I feel so humbled. I mean, like, *Wow... I mean that much.*"

With a tribute to Olajuwon, it would not have been enough to build the monument. The Rockets made sure to do it right.

Olajuwon's religion is central to everything in his life. As a practicing Muslim, he could not endorse a likeness of himself, inspiring the Rockets to go another way. Instead, a local artist,

Eric Kaposta, designed a 12-foot, 1,000-pound bronze monument featuring Olajuwon's No. 34 uniform and a paragraph listing his career achievements. The monument rests on a red granite foundation listing career milestones.

"This is a great moment in Rockets history," then-Rockets owner Leslie Alexander said at the unveiling. "There has been no greater player in Houston sports history than Dream. He's a great guy also. I wish you all knew him as well as I did.

"Once I saw what they did for Michael Jordan [in Chicago], I knew we had to do that for Dream. We want to have a tradition of winning and people knowing that when they come here, it's a place to be."

It all comes together to the point that it is a striking reminder of Olajuwon's greatness. It does not show him blocking a shot or performing a Dream Shake. There is no picture of him. Instead, it honors who he is, along with celebrating what he did.

"It took a long time, us sort of negotiating with Dream about what he would accept and what he wouldn't accept," Alexander said. "What we finally arrived at is something that we think is beautiful but [is] acceptable to Dream."

It was more than acceptable. It remains a respectful, must-see celebration, and, as Olajuwon said, "beautiful."

"A statue is against my faith and they recognize that and we worked to be creative," Olajuwon said. "What are the things that we can do that can make it more acceptable and still accomplish the goal? I think we accomplished that.

"It's beautiful. I feel so honored that they've given me this gesture."

88 Build a Rockets Library

Having gotten off to a good start, there are many fine additions to add to a Rockets-themed literary collection, covering the history of the franchise, biographies of the star players and coaches and even children's books.

An ideal companion to this offering would be *Houston Rockets: Celebrating 50 Seasons*, written by Fran Blinebury, Jeff Balke, Jonathan Feigen, Jenny Dial Creech, Matt Thomas, Sean Pendergast, Kelli Anderson, and Ian Thomsen in 2016, and bringing a good mix of storytelling and coffee table–worthy art.

The Houston Rockets Basketball Team by William W. Lace, released in 2000, offers a history of the team with an emphasis on the championship teams.

A year later, Aaron Frisch released *The History of the Houston Rockets*, a children's book with the requisite mix of story and photographs.

The biographies will fill a Rockets library wall.

A Rocket at Heart: My Life and My Team by Rudy Tomjanovich and Robert Falkoff (1997) and *Living the Dream: My Life and Basketball* by Hakeem Olajuwon and Peter Knobler (1996) offer a great start.

In 1984, Bert Rosenthal produced *Ralph Sampson: The Center for the 1980s*.

Two decades later, another Rockets giant, Yao Ming, teamed with Ric Bucher on *Yao: A Life in Two Worlds*, detailing much of Yao's unique road to the NBA.

The Tao of Yao: Wit and Wisdom from the Moving Great Wall Yao Ming by Douglas Choi (2003) is a fun read.

In 2014, Clayton Geoffrey's produced a pair of books about Rockets guards, *Tracy McGrady: The Inspiring Story of One of Basketball's Greatest Shooting Guards* and *James Harden: The Inspiring Story of one of Basketball's Premier Shooting Guards.*

No offering, however, can be more inspiring than *Winning a Day at a Time*, John Lucas' 1994 biography on his career and battles with substance abuse.

Speaking of autobiographies, *They Call Me "The Big E,"* by Elvin Hayes was published in 1978 and covers Hayes' life from the Louisiana cotton field to his religious conversion. *Clyde the Glide: My Life in Basketball* offers Drexler's story through 2004 and more than a few thoughts about issues around the NBA.

To round out the collection, several books will cover issues that helped change the NBA.

The Punch: One Night, Two Lives, and the Fight That Changed Basketball Forever by John Feinstein is a very good read from 2002, even for those that know the story of the punch that nearly took Rudy Tomjanovich's life.

Tip-Off: How the 1984 NBA Draft Changed Basketball Forever by Filip Bondy (2008) tells of the draft that brought Hakeem Olajuwon to the Rockets and changed the franchise forever, and includes several potential trades that never quite were made.

Finally, Jack McCallum's inside look at the basketball revolution Mike D'Antoni ushered in with the Suns, *Seven Seconds or Less: My Season on the Bench with the Runnin' and Gunnin' Phoenix Suns*, will shed light on the Rockets coach and his ground-breaking offensive philosophies.

89 Sit with the Red Rowdies

Joining the Red Rowdies is not for everyone. It's not even an option. Fans must win an audition to earn membership in the fan group, earning the right to dress up, stand, sing, and shout through Rockets home games.

Anyone, however, can sit in the general vicinity of section 114 in Toyota Center and get the idea.

The Red Rowdies are a band of fans selected to be a home-court cheering section, given tickets in exchange for their steadfast devotion and volume.

They began in 2006, when former Rockets coach Jeff Van Gundy wanted to improve the home-court advantage after a season in which the Rockets went 15–26 in Toyota Center. He purchased 30 season tickets and had them awarded to the winners of auditions of fans eager to make all kinds of noise. Tracy McGrady liked the change during a 2006–07 preseason game enough to buy 20 more tickets and the Red Rowdies cheering section was born.

Over the years, they have become sponsored, but the act has remained pretty much the same.

Before home games, they parade around the concourses, a warmup for the performance to come. They arrive costumed and armed with drums, cowbells, and indefatigable determination.

In the early years, the most memorable chant was to sing "Yao Ming, Yao Ming, Yao Ming," to the "Ole" tune. It has been updated to "Nene, Nene, Nene." They sing "[Luc] Mbah a Moute, clap, clap, clap, clap" or for "Splash Gordon" or "CP3, CP3."

Opponents are taunted. If James Harden makes a particularly strong move, his defender will hear, "You can't guard him." An opposing player better known for his previous team will be labeled, "Lakers [or Mavericks or Pistons, etc.] reject."

Late in wins against the Spurs, the Rowdies might sing "I-10," or when playing the Mavericks, "I-45."

The most conspicuous cheer, however, comes before the games begin. When the word "rockets" is sung in the national anthem, the Rowdies offer a shout, with much of the crowd joining them.

That leads to an ironic, but likely satisfying, result.

When Rockets fans familiar with that tradition time that shout just right during the anthem at Rockets road games, they can often

Members of the Houston Rockets Red Rowdies fan club cheer before a 2013 game against the New Orleans Pelicans at Toyota Center. (Troy Taormina/ USA TODAY Sports)

get home fans to mistakenly think they are celebrating the vocal stylings of that night's anthem singer to chant along. It takes more of a cheer than the Toyota Center shout, but it often works.

Either that, or fans can grab a seat near section 114 and sing along.

90 See the Long and Short (and a Few in Between) of the Hall of Fame

The elevator door opened like a stage curtain, perfectly timed, revealing the scene as if crafted in a script.

Yao Ming, the humble 7'6" Hall of Famer-to-be stood on one side. Calvin Murphy, the boisterous 5'9" Rockets icon, stood on the other.

At that moment, and in the photo shoot they had planned for that afternoon of Yao's Hall of Fame induction in Springfield, Massachusetts, the tallest and shortest Hall of Famers ever, and the only two Hall of Famers to have spent their entire careers with the Rockets, came together perfectly as Murphy let out a characteristic shout, "My brother!"

Murphy has been a fixture at the ceremonies since his own initiation in 1993, but especially in the years he is joined in Springfield by fellow Rockets.

A Rockets fan that makes his way to the Naismith Basketball Hall of Fame will find 14 former Rockets, from franchise icons to several who stopped by after legendary careers. They will also see an omission as conspicuous as it is egregious, with Rudy Tomjanovich inexplicably excluded despite leading the Rockets to two championships, the United States Olympic team to a gold medal, and excelling through his own career as an All-American and All-Star.

Rick Barry came first, inducted in 1987, seven years after his career ended with two seasons playing for the Rockets after his championship run with the Golden State Warriors and seasons in the ABA.

Elvin Hayes, the former University of Houston star who was the No. 1 pick of the 1968 NBA Draft by the San Diego Rockets, was inducted in 1990. Hayes spent the first four and final three seasons of his career with the Rockets, retiring in 1984. He is the ninth-leading scorer and fourth-leading rebounder in NBA history and holds a special place in Rockets history as part of the inspiration to move the franchise to Houston and the reason Rockets owner Tilman Fertitta became a Rockets fan as a child.

Murphy, Hayes' teammate in San Diego and Houston, was inducted three years later, having averaged 17.9 points and 4.4 assists in 1,002 career games, still one of just two players (with Avery Johnson) shorter than 6' to play in 1,000 or more NBA games.

Alex Hannum became the first former Rockets coach inducted, in 1998, though he never coached in Houston after two seasons with the San Diego Rockets after his championship seasons with Philadelphia and St. Louis.

Moses Malone also won his championship in Philadelphia, but when he was inducted in 2001, he had built plenty of Hall of Fame credentials in Houston. That included two of his three MVP seasons, his stunning 1981 postseason when he took a team with a losing record to the NBA Finals, and his final season with the Rockets when he scored at least 30 points in a franchise record 13 consecutive games. Nearly as incredibly, he played 13 more seasons, though he always called Houston home until his passing in 2015.

Just as Malone ended his career with many stops after Houston, Clyde Drexler began his career elsewhere, building a Hall of Fame resume in Portland, before returning to his hometown to win his championship and induction in 2004.

Drexler's teammate in his final seasons, Charles Barkley was inducted two seasons later, also with much of his resume writing in previous stops prior to his four seasons with the Rockets.

The most legendary (and greatest) Rockets player of them all, Hakeem Olajuwon, was inducted in 2008, having established himself as one of the greatest players in NBA history, the blocked shots record holder in the top 10 for scoring, rebounding, and steals. But to Rockets fans, no number stands larger than the two championships he brought to Houston, the first major team sports titles in the city's history, starting with 1994 when he became the first player in NBA history to be the MVP, Defensive Player of the Year, and Finals MVP in the same season.

That led to a few players with Rockets ties going into the Hall for their work with other teams. Scottie Pippen, who spent one lockout-shortened season in Houston between his championship seasons with the Bulls and the close of his career with the Trail Blazers, was inducted in 2010. Tex Winter, the Rockets' first coach in Houston, was inducted in 2011 for his championship work as an assistant with the Bulls and Lakers, and his creation of the Triangle offense.

Ralph Sampson also spent years elsewhere, but when he was inducted in 2012, reuniting the Twin Towers in Springfield, there was no question that his finest NBA days were with the Rockets. Sampson was a four-time All-Star and a key to the Rockets' run to the 1986 Finals.

Another member of the Rockets' long line of centers went into the Hall next with Dikembe Mutombo's induction in 2015, having spent the final five seasons of his 18-year NBA career in Houston, where he moved to second all-time in blocked shots.

That put Mutombo in position to be there with his friend Yao when Yao was inducted in 2016, with Yao celebrated as an eight-time All-Star, five-time All-NBA Team selection, and global icon.

Finally, Tracy McGrady, who split his best seasons between Orlando and Houston, was inducted in 2017, representing the hometown area of his youth and the hometown he chose ever since. A seven-time All-Star and All-NBA selection, McGrady averaged 22.7 points, 5.6 assists, and 5.5 rebounds with the Rockets.

91 Attend the Sloan Conference

When Rockets general manager Daryl Morey co-founded the MIT Sports Analytics Conference, he not only did not know how far it would come, he could not have imagined its stunning growth.

The use of sports analytics then was cutting-edge and would be considered controversial before it became as much a part of professional sports as stretching before workouts or drinking fluids after.

There are those that remained frightened by the idea of analytics and what they assume the word and movement mean, but they are decreasing in numbers, left to sound as out of date as if advocating for the two-hand set shot rather than this foolish new idea of jumping. But when Morey and Jessica Gelman, the CEO of Kraft Analytics Group, founded the Sloan Conference, the use of analytics was still new, the conference small.

It has mushroomed to proudly declare itself the largest student-run conference in the world, an enormous forum for sports industry professionals, drawing between 3,000 and 4,000 spectators and participants each year to Boston.

It has grown so much since the inaugural conference in 2007 that it has moved from MIT to convention centers. It has drawn nearly 200 professional franchises. By 2018, it had become such a go-to event that former president Barack Obama was a participant.

"It's exciting. Through a lot of effort by MIT students and others, it's really become something," Morey said. "Jessica Gelman and myself, we were teaching a class at MIT. When I took the job in Houston, obviously, teaching a class wasn't going to work. I couldn't fly back to MIT and teach a class for 11 weeks. So it really started like a class over a weekend. It just exploded from there.

"I think people go because it works. I don't think it's very controversial that using data to make decisions is a really, really good idea."

For a fan of the Rockets, having heard for years about the Rockets' use of analytics, the conference is a chance to get an understanding of how data can be applied to decision-making and, as Morey has often said, how it is not.

Morey has always considered the search for more information central to doing his job. That involves the use of data and the pursuit of greater, more revealing statistical analysis. But part of "more" has always been the use of traditional scouting, as well, with Morey and his staff spending much of each basketball season in gyms and arenas around the world for traditional evaluations.

Yet, analytics have been so central to Rockets decision-making for so long, the term gets tossed around routinely. Though fans cannot stroll into the Toyota Center offices or conference rooms, they can attend the Sloan conference and get a deep understanding of how analytics are used and where they might be taken next.

Tickets—$250 for students and $600 for general admission in 2018—sell out quickly. There are additional, more expensive tickets also available.

In addition to industry leaders discussing applications of analytics in the panels, there are competitions for research papers, startups, and a "Hack-a-thon" competition.

The event has grown so important and influential, panelists have included owners, general managers, and commissioners from every major sport, former coaches and players, agents and media personalities, and now, a former president of the United States.

"Obviously, I'm biased, but I think anyone that comes will take something out of this," Morey said. "There's more high-level panel speeches, then there's the nitty-gritty, the competitive-advantage sessions where executives in sports talk about how they do their jobs. There's something for everyone."

92 The Short Season with Scottie Pippen

In the mad rush of moves to fill rosters at the end of the 1998 NBA lockout, the Rockets did what they often had before and have since. They made the big splash, landing the big name sure to bring hope and headlines.

The one season with Scottie Pippen, however, had the Rockets living the old line about the best days of boat owners: the day they buy a boat and the day they sell it.

With the Rockets and Pippen, the six-time champion who departed Chicago in the breakup of the Bulls, it never worked.

Pippen arrived on a wave of optimism and promise, and in a white stretch limousine that seemed to scream stardom.

"I'm very happy to be here," he said once the sign-and-trade deal and five-year, $67.2 million contract were approved. "I realize what this franchise means. I want to bring a championship to the city of Houston. There's been a lot of hard work over the last few hours to try and get this deal done. I just hope we put as much hard work on the floor this season. I'm just looking forward to the season."

Olajuwon's window was closing. The Rockets had tried to stretch his years of excellence by adding Charles Barkley to take turns in the low post and help on the boards, but he too was near the end. Clyde Drexler had just retired, ending his Hall of Fame career with a 41–41 season and a first-round loss to the Jazz.

Pippen, however, did not blend in as much as try to direct how things be done. There were positives in that. He influenced Barkley to join his morning "Breakfast Club" workouts. There were tensions. The Rockets spent the season lamenting the marathon shootarounds when Pippen would stop the sessions to suggest how things should be done, and specifically how they were done with the Bulls.

There were successes, too. The Rockets went 31–19 in that lockout-shortened season. Olajuwon was a third-team All-NBA pick. Barkley was second in the NBA in rebounding, averaging 12.3 per game. Pippen was a First-Team All-Defensive Team selection for an eighth-consecutive season, though in his first season after back surgery, he was far from the defender he had been and not all he would be in the coming years.

Pippen was frustrated with his role in the Houston offense— which was built around the post-up moves of Barkley and Olajuwon—and preferred to play in a more up-tempo style. He averaged 14.5 points per game, his lowest since his second year, and he made a career-low 43.2 percent of his shots. He also averaged 6.5 rebounds and 5.9 assists, but always seemed out of place.

By Game 1 of the postseason, he slipped and lost the ball in the final minute with the Rockets protecting a lead. Kobe Bryant scored. The Rockets lost. Pippen blamed Barkley for fouling

Shaquille O'Neal earlier, perhaps offering a glimpse at the rift that would become glaring in the weeks to come.

As reports surfaced that Pippen was interested in a trade to the Lakers to reunite with Phil Jackson, Barkley repeated comments he had made in Houston that Pippen owed the Rockets an apology for his interest in another team.

This time, the comments got to Pippen, who said he wouldn't apologize to Barkley with a gun to his head and added that Barkley owed him an apology for making him play with Barkley's "fat butt." He even added that Michael Jordan had warned him that Barkley would never win a championship, then labeled Barkley as selfish and not dedicated.

"For him to want to leave after one year, it disappointed me greatly," Barkley said. "The Rockets went out of their way to get Scottie and the fans have treated him well, so I was just disappointed in him."

By then, former Rockets general manager Carroll Dawson was working on a deal to send Pippen to Portland, but was trying to bring back greater return than the eventual deal for Stacey Augmon, Kelvin Cato, Walt Williams, Brian Shaw, Ed Gray, and Carlos Rogers. When Pippen's comments surfaced, negotiations were over and Dawson took the deal on the table.

"We're moving forward," Rockets coach Rudy Tomjanovich said. "I think we've taken a negative situation and tried to turn it into a positive."

If nothing else, however, the Rockets' one short season with Pippen was eventful and memorable.

"I enjoyed my time in Houston," Pippen said the next season. "I guess I opened my mouth too much. It wasn't as big as Charles' so I ended up getting kicked out of town.

"But it worked out for both sides."

93 Aaron Brooks

When Daryl Morey made Aaron Brooks his first draft pick as Rockets general manager, most others saw what Brooks was not.

He wasn't tall, or anything close to it, needing to lie a bit to claim to be 6'. He was not a playmaking point guard. He was not the sort of pick likely to make much of a splash, much less be the sort of draft selection that Morey would always happily be able to cite as his first.

Morey saw what Brooks was. He was a guy that could fall out of bed and put the ball in the basket. Despite anything he lacked, he could also get his shot.

By the 2008–09 season, Brooks had proved himself, and a year later, would even add his signature moment.

"What made us decide to draft him was he was a guy who was counted out—too small, doesn't pass the ball enough, won't make it in the NBA," Morey said. "We felt like he had the talent to do it. He's obviously shown that."

The Rockets finally broke through to win a playoff series for the first time since the Hakeem Olajuwon days, beating Portland, where Brooks was still celebrated as a former Oregon Ducks star.

Yao went out in Game 3 of the next series against the Lakers, but Brooks led the Rockets to Game 7, stunning the Lakers in Game 4 when the Rockets' situation seemed hopeless following the news of Yao's injury. Brooks put in a buzzer-beating alley-oop as if to announce the Rockets would not go quietly.

That was fitting for a player who had refused to give in to doubts. He had begun his career the odd man out in a backcourt crowded with Steve Francis, Mike James, Rafer Alston, and Luther

Head. He was sent to the Development League as a rookie before that became the Rockets' routine for draft picks with potential.

Brooks was the 2009–10 Most Improved Award winner, with his scoring average jumping 8.4 points per game as the Rockets went 42–40 in a season Yao Ming had to sit out.

Things did not go as well throughout his tenure.

The Rockets had traded Alston for Kyle Lowry at the 2008–09 trade deadline. By the 2010 training camp, Brooks was the 10th highest paid player on the Rockets roster and not happy about it, particularly when Lowry, his backup, received a new contract that dwarfed his. The Rockets chose to let Brooks become a restricted free agent, rather than work out a contract extension, but Brooks was open about his displeasure.

In the season's fifth game, he landed on Manu Ginobili's foot on a halfcourt heave to beat the halftime buzzer in San Antonio and missed 25 games with a sprained ankle. He struggled badly when he returned.

By the spring, when Brooks left the court entirely when he was pulled for a game in the fourth quarter, he was suspended for a game and eventually traded for Goran Dragic, giving both a chance to start over.

That, however, was not the end of his Rockets tenure. He signed on as a free agent in March 2013 and again that summer to be a backup, showing there were no long-lasting hard feelings and getting Rockets fans to show that he remained a fan favorite.

That encore stint with the team did not last. Brooks was traded to Denver to give him a chance to play more than he was in Houston and to earn another contract.

But he will always be Morey's first pick and one of his best, having gone from overlooked to an overachiever. After his initial stint with the Rockets, Brooks played in Sacramento, Denver,

Phoenix, Indianapolis, Chicago, and Minnesota, and for one season during the lockout, in China. But his run in Houston remained

"It's just special, man," Brooks said of his Rockets tenure. "Lot of good memories. It's Houston, where I kind of feel like I was raised."

94 Robert Reid

Though it does not seem possible now, Robert Reid was once considered a long shot, if he had any shot at all.

Long before he would twice help the Rockets to the NBA Finals, before he became a bridge from the 1970s teams to the teams of the '80s and all they have come to represent in Rockets history, before he reached unquestioned franchise icon status, Reid was not expected to make the Rockets roster.

Perhaps it is fitting that a player so integral to teams that exceeded expectations began his career that way. It is also telling about Reid's place in Rockets history that he immediately was connected to, and respected by, some of the franchise's all-time greats.

Reid was then a second-round pick out of St. Mary's in 1977, the 19th player on a roster with 15 guaranteed contracts that would have to be trimmed to 11. He played with Moses Malone, was pushed by Mike Newlin, and harassed by Calvin Murphy, the veteran who claimed the rookie at a time of rookie initiations. He had been brought in primarily to push Rudy Tomjanovich in practices.

Reid, however, had exceled in the Los Angeles summer league, giving him confidence that he belonged. He made that team and, with the Rockets off to an 8–12 start, became a starter. That season fell apart soon after the punch in Los Angeles that felled Tomjanovich. Reid, however, remained essential, so much so that even after he retired, walking away from the NBA lifestyle, the Rockets convinced him to return.

He had carved out a niche as a player that would excel at four positions.

"Whatever they wanted me to be, that's what I was going to do," Reid said.

The exception was in the Rockets' run to the 1981 Finals, when Reid played entirely at small forward, looking to shoot as Murphy and Tomjanovich had before him.

Just two seasons after that Finals run, however, Reid retired. He moved to Miami, happily worked in a clothing store, considered basketball behind him. But when the Rockets won the coin toss to draft Ralph Sampson, new Rockets coach Bill Fitch and general manager Ray Patterson convinced Reid to return to help mentor Sampson and Rodney McCray.

With one more lost season and won coin toss, the Rockets added Hakeem Olajuwon and by 1986, were back in The Finals, with Reid cementing his legacy as a do-everything Rockets stalwart. John Lucas had been kicked off the team after a substance abuse relapse with Fitch making the decision that Lucas would later say saved his life after Reid and Allen Leavell spoke up at a team meeting to say Lucas needed help.

Though the Rockets were flush with guards, Reid became the sort of steady, veteran leader he had joined nearly a decade earlier. Before Sampson's iconic shot to beat the Lakers, Reid sank the three with 15 seconds left that made the Game 6 upset possible.

He reveled in the camaraderie of the team, in contrast to the team he had left. He had started just five games in the regular season, but late that season, Fitch moved Reid to the point and into the starting lineup for the playoffs. He averaged 14.9 points and 6.9 assists in the postseason as the Rockets returned to The Finals and another meeting with the Celtics.

The Rockets of the '80s were never the same. Mitchell Wiggins and Lewis Lloyd received drug suspensions. Sampson was hurt and never the same before he was traded to Golden State, ending the Twin Towers experiment. Reid played two more seasons in Houston, with the Rockets winning just one playoff series, before he was traded to the Charlotte Hornets.

Reid retired after three more seasons, convinced that if the 1986 Rockets had been able to stay on the floor, they'd have been champions. But Reid's place in Rockets history was already secure, not just as one of the keys to The Finals teams, but as the epitome of a player doing whatever was necessary to succeed.

95 Allen Leavell

At a time in Rockets history filled with uncertainty and rapid-fire change, both planned and very unexpected, Allen Leavell was the constant.

Partners in the Rockets backcourt came and went. He teamed with Calvin Murphy through the end of Murphy's Hall of Fame career. He spanned the careers of John Lucas, Allen Wiggins, and Lewis Lloyd. He was a key player on the 1981 and 1986 NBA Finals teams.

Leavell was always there, always reliable as a blindingly quick point guard that set up star teammates.

A fifth-round pick in 1979, Leavell played 700 games over 10 seasons, averaging 9.5 points and 4.8 assists, bringing consistent defensive intensity to a high-scoring era and not only accepting a role playing with headliners, but embracing it.

"I had the opportunity to play with six or eight Hall of Famers," Leavell said. "That says it all."

Leavell retired second in franchise history in assists, since surpassed by James Harden. But as with so much about the 1986 Finals team, his career was also marked by what could have been had things been different with a team that came apart with drug suspensions.

After Lucas was released, Leavell moved up as the starting point guard and excelled, until he broke his wrist in San Antonio. He returned in time to play a key part in the Rockets' run to The Finals, grabbing the rebound and calling time out before Ralph Sampson's game-winner against the Lakers, always filling whatever role was needed.

"I love Houston... I put in my heart and soul with the Rockets," Leavell said. "I really did. I'm just happy to have been a part of it.

"To come out of [Muncie, Indiana] and make it here, it was a dream come true for me and my family."

96 The Shark

There are many ways to recall Mike Newlin's time with the Rockets, from his hard-driving competitiveness to his soft free throw shooting touch, his erudite manner to his role establishing the Rockets' foothold in Houston.

There was another way, the first way he was described, that might encompass all of that.

Newlin was quickly labeled by Billy Goldberg, the owner that brought the Rockets to Houston, as "the first Rocket." While that might be about the timing of his first contract, the title also seemed to represent the qualities he demonstrated when professional basketball first arrived in Texas.

Newlin had been drafted out of the University of Utah (where he was magna cum laude with a degree in English) in 1971 by the San Diego Rockets, weeks before the Rockets' move to Houston became official. His was the first Houston Rockets contract approved by the NBA.

Newlin was proud of the label, but he also encompassed the image the Rockets wanted for those early teams, with a selfless, determined playing style that meshed well with the stars of the time, Calvin Murphy and Rudy Tomjanovich, and at the end of his career, Moses Malone.

"I developed kind of an aggressive game," said Newlin, a 6'4" shooting guard who played eight of his 11 seasons with the Rockets. "I was just a hustler. Basketball was a great collision sport and I enjoyed the physical contact. Calvin Murphy, Rudy Tomjanovich, and Moses Malone were three of my teammates. One thing I learned about them—never, ever, not once did any of those guys not hustle. It was a pleasure to play 10 years with those guys.

"It was really an amazing thing to watch the emergence, the growth, and now the blossoming of a major franchise in Houston. It was fun to be part of the beginning."

Newlin averaged 14 points on 46.1 percent shooting and 4.3 assists with the Rockets, roughly matching those numbers in his three playoff seasons, advancing to the 1977 Eastern Conference Finals.

Newlin loved the interaction on the floor, the unspoken communication at high speed, but he also prided himself in the individual work required to hone his craft, particularly at the line, where he made 87 percent of his free throws in his career.

He remained in the Houston area, did some broadcasting on Rockets games and talk radio, mastered four languages, and was a great success with his company, Camelot Deserts, and in real estate.

"I never relied on anything I did in the NBA to make my life a success," Newlin told the *Deseret News*. "It was just living up to my God-given talents. You shouldn't extract from that to give you satisfaction for the rest of your life. The glory evaporates. The applause dies down. The sun goes down."

Yet, for all the ways his career is remembered, he is primarily known for simply being a Rocket, an identity he had from the day he arrived, never lost, and always embraced.

"Being in Houston, you're never not a Rocket," Newlin said. "Even if you're not acknowledged, you're still a Rocket. It's a circular argument. I can't get away and I don't want to get away. It's kind of nice."

97 Rudy T and the Olympics

The celebration when the gold medals were draped on necks was not that different from most others before or since, except that it was not shared the way it deserved. The triumph was not understood. It is now.

Rudy Tomjanovich's success as the USA Basketball coach, first in the World Championships and then two years later in the Olympics, might not have been as appreciated in its time when beamed back to the United States. Fans, and even the basketball community that had not caught up to the way the basketball world had changed, did not understand.

That would come when the reality that was somehow missed at the time hit back hard in the years that followed. But those that were there knew. They knew the challenge that the United States Olympic team faced in Sydney. They especially knew of the near-impossible task a band of undrafted and unsigned fringe players took on in Athens.

Most of all, they knew how two of Tomjanovich's greatest coaching jobs—in some ways like his championship seasons with the Rockets—were monumental, though not fully appreciated until given the benefit of time and perspective.

The odds were so stacked against his World Championships team in Athens that finishing with a bronze medal might have been his greatest accomplishment.

With the roster wrecked by the NBA lockout, Tomjanovich took a team of players that either hoped to one day play in the NBA or had given up that dream, knowing they would never share the floor with the stars that had backed out of the 1998 World Championships and convinced former stars to also sit out to support their cause.

Mateen Cleaves, the point guard that starred at Michigan State, sprained his ankle and was lost for the tournament. Tomjanovich took a team led by David Wood, Jimmy Oliver, Jimmy King, David Hawkins, and Brad Miller to Athens at a time when USA Basketball was still struggling to conquer the European way of playing.

In a few years, even the awesome star power of NBA talent would not be enough, but in 1998, Tomjanovich did not even have that.

Instead, he inspired a team to play with his own sort of defiant determination, reaching the point that, in the Semifinals, the United States led Russia by 10. Tomjanovich's young team cracked in the final three minutes, overcome by mistakes and some stunning, unforgettable calls. But as crushed and wounded as that team was, Tomjanovich got it to regroup in time to beat Greece in Athens and win the third-place game, taking one of the most remarkable bronze medals in USA Basketball history.

By 2000, he took a team of NBA stars to Sydney for the Olympics. The team was in transition, from the first two Dream Teams, to a team led by Vince Carter, Gary Payton, Tim Hardaway, Antonio McDyess, Kevin Garnett, and Alonzo Mourning (who had to leave during the tournament for the birth of his daughter, Sydney.)

Those Olympics were the epitome of a no-win situation, with the USA struggles dramatically misunderstood at a time the United States team was expected to roll easily. In the Semifinals, the USA team edged Lithuania by two, winning only when Sarunas Jasikevicius' three at the buzzer fell short. The USA team needed to take over down the stretch to take a 10-point win against France for the gold medal.

"This was not a party at the beach for us," Tomjanovich said, though few understood. "Just because we are the United States does not mean we automatically will win.

"We have been down in the trenches and have had to battle hard. We have won, but people still feel we have failed because we have not won by large margins, as at previous Olympics. People expect us to rule all the time but it's not like that any more. We are in a no-win situation."

Tomjanovich's USA team went 8–0, but is remembered most for Carter's leap over 7'2" Frederic Weis, perhaps the greatest in-game dunk ever. Most did not understand at the time that the world had closed the gap and the United States' failure to understand the international style was a dangerous flaw.

Those lessons became vividly apparent in the 2002 World Championships in Indianapolis and 2004 Olympics in Athens. But before the United States lost, Tomjanovich won, knowing before most of the rest of the basketball world what a triumph it was.

"When it was over, I hugged the guys from USA Basketball," Tomjanovich said. "I thanked them for their help and their support. And I told them, 'I don't want to ever do this again.'"

98 Harvey

The waters rose to levels previously unthinkable, even unimaginable. Hurricane Harvey had drenched the nation's fourth-largest city and the region from Galveston to The Woodlands, Katy to Beaumont, soaking every town and neighborhood in between and many far beyond.

It destroyed homes and changed lives forever. Yet for all the ferocity and volume of the deluge unlike any other, Harvey could never dampen the spirit of a city that would not surrender.

Harvey hit hard. Houston did what it always does. Strangers reached hands out to strangers to lift one another back up. Volunteers manned boats and filled the rivers that had been streets and neighborhoods in rescue efforts that lasted for days. Others worked the shelters where nearly 37,000 were housed and cared for.

Harvey would dump nearly 52 inches of rain, with areas beyond the city reporting up to 60 inches. It claimed the lives of four dozen victims, flooded 50,000 homes, impacted more than 13 million people in Texas, Louisiana, and Mississippi, and as far off as Tennessee and Kentucky. It damaged 203,000 homes, destroying 12,700, with 17,000 people rescued. It caused $125 billion in damages. Nearly 30 percent of Harris County was submerged. The ecological damage will be felt, and won't be fully assessed, for years.

Yet, most of all, and perhaps most enduringly, it revealed the implacable, indefatigable spirit and resolve of the people of Houston, a sprawling, spectacularly diverse city accustomed to facing challenges.

The worst storm in United States history hit and kept on hitting. A city and region familiar with the trials and tragedies of catastrophic weather events, from the devastation of Tropical Storm Allison to the more recent Memorial Day floods, had known hurricanes. It had become home to the Katrina transplants. It took the hit delivered by Ike and learned the lessons from the evacuation nightmares of Rita.

Harvey was different. Harvey came to town and stayed, like the Houston transplants that arrive considering themselves to be from somewhere else and then never want to leave.

Harvey hovered, drenching southeast Texas and overwhelming the bayous and reservoirs. A second band formed 100 miles to the southwest, merging with the first. Houston was hit by a storm considered a once-in-500-years event. And then it was hit by another. In the early hours of Sunday, August 27, a third band of storms formed in the west and moved toward the region.

From August 25, when Harvey hit Port Aransas, to September 3, when it reached the Texas-Louisiana border, Harvey brought its worst and brought out Houston's best.

Weeks before the start of training camp, the Rockets were scattered around the country, but made donations, nearly all with no announcement, and appearances at the shelters.

Former Rockets owner Leslie Alexander donated $4 million and then days later increased it to $10 million, with mayor Sylvester Turner's office acknowledging the donation. James Harden arrived when flights resumed and visited with the volunteers and evacuees at the George R. Brown Convention Center and donated $1 million to the mayor's relief fund.

Toyota Center served as the convention center's overflow shelter with Rockets staff living in their offices for days so that they could remain on site to serve those sheltered in the arena.

In the months that followed, Rockets players continued to make appearances with and donations to groups struggling to recover.

Normalcy returned. The Astros gave the region a joyful release with the World Series championship. The Rockets had the best regular season in franchise history. But the greatest triumph might have been by the thousands of anonymous heroes who manned the boats, served the meals, healed the wounds, and have been rebuilding the city ever since. In the end, Harvey was the most formidable of foes, but Houston's usual indomitable spirit and strength won.

99 And the Award Goes To

When the NBA announced the finalists for the 2018 awards, there was no surprise to have three Rockets players listed among the top three for the NBA's major awards.

That comes with a 65-win season. For the second consecutive season since the league went to its made-for-TV presentation event, the Rockets would be all over the event, leading to James Harden taking the Most Valuable Player Award after finishing as the runner-up in two of the previous three seasons.

There was a time, however, when the Rockets had trouble breaking through with Tom Nissalke, the 1977 Coach of the Year, the first to take home the hardware.

That began a brief run, though the next few awards could not be celebrated for long.

Moses Malone won the Most Valuable Player Award in 1979 and again in 1982, but he departed for Philadelphia for the 1982–83 season.

Ralph Sampson was the 1984 Rookie of the Year, but his time in Houston lasted just a bit more than four seasons.

Don Chaney was the 1991 Coach of the Year, but like Nissalke, he was soon fired, replaced by Rudy Tomjanovich the season after he won the award.

As with most things with Rockets history, Hakeem Olajuwon would deliver celebrations that would last.

Olajuwon was the Defensive Player of the Year, the only Rockets player to win that award, in 1993 and 1994. He added the MVP in 1994, when the Rockets won the first of consecutive championships (and Olajuwon added back-to-back Finals MVP honors.)

Also as with many things in Rockets history, there was a lull between the championship years and more celebrations.

Steve Francis broke through, offering hope for a revival, as the 2000 co-Rookie of the Year, finishing in a tie with Elton Brand. But Francis would be dealt after five seasons.

Aaron Brooks was the 2010 Most Improved Player, but played parts of just two more seasons in Houston before he was traded, though he would return for parts of two more seasons.

Finally, the Mike D'Antoni era brought acclaim, awards, and the best regular-season in franchise history.

D'Antoni became the third Rockets coach to win Coach of the Year, taking the award for the 2016–17 season, his first with the Rockets. Eric Gordon, also in his first season in Houston, was the Sixth Man of the Year in the first season of his career coming off the bench full time.

Finally, with Clint Capela a finalist for Most Improved and Gordon to repeat as Sixth Man of the Year, Harden took home the big award, completing his record-setting, best season of his career with the 2018 Most Valuable Player.

100 2017–18

The Rockets had only one real goal. Any other aspirations along the way, from James Harden winning the MVP to accumulating the most victories in the NBA or franchise history, were to service the pursuit of a championship.

More than strive for the title, as many teams do or at least claim to, the Rockets came to believe they would be champions. Right up to those closing minutes, when the three-point shooting that had come to define their style and rewrite record books betrayed them at the worst time possible, the Rockets believed.

They had taken aim at the Golden State Warriors and did not care who knew it. General manager Daryl Morey confessed to his "obsession" and his players called out the champions as no one else dared to.

They became the best team of the 2017–18 regular season. It took one of the greatest teams of any season to conquer them.

In the end, that belief made the defeat more demoralizing. The Rockets refused to consider the accomplishments to salve the pain, but time will allow the successes to emerge, if not satisfy.

"The year has been unbelievable," Rockets coach Mike D'Antoni said. "The locker room has been great. I'm just really super lucky to be able to coach these guys.

"You don't buy heart at the supermarket. It's definitely a privilege. To be in this position, and to be able to coach these guys, really lucky."

Ultimately, there was bad luck, the sort that changed everything. Chris Paul strained his right hamstring in the final minute of Game 5 in the Western Conference Finals, a game in which he had propelled the Rockets to a 3–2 series lead against the Golden State Warriors in the collision course showdown that seemed destined since Paul engineered the trade to join forces with James Harden.

Paul limped off the floor as if he knew he would not be back in the series. He wasn't. The Rockets built a 17-point lead in Game 6 and lost when the offense crashed in the second half in Oakland. They built a 15-point lead in Game 7 and lost when the three-point shooting that had helped define them for two record-setting seasons abandoned them in Houston.

The Rockets had been built to take on the Warriors and did not care who knew it in the season-long quest to get that Game 7 on their home floor.

The Rockets built the best record in the NBA and in franchise history with the ultimate goal in mind. With a pair of 4–1 runs past the Timberwolves and Jazz to reach the Conference Finals, the Rockets won more games than any Rockets team ever had. Paul had advanced further than in any of his previous 12 seasons, but the Rockets' aspirations had been clear.

"The ultimate goal is to hold that trophy up, so until we do that, there's no celebrations," guard Harden had said when the Rockets were assured the top record in the NBA for the first time in franchise history.

"We all know," Paul said, "we will be judged by the postseason."

There was more to the Rockets' 2017–18 season than falling five wins short of a championship. Harden was a unanimous All-NBA First-Team selection. The NBA assists leader in 2016–17, he was the scoring champion a year later, joining Michael Jordan as the only players to have averaged at least 30 points, eight assists, five rebounds, and 1.7 steals in a season. He was the only NBA player with multiple 50-point games, scoring at least 50 in four games, including the only 60-point triple double in NBA history.

The mix of Harden and Paul in the backcourt was seamless and devastating, with the Rockets going 50–8 in games Paul played. Paul averaged 18.6 points and 7.9 assists and 5.4 rebounds. More than that, they meshed immediately, as if there never was reason to doubt.

"I don't mean to sound too mushy or whatnot, but it was like love at first sight," Harden said. "Once last summer hit and we just started hanging out and how competitive he really is and how much he loves putting that work in, being in the gym in the same way. So, it kind of just made sense. Obviously everything else from off the court, hanging out, bowling—he loves to bowl—dinner. It was meant to be. And then when you add other guys around it, it kind of brings us together."

Rarely has a team been more together. Two seasons removed from the dysfunctional, tension-filled slide to 41–41, the Rockets developed remarkable chemistry. Harden said "I've never been happier." But many felt the same way.

"I can't describe it," forward P.J. Tucker said. "We talk about it to other people and it's like a feeling. You can't describe it when you're on a team like this. That's weird to say, being a 12-year veteran. To be on a team like this with so many veterans, so many guys that get it and a coach that gets it, a front office that gets it. You never have to question motivation or if people are here for certain reasons. You don't have to question anything. It's a rarity."

The Rockets' winning streaks of 17, 14, and 11 games made them the sixth team in NBA history with three winning streaks of at least 10 games. Their 31 road wins were the sixth most in NBA history. Their point differential of 8.5 per game topped the league.

Tucker, the off-season addition overshadowed by the trade for Paul, his childhood friend, became a starter, infusing the Rockets with his defensive ferocity and determination. The Rockets went from the 18th-ranked defense in 2016–17 to sixth in 2017–18, and third after Tucker became a starter.

Luc Mbah a Moute fit nearly as well, coming off the bench to solidify the defense before his second dislocated shoulder injury, suffered in the penultimate game of the regular season on a dunk in Los Angeles, left him ineffective in the postseason.

Eric Gordon, the reigning Sixth Man of the Year, was a finalist for the award in 2017–18, but also excelled as a starter in the 30 games either Harden or Paul missed.

Gerald Green was a sensation, signed off his couch in late December when Paul and Mbah a Moute were out with injuries and days before Harden would go out. More than just bringing his usual fearless shooting, Green literally wore his affection for his home town on his sleeve, wearing his Houston-themed throwback uniforms to every home game and using his love for Houston to fuel his play just as it drove his Harvey rescue efforts before the season began.

Clint Capela improved so greatly that, by the time he outplayed Karl-Anthony Towns and Rudy Gobert in consecutive playoff series, he was often considered part of a Big Three with Harden and Paul. Capela, who led the NBA in field goal percentage in the regular season and playoffs, was such a force and fit as a rim-runner on one end and protector on the other, the Rockets went 42–3 in games he, Harden, and Paul all played, outscoring teams by 11.5 points in the games they were on the court together and losing those three games by an average of 3.67.

Harden especially reached another level, from joining Kareem Abdul-Jabbar and Wilt Chamberlain as the only players to score at least 20 points in each of his team's first 35 games to joining Oscar Robertson as the only players with 2,000 points and 700 assists in three straight seasons. Harden and Elvin Hayes are the only Rockets to lead the league in scoring. He and Moses Malone are the only Rockets players to average 30 points per game.

"I know I said he was the best offensive player I've ever seen," D'Antoni said. "There was discussion about that. I don't know how you get better than that. He has so many moves and so many things that he does, how do you guard him?"

He was never stopped, but he could not finish those final playoff games, unable to carry the Rockets through their second half collapses, which kept the Rockets from that one goal that influenced everything else.

They did not succeed with that. All the other successes tended to tease with what could have been. Time, however, will bring perspective, if it had not already.

"I read something the other day," D'Antoni said before the playoffs began. "'Sure, James Harden should be the MVP. Sure, Chris Paul and James have been great. Sure, they set a franchise record for [wins]. But they'll be ultimately judged by if they win a championship or not.' Really? It doesn't diminish what these guys have done.

"The way I celebrate it is I enjoy every fricken' day I go in the locker room with these guys and go on the court and all the games they've won and all the trips we've made back from games on the road. That's what's enjoyable."

The season ended with disappointment. That did not change the seven months that preceded the final loss. The goal was not achieved. The loss was painful. Just as the success was driven by championship aspirations, the belief in those hopes made defeat more crushing. Still, it was a remarkable season.

"I couldn't be prouder," D'Antoni said. "So we'll go back and nitpick things and try to get better next year, but just a good group of guys all year, all year."

Acknowledgments

After two decades covering the Rockets for the *Houston Chronicle*, nearly 40 percent of the franchise's history and more than half of my career, there are a great deal of people I have to thank, many that likely have no idea of how helpful they were on this project or along the way.

With that in mind, I must start with Ralph Sampson. When Sampson was the player of the year at the University of Virginia and I was covering the police beat at the University of Delaware, the guy that was supposed to cover the Delaware men's basketball team decided to play one more year of college lacrosse. We needed someone to fill in because the great Ralph Sampson was coming to town. I was playing basketball every day then, so I was asked to cover the game.

I've been a sportswriter that has loved covering basketball—and especially the past two decades of Rockets basketball—ever since.

I must thank Dennis Jackson for mentoring me in those days in ways that many around me have heard about for years. Many thanks to Dan Cunningham for bringing me to Houston and putting me on the Rockets beat, to Fran Blinebury and Eddie Sefko for showing me how it's done, and Reid Laymance for his support and influence, along with greenlighting this project.

A great deal of the stories you have read if you have gotten this far come from the years spent around the Rockets and the NBA, from Rudy Tomjanovich and Carroll Dawson to Mike D'Antoni and Daryl Morey. The assistance of Rockets players has been so extraordinary, the great Sam Smith, when advocating for better cooperation around the league, once lamented, "We can't all work in Houston." I have.

I must acknowledge the aid of the *Houston Chronicle* archives, the fine book *Celebrating Fifty Seasons*, and the Rockets 50th anniversary video series.

Thanks to the great many friends and colleagues at the *Chronicle* and to Tracey Hughes and the media relations department at the Rockets.

Most of all, to my family. My parents and brother were endlessly supportive with my dad forever insisting that I provide a book with my name on it for his shelf. Daniel, Emily, and David are my joy and inspiration. Kathy, the best teammate I could ever have and better than I deserve, never ceases to amaze me as she makes everything possible.